On Time at Winchester College

-

Sundials and Clocks

Winchester College Clock.

1920 Photograph by R.P. Howgrave-Graham (1880-1959), Keeper of the Muniments of Westminster Abby, archaeologist, horologist, and accomplished photographer.

On Time at Winchester College Sundials and Clocks

Paul R. Secord

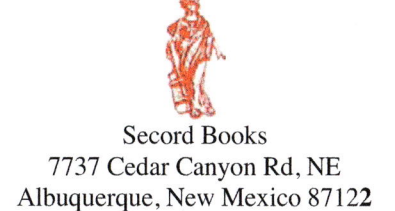

Secord Books
7737 Cedar Canyon Rd, NE
Albuquerque, New Mexico 87122

© September 2021 by Paul R. Secord
All Rights Reserved

No part of this book may be reproduced in any form or by any electronic or mechanical means including information storage and retrieval systems without the permission in writing from the publisher, except by a reviewer who may quote passages in a review.

Cover: The 17th century painted glass sundial at Winchester College, this image has been digitally restored by the Author.

Backpiece: A 1920 photograph through the passage at the Winchester College Sick House with the c.1780 "Watkins of London" sundial in the background. The inscription over the entrance reads "Bethesda" meaning "house of her mercy" in Hebrew.

ISBN: 9798458375580
Library of Congress Control Number (LCCN): 2021916820

Secord Books are printed by Amazon.com and may be purchased through them in hardcopy and eBook format.

CARPE DIEM
Ovid Odes 1.11

*Tu ne quaesieris, scire nefas, quem mihi, quem tibi
finem di dederint, Leuconoe, nec Babylonios
emptaris numeros. Ut melius, quidquid erit, pati,
seu pluris hiemes seu tribuit Iuppiter ultimam,
quae nunc oppositis debilitat pumicibus mare
Tyrrhenum: sapias, vina liques, et spatio brevi
spem longam reseces. Dum loquimur, fugerit invida
aetas:* **carpe diem**, *quam minimum credula postero.*

*You mustn't ask, it is not lawful to know, what end to me, which to you
the gods have given us, and don't tempt the Babylonian kabbalah,
Leucònoe. How much better it is to endure what will be,
Whether Jupiter has granted us many winters or whether this is the last one
that now wears out the Tyrrhenian sea on the opposite cliffs:
be wise, filter the wine, cut back long hope,
as life is short. While we speak, envious time has already fled:*
seize the moment, *trust in the future as little as possible.*

Translation by Vittoria Smorto

TABLE OF CONTENTS i

FOREWORD iv

PREFACE v

ACKNOWLEDGEMENT vi

INTRODUCTION 1

PART I: The Sundials 9
    1. The St. Michael's Church Sundial - Medieval 12
    2. The Middle Gate Sundial (no longer in existence) - 1566 16
    3. The Fromond Chantry Sundial (no longer in existence) - <1712? 18
    4. The St. Cross Vertical Sundial - seventeenth century 19
    5. The Winchester College Painted Glass Sundial Window - c.1680 21
    6. The Old Sick House Garden "London" Sundial - c.1780 26

PART II: The Clocks 28
    7. The Turret Clock - fifteenth? through twentieth century 29
    8. Longcase Clocks - 1695 and 1760 53
    9. Synchronome-Shortt Free Pendulum Clock - 1923 58
    10. Brillié Magneta Master Clock - c.1910 65
    11. Sewills Pendulum Clock - late nineteenth or twentieth century 69
    12. The Empire Clock - 1935 71
    13. The Buckland (1912) and Jacker (1972) Clocks 79

LIST of FIGURES

    Figure 1: How a Sundial Works 9
    Figure 2: St. Michael's Church Medieval sundial 14
    Figure 3: St. Michael's Church sundials location 15
    Figure 4: South side of St. Michael's Church 15
    Figure 5: Middle Gate from the Chapel Tower 16

Figure 6: 1566-67 Winchester College account..16
Figure 7: Sketch said to be a Sundial and Fromond Chantry buttress 18
Figure 8: South side of Beaufort's Tower, St. Cross...19
Figure 9: Sundial painted on the tower at St. Cross...20
Figure 10: Painted-Glass Sundial in the window of the Election Chamber 21
Figure 11: The fly in the Winchester Painted Glass Sundial.......................................22
Figure 12: Windows facing Chamber Court above Middle Gate 23
Figure 13: A Watercolour Rendering of the Winchester Glass Sundial......................24
Figure 14: Design Characteristics of a London Sundial Dial 27
Figure 15: Photographs of the London Sundial in the old Sick House garden 27
Figure 16: Winchester Empire Clock Drawing Detail..28
Figure 17: 1920 Photograph of Winchester College turret clock 29
Figure 18: Winchester College Rubic 29, line 7, 1400..30
Figure 19: Winchester College Account Roll 22087, 1403 to 1404............................31
Figure 20: Winchester College Account Roll 22162, 1498 to 1499............................32
Figure 21: Winchester College Account Roll 22165, 1501 to 1502............................32
Figure 22: Winchester College Account Roll 22220, 1644 to 1645............................33
Figure 23: Winchester College Account Roll 22221, 1646 to 1647............................34
Figure 24: Winchester College Accounts 1659 to 1660 35
Figure 25: Winchester College Accounts 1729 to 1730 35
Figure 26: Winchester College Accounts 1781 36
Figure 27: Winchester College Accounts 1782 36
Figure 28: Winchester College Accounts 1807 37
Figure 29: Winchester College Accounts 1811 38
Figure 30: Winchester College Accounts 1818 38
Figure 31: 1954 Plan of Winchester College Chapel and Satellite Photo 40
Figure 32: Winchester College Chapel and Tower in 1404..41
Figure 33: Winchester College Chapel and Tower in 1675..42
Figure 34: Winchester College Chapel and Tower in 1838 43
Figure 35: Winchester College Chapel and Tower in 1925..44
Figure 36: Verge and Foliot Escapement...46
Figure 37: The Turret Clock in 2021 47
Figure 38: The Winchester College turret clock Photograph 48
Figure 39: Anchor/Recoil Escapement 49

Figure 40: Holes and Notches Showing Reconfiguration 50
Figure 41: The Minutes Setting Dial 51
Figure 42: View from the Clock Balcony Looking at the Bells of the Spire 52
Figure 43: Longcase Clock Escapement, Pendulum, and Mechanism 54
Figure 44: Major Malcolm Robertson "The Bobber" (1882-1956), ... 55
Figure 45: William III longcase Clock - 1695 56
Figure 46: George II longcase Clock - c.1760 57
Figure 47: Synchronome-Shortt Free Pendulum Clock #61 58
Figure 48: Shortt Clock Main Dial and Subsidiary Dial 58
Figure 49: William Hamilton Shortt and Frank Hope-Jones 63
Figure 50: Advertisement for the Shortt Clock 64
Figure 51: Lucien Brillié (1865-1911) 66
Figure 52: Science School *Magneta/Brillié* Controlling Clock 67
Figure 53: *Magneta/Brillié* Clock Instruction Manual and Description 68
Figure 54: Sewills Observatory Regulator Compensation Pendulum clock 70
Figure 55: The Empire Clock in the Winchester College Moberly Library. 71
Figure 56: The Empire Clock Face and Motto 77
Figure 57: Concept drawing of the Empire Clock 78
Figure 58: The Buckland Clock 79
Figure 59: The 'Jacker' Clock 80

REFERENCES 82

APPENDIX A - Shortt Clock Documentation 88
APPENDIX B - Empire Clock Documentation 116

ABOUT THE AUTHOR 161

Chris McKay BSc CEng MIET FBHI

Horologist
Turret Clock Specialist

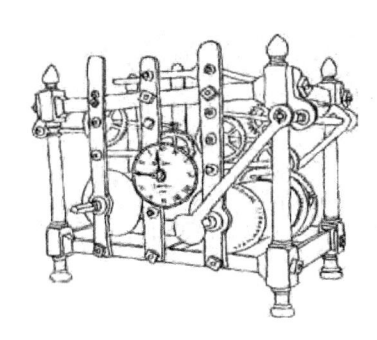

FOREWORD

If you are in a garden and turn a stone over with your foot, you may find a host of insects hiding there, or there may be nothing at all. Such it is with historical researching; you can spend a day trawling documents in an archive and find nothing but the mundane; the next day you can hit on a letter or a set of accounts that is the key to opening up your research. 'The past is a foreign country, they do things different there', so starts the book *The Go-Between* by L.P. Hartley. Researchers could spend a lifetime discovering fascinating things that really do not have much to do with the subject they are investigating, to keep focused takes some grit.

The reader will soon see just how much research Paul has put into this book. It must have started with an interest in just one clock and then rolled on to another, and another and then spilled out into sundials. Paul's work is really to be commended particularly since he lives in America and his mission to uncover the story of Time at Winchester College must have presented a great challenge. It is one thing to look at an artefact or old document, it is quite another to have to do it all by remote control, relying on scans, photographs and people on the ground close to the source.

However, despite the several thousand miles of separation Paul has unravelled a lot of information and presents it now. I am sure he has enjoyed preparing his work and I am equally sure the reader will find this potpourri of horology diverse, absorbing and thought-provoking.

Chris McKay

PREFACE

Winchester College is a private institution and not open to the public. The sundials and clocks at the College can only be viewed on prearranged tours:
<www.winchestercollege.org/visit-us>

Time keeping through the centuries at Winchester College, founded in 1382, is a fascinating story. The time measuring and reporting devices, still found at the college, are a microcosm of the history of horology. All of the ones described in this book are exceptional examples of their particular type. The College and its immediate surroundings contain examples of most of the significant advancements in time keeping mechanisms, from sundials through mechanical clocks.

ACKNOWLEDGEMENTS

The Winchester College Archives is an extraordinary resource for all manner of material concerning the College, literally spanning centuries. My thanks to their Archivist, Suzanne Foster, for providing scanned copies of the documents, as well as many of the photographs contained in the book.

The Antiquarian Horological Society (AHS) and the British Sundial Society were most gracious in offering direction, comment, and counsel during the preparation of this book. Without their considerable input it would not have been possible.

I owe a great debt of gratitude to all of the following person who review and commented on various aspects of the book. Again, without their considerable input it would not have been possible:

Marissa Addomine for Latin translations of Winchester College records.

Jake Bransgrove, Tutor in the History of Art (Edinburgh College of Art), University of Edinburgh was extremely generous with sharing his knowledge of Herbert Baker and the College's Empire Clock.

Mark Frank, an American author, collector, and authority on all things clocks, for his direction early on in helping me find my way into the world of turret clocks.

Sue Manston of the British Sundial Society for her careful reading, comments and corrections to the sections pertaining to sundials.

St. Cross Brother Clive McCleester provided photographs of the sundial at St. Cross and Brother John Leathes accurately recorded the latitude angle elevation of the gnomon.

Chris McKay, one of Britain's leading authorities on turret clocks, provided an invaluable assessment of that clock. We corresponded on a number of occasions, and his report on the turret clock has been incorporated in its entirety into the main text of this book, rather than relegated to an Appendices.

James Nye, Chairman of the AHS for his considerable contributions and corrections to the section on the Shortt Clock and the Brillié - Magneta Master Clock, as well as his review of the draft section on the Empire Clock.

Rabbi Harry Rosenfeld for his insight into the Hebrew inscription above the entrance to the Old Sick House.

Keith Scobie-Youngs, Director of the Cumbria Clock Company, Castle Workshops, Dacre, Penrith, Cumbria, a Fellow of the British Horological Institute and Accredited Conservator Restorer for his comments on the turret clock.

Lewis Walduck, of the Clock Workshop, in King's Worthy, Hampshire maintains the College's longcase clocks. He provided important insight into their history.

Heather Whitworth, Director of Smith of Derby for carefully checking company records covering their work on the turret clock.

Thanks to my wife Marcia, and friends Jennifer Coile, Gordon Bronitsky PhD, as well as Kevin Brown FSA (Scot) for their proofreading and comments on drafts of this book.

My sincere apologies if I have left anyone out.

INTRODUCTION

The abundance of superior time measuring devices at the College should come as no surprise. While the author's initial interest clocks at the College was initially focused on the prospect of finding a Medieval turret clock, having many years before becoming familiar with such a device in Winchester, an offhand comment to the Colleges archivist asking if such a mechanism was still up in the Chapel Tower quickly lead to the identification of several precision, high quality and interesting time measuring devices to be, if not rediscovered, at the very least brought to a wider attention.

A learning institution will require accurate timekeeping for several reasons throughout its history. Initially the most important of which is knowing the appropriate hour for prayers, services, and special events. Secondly, being a school, it is important that students arrive at class and various activities, such as meals, on time. Other time measuring devices fall into the various other categories include: being decorative; as commemorative clocks; or for educational purposes.

There are two appendices containing extensive background information on the 1923 Synchronome-Shortt Free Pendulum in the Science School, and the 1935 Empire Clock in the Mobley Library.

All but one of the timekeeping devices described in this book are located at Winchester College, with the vertical sundial at St. Cross, about half a mile south of the college, being an exception. This sundial represents an important type, and it is known that there was once a very similar sundial at the college, In 1970 Winchester College acquired the St. Michael church building, that incorporates in its south facing wall a sundial of medieval age. Another venerable vertical sundial, not addressed in this book, is found high on the side of a south facing buttress at the nearby Winchester Cathedral.

The time measuring devices in this book are generally organized chronologically in two parts; the sundials as Part I, followed by mechanical and electrically driven devices as Part II.

The following is a summary of the sundials and clocks described in this book.

1. Ancient Canonical Hour Sundial
medieval

This sundial, often said to be of Anglo-Saxon age, but of indeterminate age, is inserted high into the exterior wall of the reconstructed church of St. Michael's, near the Kingsgate Road. Note the crosses on some hour lines, they are believed to mark the hours when a Mass was said and are typical of such medieval sundials.

2. The Middle Gate Tower Sundial
date unknown, not survived

The perfect place for a vertical sundial used for calibration of the College's mechanical turret clock would have been on the tower located at the southwest corner of the Middle Gate facing Chapel Tower where the turret clock is located. Unfortunately it has not survived cleanings and restoration work.

3. The Fromond Chantry Sundial
date unknown, not survived

A vertical sundial is said to have been painted on the south side of Fromond's Chantry, but that it had disappeared sometime after the First World War. The sole image of it, seen above, does not relate to any locations at Winchester College and there are no College records of such a sundial.

4. Vertical Sundial at St. Cross
c.1600

A vertical sundial at St. Cross is painted on the south face of the entrance tower. Such sundials on church towers were used to calibrate turret clocks, in order to insure that the bells/chimes struck at the correct time. A similar vertical sundial was once at Winchester College, but as discussed on the preceding page, no trace of it remains.

5. Stained-Glass Window Sundial
seventeenth century

A sundial in a stained-glass window is located in a window directly above the south side of Middle Gate looking into Chamber Court. The motto reads: "Ut Umbra sic Vita Transit." There is a fly painted below the motto, evoking the saying *time flies*. The photograph below has been digitally enhanced to correct the sundials colour and "repair" cracks.

6. Sick House Garden Sundial
c.1780

This exceptionally high-quality sundial was placed in the garden of the of the old Sick House, when the garden, featuring medicinal plants. It is known to have come from a residential garden near the College, the gift of an unknown donor. The sundial is engraved Watkins, Charing Cross, London, a high-end instrument maker in London. This is an especially detailed and well-made example of a type known as a "London sundial".

7. Turret Clock
fifteenth century? - 1998

The original turret clock in the Chapel Tower, which based on accounting records at the college archives dated to 1404, has gone through many changes. The clock that is found in the tower includes many reused parts dating from most, it not every, century of its existence. These changes and improvements incorporate many of the key innovations to clocks of its type. It is a history of British turret clocks all in one machine. The 1920 photograph above is by R.P. Howgrave-Graham (1880-1959), an important historian of clocks. It was he who established the date of the Salisbury Cathedral Clock as being made in about 1386,

8. Longcase Clocks
1695 and c.1720

William III   **George II**

Found along an inner passage is a William III longcase (i.e. grandfather) clock, dated and identified on the dial as having been made by William Carr of London. The date makes it one of the earliest of this type.

A George II longcase clock, is identified as being made by Jean Gruchy (? - 1783) of Jersey, a well-known maker of these iconic clocks.

9. Shortt-Synchronome clock
1923

10. Magneta *Brillié* Controlling Clock
c.1910

This amazing clock is mounted on the wall along a corridor at the Winchester College Physics Laboratory. It is a one of only about 100 such clocks produced between 1922 and 1958. They were the pinnacle of 20th century mechanical time keeping, eclipsed only by atomic clocks, and were accurate to about one second in twelve years.

This electrically maintained pendulum controlling clock was installed in the Winchester College Science School in 1912. Originally it was a master clock that controlled a number of subsidiary clocks installed in classrooms throughout the school, all of which were synchronized to the same time.

11. Sewills Observatory Regulator
late nineteenth or early twentieth

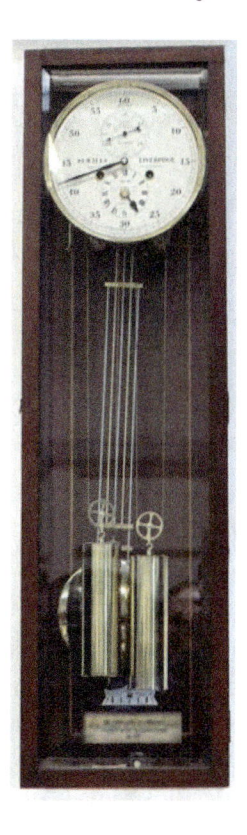

This clock, also found hanging in the in the Science School, was probably made in the twentieth century, although it could be earlier. It commemorates the years of teaching of Martin and Jennifer Gregory at Winchester College.

12. The Empire Clock
1936

This ornate wall clock is found in the College's Moberly Library. It was designed by the architect Sir Herbert Baker, as were a half dozen others in England. They represent the nationalistic nostalgic concept that "The sun never sets on the British Empire," and as such contain elaborate symbolism of the Commonwealth. While this clock is electrically driven, it has complex mechanical gearing, as well as being an early example of a synchronous clock tied into the National Electrical Grid,

13. The Buckland Clock   and   "The Jacker" Clock
1912   1972

There are two additional prominent clocks at Winchester College: the Buckland Clock installed in 1921 on the north wall of the racquet court in memory of Edward Hasting Buckland (1864-1906). A first-class cricketer, he was a Master of Winchester College from 1888-1906. The Jacker Clock, in honor of former Winchester College Housemaster Horace Arthur Jackson, "The Jacker" (1898-1907) was placed high overlooking the Flint Court in 1975. While these are both fine large wall mounted memorial clocks, they are not especially noteworthy examples of their type, both have "modern" electronic movements, and are thus touched on only briefly here.

8

Part I: SUNDIALS

The sundials/clocks presented in this book are arranged in chronological order, divided into two parts: first the sundials and secondly the clocks. However, there is some overlap, as the former persist as decorative features in gardens to this day, while there was a period in which vertical sundials were needed to calibrate inaccurate mechanical turret clocks.

A sundial is any device that tells the time of day by the apparent position of the sun. Such a device uses the suns elevation and/or azimuth in relation to the observer to determine the time.

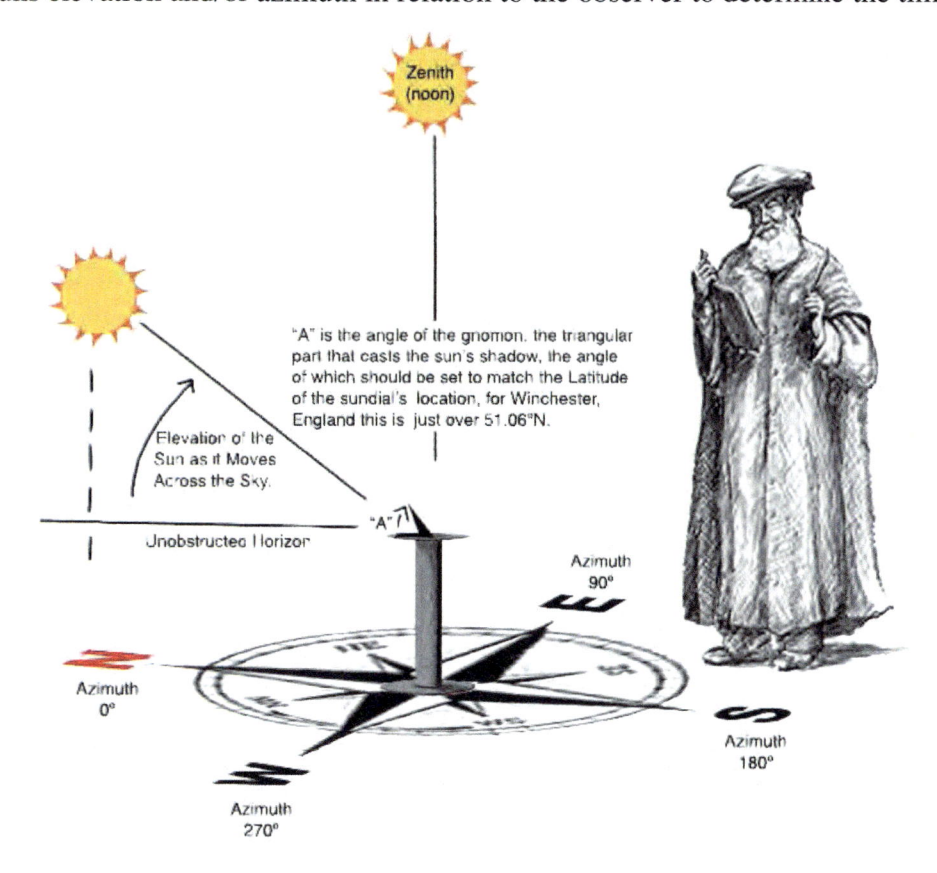

Figure 1: How a Sundial Works with a drawing of St. Cross Brother John by Joe Mildenberger, 2021.

A rudimentary sundial can be made simply by drawing a circle on the ground, and placing a stick, i.e. a gnomon, in the centre of the circle. However, as Figure 1 shows, it's a little more involved in that the circle needs to indicate some regular hour divisions oriented north/south and the positioning of the stick needs to take into consideration the altitude and azimuth of the specific location. There are numerous examples from the ancient world of using such a technique to measure time, with the world's oldest known true sundial being a 3,500-year-old one from Egypt. Accurate sundials were well known in the Greek and Roman world and canonical dials, used to indicate hours of liturgical acts, first appear in the seventh century.

There are a number of different types of sundials, but a discussion of the types goes far beyond the those addressed in this book. Here we will be limited to two vertical types, and the common horizontal or garden sundial.

The British Sundial Society is an excellent resource to further explore sundials. Their website includes a comprehensive overview of sundials through history, how they work, how they are made, a list of nearly 7,000 quality sundials throughout Britain, a bibliography of published source materials, and a variety of lectures, tours and other resources pertaining to sundials - <https://sundialsoc.org.uk>.

Vertical Sundials

Vertical sundials are often found on older churches where they were needed to keep the inaccurate mechanisms of mechanical clocks properly calibrated. Such early clocks could lose as much a half an hour a day. Instructions for the laying out of vertical sundials were published by the Italian astronomer Giovanni Padovani in 1570; around 1620, another Italian astronomer, Giuseppe Biancani, wrote *Constructio instrumenti ad horologia solaria* which describes, in great detail, how to make an accurate sundial.

One of the less common types of vertical sundials are those made of stained-glass. Most date to the latter part of the Seventeenth Century, when Puritan prejudice against colourful windows was no longer in vogue. Sundials also provided an alternative from the Biblical scenes that were more common in earlier times. They were typically installed in south-facing windows, with the gnomon fitted on the outside of the window, but the numerals were reversed so they could be read from the inside of a room. Judging from various contemporary records there must at one time have been many such dials at one time, however, the glass on which they were made was thin and fragile, and often had to be drilled in two or three places to allow for the gnomon to be fixed in position. As a result there are only thirty-six glass sundials remaining in windows in Great Britain; one of which is at Winchester College.

Horizontal Sundials

A bronze or brass horizontal sundial mounted on a plinth is a typical decorative feature of numerous gardens, hence the type is often referred to as a "garden" dial. They represent the ubiquitous sundial style. Mass-produced decorative sundials will usually be highly inaccurate, given that the gnomon, shadow lengths and hour markers are not calibrated to tell the correct time at the specific location of the dial. But that is not the case with the Winchester College sundial, which is a highly accurate scientific instrument. The instrument makers who produced such sundials were members of a heavily protected system of craft guilds.

1. The St. Michael's Church Sundial

St. Michael's church is located at the end of St. Michael's Passage just off of Kingsgate Street, across the street from Winchester College's western gate. A church is known to have been on this site since Anglo-Saxon times, but like most early churches it has been subject to many alterations over time. Aside from blocks of Binstead limestone, quarried on the Isle of Wight, set randomly through the flint walls, the sundial might be the only survival of a much older church. It is important to note that this sundial is of a reddish stone, possibly a sandstone, but clearly not the lighter Binstead limestone.

The earliest record of the Church is in a thirteenth century register of John of Pontoise, Bishop of Winchester from 1282 to 1304 when it was known as St Michael-in-the-Soke, and was a part of the eastern suburb of the medieval city. In addition to significant rebuilding in the fifteenth Century, the church was altered and extended in 1822 by Martin Filer of Winchester and further remodeled in 1882 by William Butterfield, including reseating, rebuilding of the chancel, addition of southwest porch, and inclusion of an organ chamber, as well as a vestry, that was further extended in 1898.

St Michael's became redundant as a parish church in the 1970s and was acquired by Winchester College shortly after that date. Today it is used as a chapel for Juniors at the College, as well as a music classroom and performance space.

The subject sundial is one of three sundials of its type known in Hampshire, the other two located at churches in Corhampton and Warnford. They are all vertical direct dials, in that they are perpendicular to the ground and generally face somewhat to the south, as is typical for such dials. The Winchester dial has a circular dial, 280 mm in diameter, and stands in relief on a square stone with fleur-de-lis designs in each corner.

The upper half of the dial is plain, while the line divisions of the lower half represent the early Christian method of measuring the day divided the day into eight sets of three hours each. Three lines are marked so as to form a cross, which represents the canonical hours of prayer, i.e. 9am, 12 noon and 3pm. Other lines mark the beginning and end or the three-hourly periods. This is a typical feature of such a sundial.

Today the sundial is about 4m high on the wall facing St Michael's Passage. Its original location is unknown. Although there is a hole or depression in the middle of the dial, any evidence of a fixed gnomon is long gone, assuming it even had a fixed gnomon.

It is extremely difficult, if not impossible to date early Medieval sundials, except in rare circumstances where exact provenance is known and well documented. This situation becomes increasingly tenuous the further back in time one goes. In fact, the attribution of "Saxon" applied to a sundial placed in a church wall is more than likely apocryphal.

Trying to date the St. Michael's dial only highlights the difficulties involved. A discussion of early sundials found in *The Corpus of Anglo-Saxon Stone Sculpture: Catalogue* <http://www.ascorpus.ac.uk> states that:

> *The dials from Warnford, Hampshire, and St Michael's, Winchester, must be grouped with the in-situ example from Corhampton, Hampshire, as they share the same form, a circular dial sculpted on a square stone; the same calibration; and very similar decoration, consisting of a stem ending in three leaves in each corner of the slab on which the dial is carved. On primary evidence the dial from Corhampton can be placed in the eleventh century, and a late pre-Conquest date is confirmed by the form of the leaf ornament (Ill. 438) which, as noted above, occurs widely in manuscripts, ivory, and metalwork of the tenth and eleventh centuries. This dating can be extended to the other dials of the group.*

The corner designs at St. Michaels are similar to those found on the tower-slabs and sundial, that have been tentatively dated to the early tenth century, at St. John the Baptist's Church, at Barnack, near Peterborough, 140 miles away.

Churches said to date to the Middle Ages will have typically undergone considerable rebuilding and repairs, and the earlier the structure the more extensive such changes are likely to have occurred. Hence the fact that many "Saxon" dials are in walls much younger than the date attributed to them.

In addition, most Saxon churches were simple wooden structures, making it unlikely that the not insignificant number of stone dials said to be Saxon are in fact from later periods.

So in the end about the best that can be said is that the St. Michael's Church sundial is apparently Medieval, dating from sometime between the 6th and 12th centuries. Exactly when it was made, where it was originally used, and how it came to be at its present location is unknown. But it is certainly old, and of an early and common type associated with churches.

Figure 2: St. Michael's Church Medieval sundial, note that the sundial features cross shaped marks denoting canonical hours. (photograph by Suzanne Foster, February 2021)

Figure 3: A photograph of the south side of the church showing the sundials location high in the upper corner of the building. (photograph by Suzanne Foster, February 2021)

Figure 4 : A photograph of the south side of the church as it is today. The sundial is high on the wall beyond the central door and is not visible in this image. (photograph by Jon Benn, January 2021, Google Maps posting)

2. The Middle Gate Sundial

The perfect place for a vertical sundial used for calibration of the College's mechanical turret clock would have been on the tower located at the southwest corner of the Middle Gate facing Chamber Court and the Chapel Tower where the turret clock is located. A photograph taken from the roof of the Chapel Tower, presented below, clearly demonstrates why this was the case. Unfortunately, this tower, being of limestone blocks facing south has been subject to considerable weathering and, of necessity, has been repaired. The result is that all traces of any former painted surface has long vanished.

Figure 5: The Chamber Court showing the south side of the Middle Gate from the Chapel Tower. A vertical sundial was once painted, probably quite high, on the tower of this gate. (photograph by Suzanne Foster, March 2021)

The College accounts for the year 1566-67 contain the following references to the sundial painted on the Middle Gate.

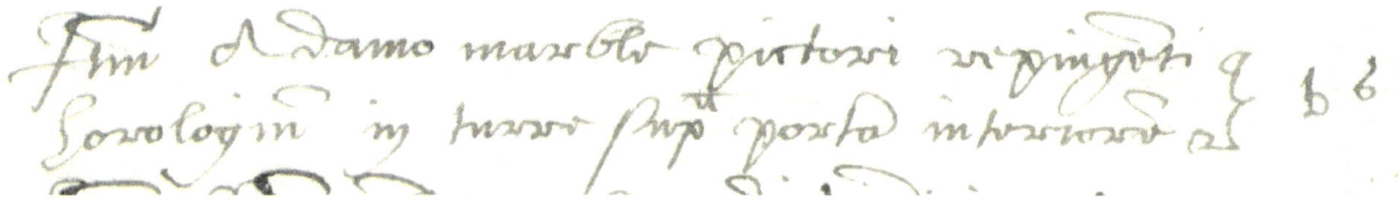

Item pro diversis expensis factis circa novum horologium pictum in muris supra portam collegii interiorem, ut patet per particularia . . . xxijs. iijd.
Also, for various expenses incurred on the new clock painted on the wall above the gate of college, according to the particulars.. £22.3.

Figure 6: The 1566-67 Winchester College account referring to a sundial painted on the Middle Gate. (Winchester College Archives)

It seems more than likely that there was a sundial painted at this location at the same time the turret clock was installed in 1403. Certainly, a sundial would have been needed to calibrate the turret clock at the time of its daily winding. Unfortunately, the 1566 record is the first mention of a sundial facing the Clock Tower that has been found.

3. The Fromond Chantry Sundial

A vertical sundial is mentioned in a handwritten note dated 1941, by Lennard Forsyth relating a conversation with Winchester College historian Herbert Chitty, as having been painted on the furthest east buttress on the south side of Fromond's Chantry in the centre of the cloisters, but that it had disappeared sometime after the First World War. Unfortunately, no photographs of this sundial were located. A sketch identified as "Sundial in Cloister Gardens, Winchester College Dated 1712" is found in Henslow's *Ye Sundial Booke* of 1914 and shows a sundial on a bay from the wall with four windows above the dial. This is clearly not a buttress and does not match a specific location at any other site at Winchester College. So the fate, and indeed possible location of this sundial, is unknown. An inventory of sundials in Britain, maintained by the British Sundial Society, does not list any vertical dials dated 1712.

Figure 7: l. This sketch from Henslow's *Ye Sundial Booke* of 1914, is said to be of a Winchester College Sundial. However the setting is not Fromond Chantry, and r. a photograph of the most southeasterly buttress of Fromond's Chantry show indication of a sundial. (photograph by Suzanne Foster, March 2021)

4. The St. Cross Hospital Vertical Sundial

The vertical sundial at St. Cross, a separate church and almshouse about a half mile south of Winchester College, is painted on the south side of Beaufort's Tower stair turret overlooking the central quadrangle. Although the tower was constructed in 1445, the sundial is thought to date from the Seventeenth Century. It has a thin iron sheet gnomon and shows the hours between 6am to 5pm in half hour increments. Full-length half-hour lines extend from a circle at the base of the gnomon. There is a 6am line drawn above the horizon, with XII for Noon and IIII for 4pm. The Winchester College painted tower sundial would have been very similar to this one.

Figure 8: The south facing side of Beaufort's tower, the sundial's gnomon is just visible (photograph by Brother Clive McCleester, March 2021).

Figure 9: Sundial painted on the tower at St. Cross (photograph by Brother Clive McCleester, March 2021), and a detail of a photograph from the mid-nineteenth century shows the gnomon. (wellcomecollection.org, 2021).

5. The Winchester College Painted Glass Sundial Window

This square vertical sundial is painted within an ornamented oval on a south facing glass window in the room directly above the Middle Gate. Unfortunately, the gnomon is now missing, and the face has faded and cracked. However, it remains essentially *in situ*, although the window where it is installed was "modernized" to a sash style in 1812 and returned to its former Medieval appearance in 1924. In both of these moves the frame was reglazed, and the dial repositioned in the window.

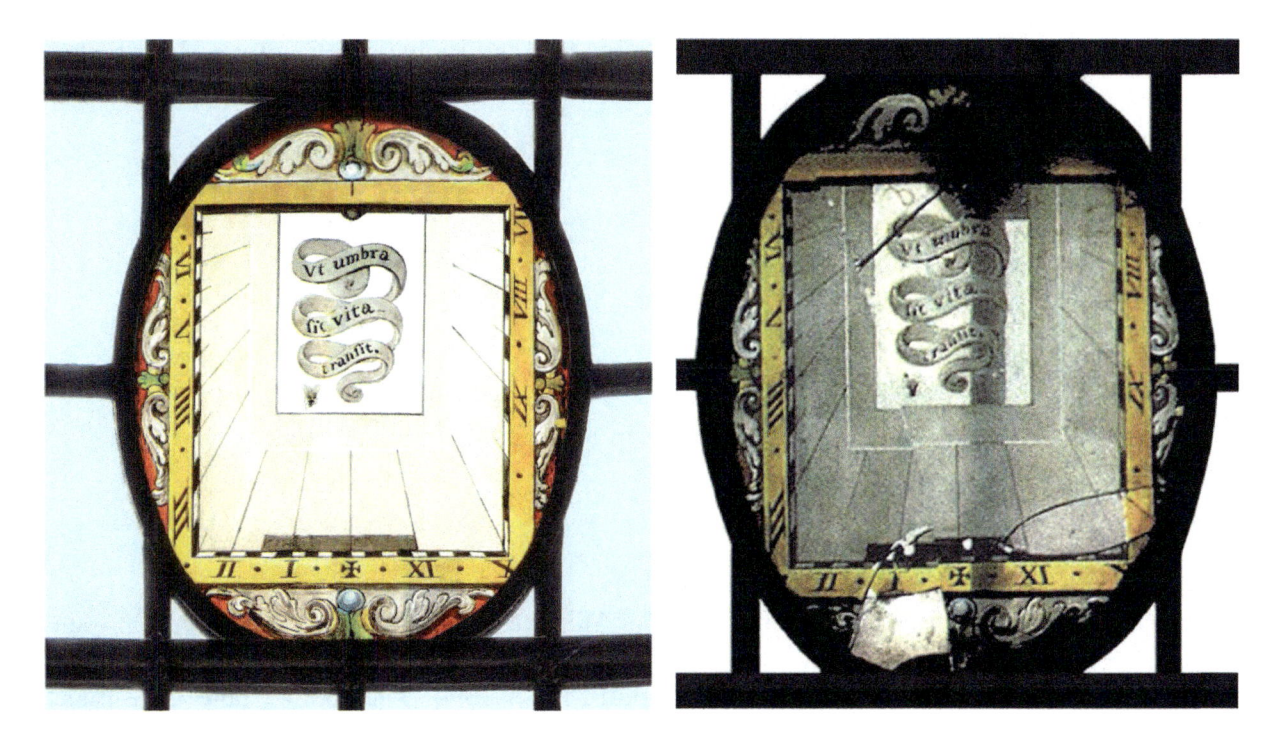

Figure 10: The Winchester College Painted-Glass Sundial in the window of the Election Chamber, digitally restored and as it appeared in 1988. At some time in the interim it was cleaned and the patched area repainted, as can be seen on Figure 12, pg 23 (l. by Suzanne Foster, March 9, 2021, digital enhancement by the Author; r. by Christopher Daniel 1988).

The motto reading *Ut Umbra sic Vita Transit* [As A Shadow, So Life Passes] is found in a scroll, uncharacteristically, located in the upper portion of the centre of the sundial dial. Such mottos are usually placed at a dial's perimeter. The Winchester dial has hour lines and half-hour marks, divided into hour blocks, with increments from 7am to 6pm. Noon is indicated by a cross pattée.

An amusing characteristic of some glass window sundials of the period is a fly painted somewhere on the dial, in this case to the left at the base of the motto. The fly evokes the saying "time flies", and is alluded to in a number of mottos such as these translated as: *Behold we fly, While you watch I flee, I fly while you slumber, No flying from death, Fly idleness, Seize the flying hour,* and *Our life's a flying shadow,* to name a few from the Seventeenth and Eighteenth Centuries (Leadbetter: 1769).

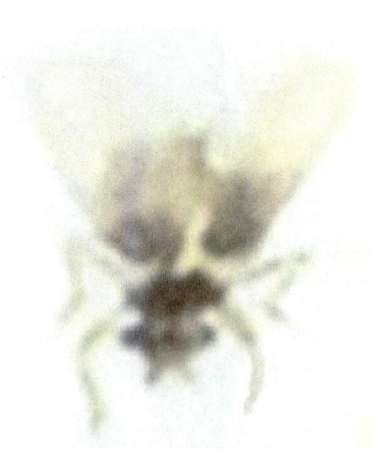

Figure 11: The fly in the Winchester Painted Glass Window. (photo by Suzanne Foster, March 2021)

Preliminary construction work on the buildings of Winchester College was began in 1386 and living quarters were ready for occupancy in early 1394. Warden John Morys was the first to occupy the three-room quarters above Middle Gate in mid-March 1394. The room where the subject sundial is located was the Warden's private hall/study and contained two tables and chairs. Windows, face into the Chamber Court and look directly towards the Chapel.

In 1604, Warden Bilson, the first married Warden, moved from the Middle Gate quarters into new lodgings at the Outer Court. By 1617 the previous Warden's Hall, where the sundial is located, is referred to as the *Camera Electionis,* and was used specifically for Elections, i.e. admittance, to College. In 1892 the Election Chamber was converted for use as lodgings by the College Tutor.

By 1908 the College Tutor rooms were moved, and the books of the Fellows Library were transferred into this room, which, in 1922, officially became the War Memorial Library. In 1996 the room was refurbished, although the books were apparently removed sometime before the refurbishing. Today (2021) it is used as a television room for the scholars.

Significant alterations to Winchester College were made by John Nicholas after he became Warden in 1679. It therefore seems likely that the two painted glass windows, one his coat-of-arms and the other the sundial may well have installed around that time. A 1980 letter from the National Maritime Museum in London commenting on the Winchester sundials states that the window dial "certainly must have been intended as a working dial and not an ornament".

Figure 12: Windows facing Chamber Court above Middle Gate, originally the Warden's Lodgings and subsequently the Election Chamber and War Memorial Library, showing the oval window with Warden Nicholas's coat-of-arms at the upper left and painted glass sundial at the upper right window. (photograph by Suzanne Foster, 2021)

The maker of this sundial is unknown, as is the exact date of its installation, which is most unfortunate - and atypical - given the excellent accounting records preserved in the College archives. Although Henry Gyles of York (1645-1709) is sometimes credited as the painter of the Winchester College dial, this is unlikely given that his work is generally restricted to the northern part of England, and that craft guild restrictions prevented him from working in London. In addition, there are various stylistic differences between Gyles' work and that of London glass-painters, see Geoffrey Lane's article on *The Tyttenhanger Sundial* posted on the Vidimus.org website on 12 April 2012.

The most likely maker of the Winchester glass sundial is John Oliver (1616-1701), a follower of the Baptist Sutton (c.1600-1667) school of glass painters in London. Oliver was a prominent glass-painter, who was a member of the "London Company of Glaziers and Painters on Glass" guild.

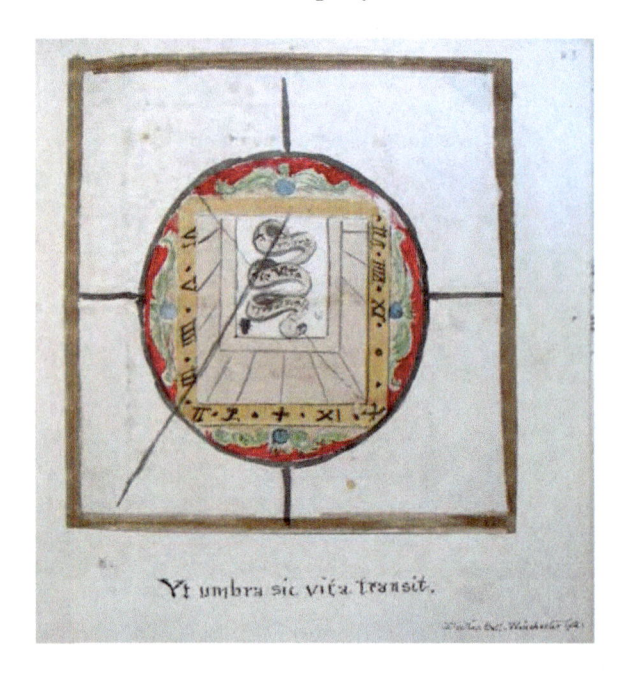

Figure 13: A watercolour rendering of unknown origin of the Winchester glass sundial painted sometime between c.1617 and 1892, as it refers to the Election Hall, and shows a diagonal crack from the upper left to the lower right. The original source of this painting is unknown.

In his 2005 article on seventeenth century London glass sundial makers, Geoffrey Lane comments that such dials typically include the following features, all of which are found on the Winchester College dial:

1) The chapter-ring is done in yellow-stain (to resemble a clock-face) and has black Roman numerals (normally Roman) interspersed with black dots marking the half hours, typical of painting by Oliver, but not of Gyles.

2) The number XII, the meridian, is replaced by a cross of the type known in heraldry as a cross pattée.

3) The central area is painted matte white or a pale shade on the back (a method borrowed from inscription panels) to show up the hour-lines and the shadow of the gnomon.

4) The hour lines are interspersed with very short half-hour lines drawn against the outer edge of this zone, which is typical of Oliver and not Gyles.

5) The quarter-hours are marked by a black-and-white scale along three sides just inside the chapter-ring.

6) The gnomon (on the outside) is directly attached to the dial by holes drilled in the glass – normally one near the top and three below. The lower holes are hidden in a black strip painted alongside the quarter-hour scale, or on the outer edge of the chapter-ring.

7) The inner field is usually enlivened with a fly, spider and fly, or other small creature. A realistic fly, as is the case with the Winchester College sundial, will have the legs painted on one side of the glass and the body on the other, resulting in the extraordinarily life-like appearance of the fly.

6. The Winchester College Old Sick House Garden "London Sundial"

This bronze sundial is in the garden that featured medicinal plants at the old Sick House (the college infirmary). It originally came from a house on Kingsgate Street, adjacent the College and was gifted by an unknown donor in 1910, perhaps a science don at the College?

The original part of the Sick House was built in 1640 by Warden Harris, who called it 'Bethesda,' meaning "house of mercy" or "house of grace," which is inscribed in Hebrew characters over the door, as seen in the photograph on the back cover of this book. In modern Hebrew there's the word *chesed*, but not *chesda*. The Sick house inscription reads *Beit Chesda*, the feminine form of Bethesda which therefore means "The House of Her Mercy", so as translated this may be a reference to the Virgin Mary, in Hebrew.

The sundial is engraved "Watkins of Charing Cross, London." Francis Watkins (c. 1723 - 1782) was one of the finest London instrument makers of the Eighteenth Century. He is known for the exceptional craftsmanship of various scientific instruments and was the maker of the 18-inch specially designed telescope used on Captain James Cook's 1769 expedition to Tahiti to record the transit of Venus. Watkins began his apprenticeship in 1737 with Nathaniel Adams, as well as others, and began operating under his own name in 1747 at the sign of Sir Isaac Newton's Head, 4/5 Charing Cross. He retired in 1784 and was succeeded by his two nephews. The business continued as a family run operation, until it was sold in 1856 to the Elliott family.

The identification of the Winchester sundial solely as Watkins argues for a date of manufacture of around 1780, which also fits stylistically with the instrument. It is an especially detailed and well-made example of a type known as a "London Sundial." Such sundials are typically set to latitude 51°30′ N, the latitude of London. The Winchester sundial is set to 51° - the latitude of Winchester and was therefore a custom order, specific to its location in a garden on Kingsgate Street opposite Winchester College.

The British Sundial Society record for it states that "it shows 4am to 8pm in Roman numerals, and is divided in 30, 15, 10, 5 and 2 minutes, and also, very unusually, to single and even half minutes". The design characteristics and quality of engraving is nearly identical to a London Sundial, dated 1812, made by Whitehead & Sons, London for a one located in Belper, Derby and thus set to latitude 53°03′ N.

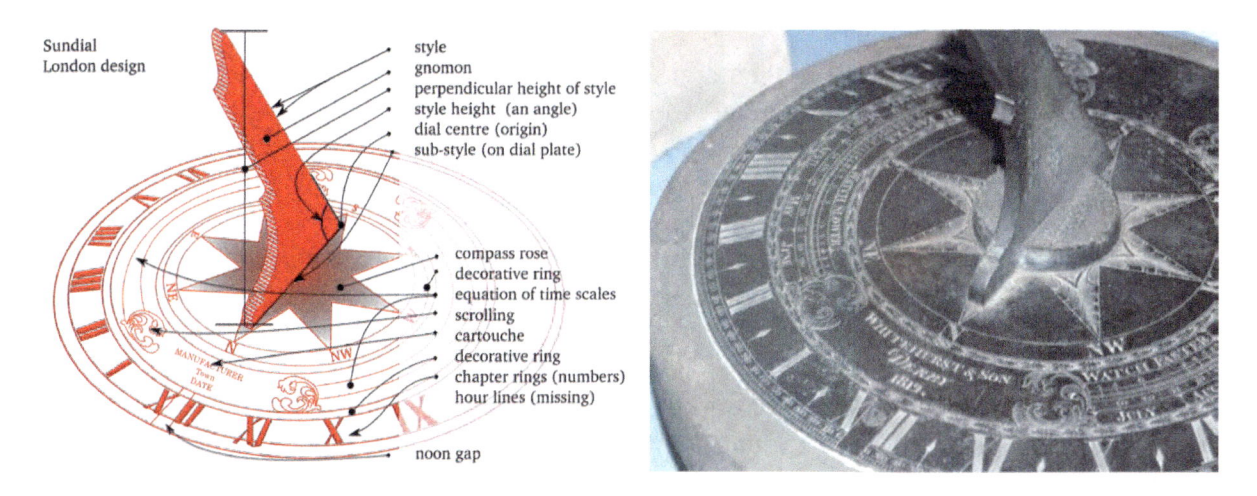

Figure 14: The design characteristics of a London Sundial and a photograph of an 1812 Whitehurst & Son of Derby sundial set for the town of Belper, Derbyshire. (courtesy of the Derby Museum and Art Gallery) It is included here because the dial of the similar Winchester sundial is nearly unreadable because of weathering.

Figure 15: Photographs of the Winchester College London Sundial in the old Sick House garden. (photographs of the Winchester sundial by Susan Foster, March 2021)

Part II: CLOCKS

The word "clock" is a derivative of the Latin work *clogga*, meaning bell. There are related words in many European languages that originate from the Low Countries, i.e. the Netherland, Flanders, and Luxembourg, resulting in the English word that came from Middle Low German and Middle Dutch. All of these early forms of clock mean bell.

In this book clock is used in the *horological* sense for a mechanical device use to keep time. Although several of the examples described here are electrically assisted, they all have significant mechanical components.

To a great extent the clocks, as well as the sundials, found at Winchester College represent a microcosm of the history of time keeping devices. The turret clock, in and of itself, with its many centuries of changes and improvements contains most of the key features found during the development of mechanical time measuring mechanisms.

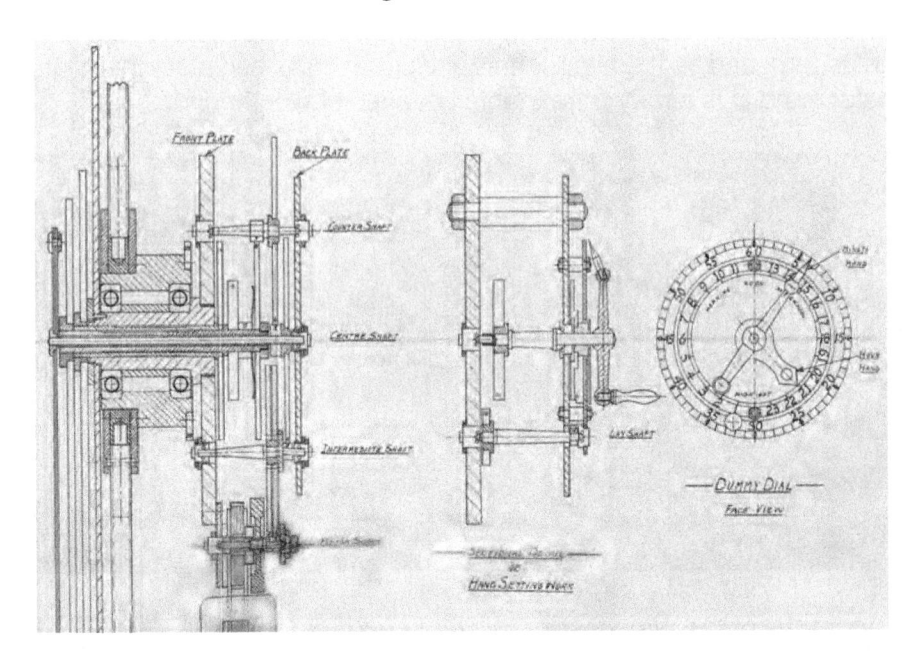

Figure 16: Sectional Detail and Hand Setting Work for the Winchester Empire Clock 1935, see Clock #12.

7. The Winchester College Turret Clock

The discussion that follows owes considerable debt to the research efforts of Winchester College Archivist Suzanne Foster, and the expert evaluation of the clock by Mr. Chris McKay. Both undertook the daunting task of climbing high into the chapel tower and maneuvering into tight and precarious spaces to allow for much of the information presented here.

Figure 17: The Winchester College turret clock from a photograph found in the notebook/scrapbook of Winchester scholar Charles Guy Stevens (1903-1955?) who was at the college from 1916 to 1922. The book contains his own photographs, a few commercial images, and others by friends, perhaps a boy named Robert Marston Deanesly (1904-1991). Note the clock's winding crank. (Winchester College Archives G255/1)

An Overview of the Clock's History

There has been a clock in the Winchester College Chapel Belfry for hundreds of years. The first reference to a College clock occurs in account records from 1403-04, and it seems likely that William Wykeham apparently made provision for the clock prior to that.

A review of College account records, along with a look at past College histories and documents, proved not as productive in clarifying the history of the clock as had been hoped. Herbert Chitty, Bursar of the College in the first quarter of the twentieth century, and an excellent historian of the College, wrote a comprehensive article on the bells: "The Winchester College Bells and Belfries" in proceedings of the Hampshire Field Club & Archaeological Society, Volume 9, Part 1, 1920 which is free of charge for download as a .pdf file on the Internet. This will prove of great interest to the campanologist and is the definitive work on the subject, but only refers to the clock in relation to the bells and chimes.

The following is chronological summary of what was found in the College muniments and in other material specific to the history of the subject clock and the tower in which it was/is installed:

1387   The Chapel and Tower foundation stone laid.

1395   The Chapel is consecrated, but not ready to be used.

1400   In William Wykeham's Statutes for the College (Rubric 29) there is a phrase for specific fixing the hour for matins by a clock in the Chapel, that reads:

. . . **interquartam et quintam pulsationem campane sive horologii pulsent ad Matutinas. . .**
. . . and that every day between the fourth and fifth strike of the bell or clock, they are to ring for Matins . . .

Figure 18: Winchester College Rubric 29, line 7, 1400. Winchester College Archive.

1402   The Chapel is completed and ready for full use.

1403-04   A turret clock is purchased and installed. Probably a gift of William of Wykeman, the year he died. Unfortunately there does not appear to be a record specifically describing the purchase, installation, or maker of the clock.

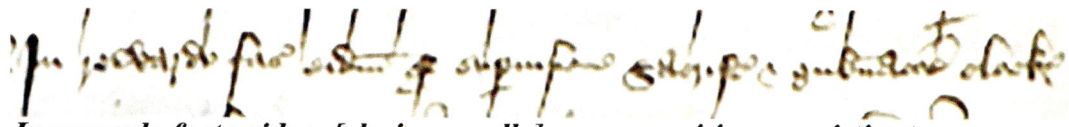

In rewardo facto eidem [clerico capelle] pro supervisione sacristie et guberhacione clockis.

In payment for the clerk of the chapel for survey of the room guberhacione(sic) clock.

Figure 19: Winchester College Account Roll 22087, 1403 to 1404 (2). (Winchester College Archive)

1409-10   Possible records pertaining to a clock, but the accounts are not clear.

1413-14   There is a possible record pertaining to a clock, however it is not clear.

1446-07   There is a statement in the accounts that relates to the purchase of cordage, as well as a wheel to ring a new bell, but nothing specifically to a clock.

1476-82   Work on a new Chapel Bell Tower is begun in 1476, about three years after construction of the Chantry had begun and was more than likely completed by 1481. This would have necessitated reinstallation of the clock, bells, and chimes. Unfortunately, the College accounts for this period are incomplete and those that do survive provide few details, nor do they mention a clock.

1498-99   This notation is for a payment of sixteen shillings to Wethym de Wyfe for the maintenance of the clock. It is not clear if this is meant to be the twelfth payment to him, or work over twelve weeks.

In solutis pro xii Wethym de Wyfe pro orolagio, xvid . . .
Payment 12 to Wethym de Wyfe for upkeep of the clock, £0.16 . . .

Figure 20: Winchester College Account Roll 22162, 1498 to 1499. (Winchester College Archive)

From the sixteenth century on, the College Accounts contain many references to a clock *(horologium),* besides the few which are listed here. These references all relate payment of a clerk/attendant for the clock's daily winding and calibration, quarterly oiling, and other adjustments. The fully wound clock would only run for 30 hours and would lose about 15 minutes a day, thus requiring constant observation and adjustment based on readings of a sundial once located above the Middle Gate opposite the clock tower. Accounts of 1644-45 refer to the clock being wound by choral staff *Queristers*, however at some unidentified later date this became the job of the College Porter. Perhaps the individual paid to wind the clock in recorded in the accounts of 1781-82 and 1783-84 was the Porter.

1501-02 This account is a record of payment to a smith, presumably a blacksmith, for repair of the clock.

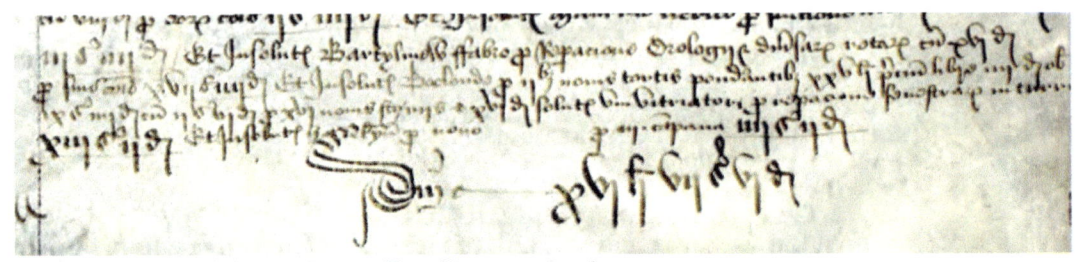

. . .Barthlmew fabro ad supellectilem orologia . . .
. . .Bartholomew, a smith for repairing the clock. . .

Figure 21: Winchester College Account Roll 22165, 1501 to 1502. (Winchester College Archive)

1578   The tenor bell, cast by John Cole in 1572, . . . *broke away from its moorings, and came hurtling like a bomb down through the clock chamber, the bell-ringers' chamber, and the vault of Thurbern's Chantry, bang onto the Chapel floor.* This implies that the clock was below the bell chamber, rather than above it, as it is today The repair of the bell is recorded in the College accounts of Custus Capelle 1578-79.

1644-45   These College accounts pertain to the maintenance of the Chapel and Bell Tower for an entire year, by term. They include specific references that *Clerks are to attend to the Chapel and keep the bells and clock* . . . The word for clock, *Horologÿ*, appears in the first and last line of these accounts.

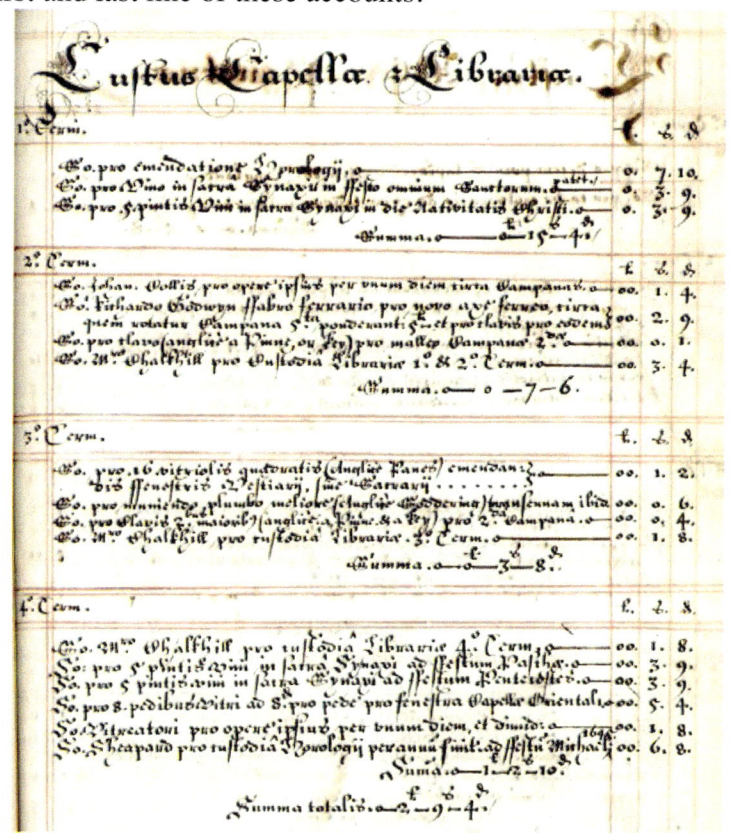

Figure 22: Winchester College Account Roll 22220, 1644 to 1645. (Winchester College Archive)

Warden John Harris (1588-1658), in 1645 during the period of the Civil War and the Commonwealth, was questioned about the functions of the choral staff. This staff was comprised of *Queristers,* a dozen or more boys, whose duties were to sing in Chapel, wait tables in College Hall, as well as serve as clerks running errands and various chores. They were selected from local boys and in return for their service and were eligible to receive a free education. The first clear reference to them comes in the Founder's Statutes of September 1400. Harris commented that the duties of the *Queristers* were as follows:

> *Their office is, to attend in the Chappell, to see it swept and kept cleane, to keep the bells and the clock and to wait upon the ffellowes at table.*

This indicates that one or more of these boys had the job of maintaining the clock, i.e. seeing that the time was correctly calibrated and that it was wound daily.

1646-47 The accounts for the third term of this year include £1.0.0 to a payment Powell for repair of the clock.

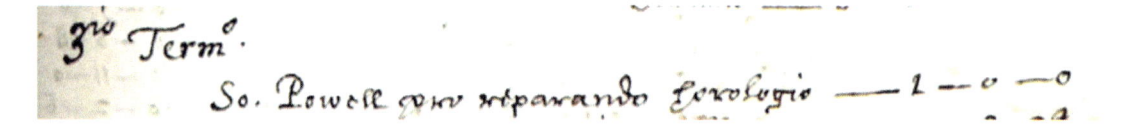

Figure 23: Winchester College Account Roll 22221, 1646 to 1647. (Winchester College Archive)

1660 During the fourth term of this year the clock was rebuilt and apparently reconfigured, using old parts in many places. In his 1892 book, *Annals of Winchester College*, T. A Kirby writes that: *It* [the College Clock] *exhausted the patience of the Society, and in the year 1660 it was replaced by the present clock, which, like its predecessor, has no face, and is wound daily.* This may well have been the time, describe later in this section, that the clock was converted to a pendulum and anchor escapement mechanism, as well as from a two-train to a three-train movement. This was a significant series of upgrades and would have essentially constituted a "replacement" of the clock.

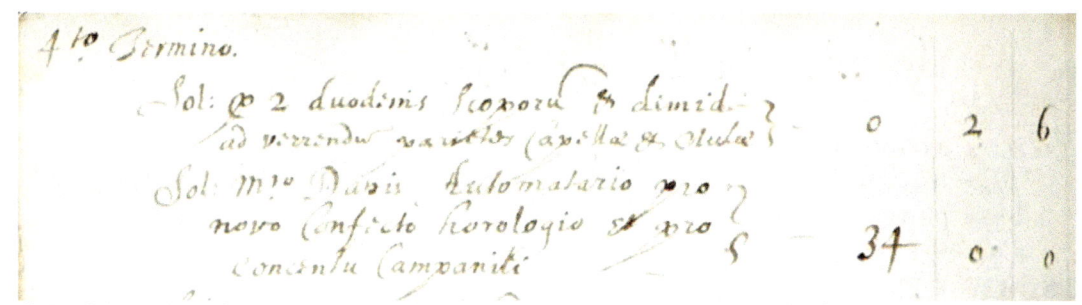

Sol. Msr. Davies automatario pro novo confedo horologio et pro concentu campanili xxxiiijll.

Payment to Messr. Davies clockmaker for the new [confedo ?] clock and bell chiming apparatus) and for the chimes of the belfry £34.

Figure 24: Winchester College Accounts 1659 to 1660. (Winchester College Archive)

1720   A report by Smith of Derby in 1998 during repair and maintenance work on the clock makes note of finding a date of 1720 on an unidentified part inside the clock. Unfortunately, this date was not relocated in a 2021 inspection.

1729-30   A payment of four guineas is made to a Thomas Holloway for work on the clock

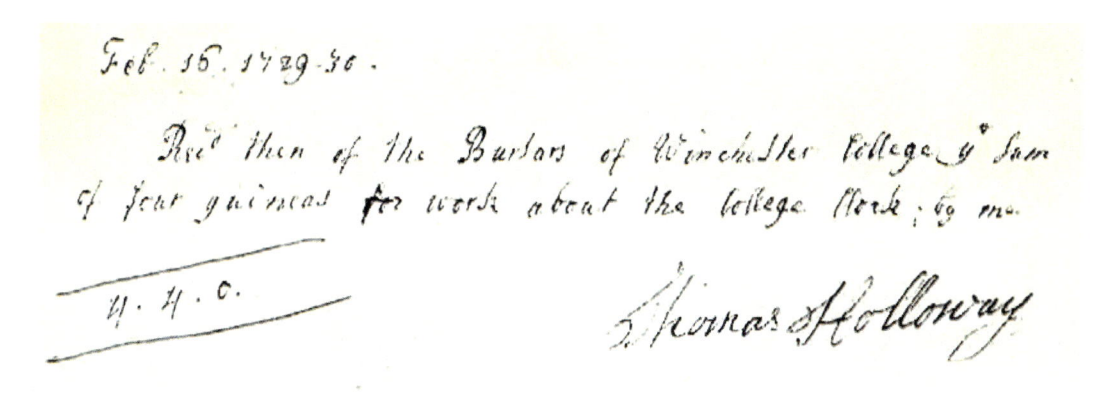

Figure 25: Winchester College Accounts 1729 to 1730. (Winchester College Archive)

1740 An Oxford mason, named Townsend, was paid £21 for his counsel and work on the tower which included iron ties to stabilize the Chapel and Tower.

1772 The Chantry is cut in half by a solid block of masonry built up to the vault between the bays, but the tower is still so insecure that the bells can't be rung and only the chimes are used from then on.

1781-82 Richard J. Lanfield paid William Lewes £7.7.0 for one years' daily winding of the clock.

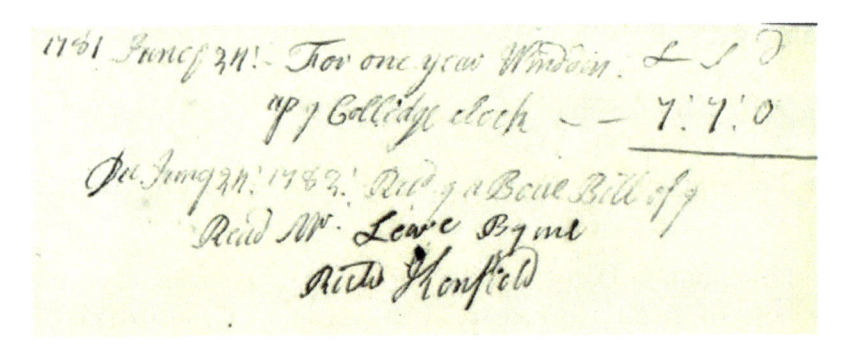

Figure 26: Winchester College Accounts 1781. (Winchester College Archive)

1782-83 Richard J. Lanfield paid William Blackston £7.7.0 for one years' daily winding of the clock.

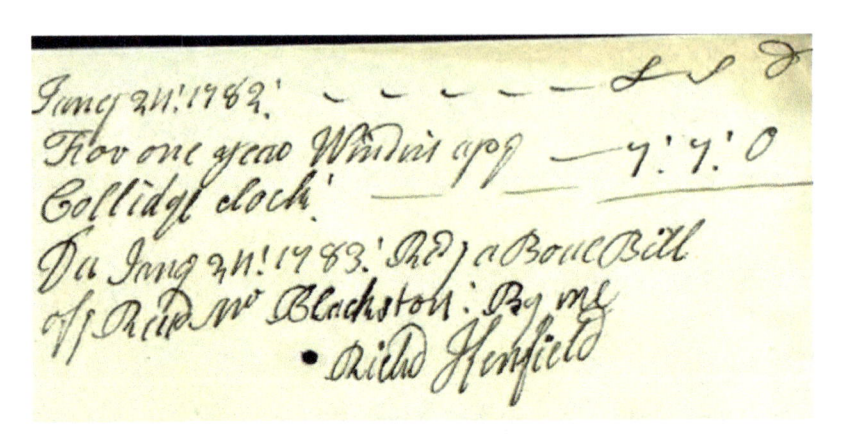

Figure 27: Winchester College Accounts 1782. (Winchester College Archive)

1807-18   Cleaning and repair work of the clock is made by Mr. J.E. Compton:
1807 for £6.16.6 entailing a new pully and frame for the striking mechanism, and repair to the hammers of the quarters.
1811 for £6.16.6 to clean the clock and put in new pins for the striking part of the hammers; and
1817-18 for £12.12.0 to cover one year's cleaning of the clock and repairing the striking, time and quarter parts, as well as replacing all of the wires that control the hammers.

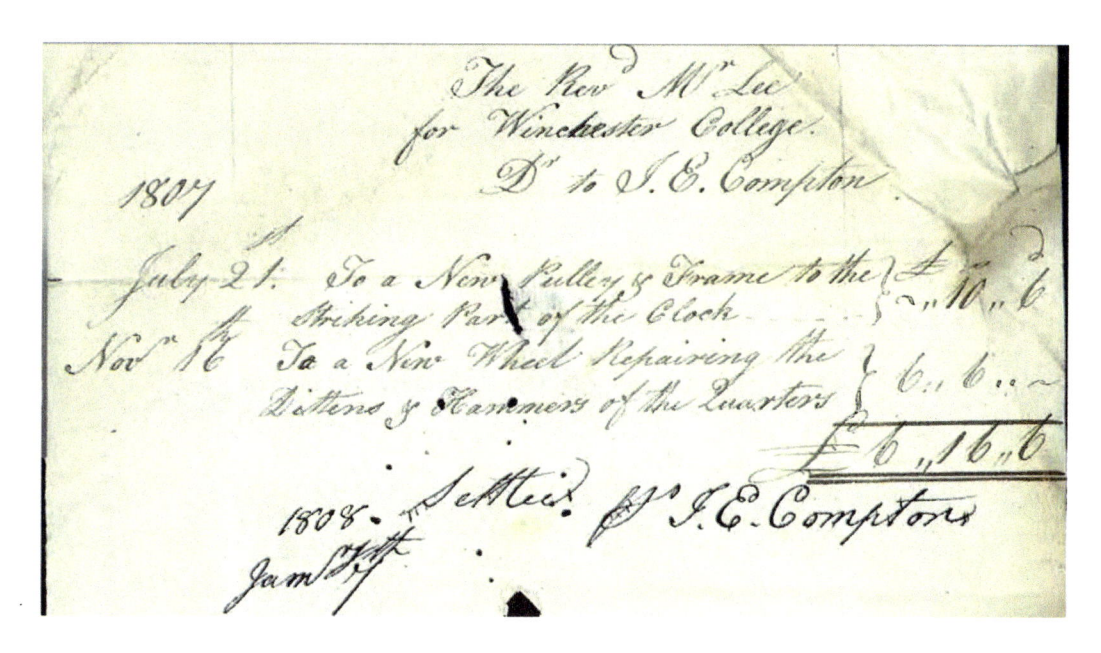

Figure 28: Winchester College Accounts 1807, Winchester College Archive.

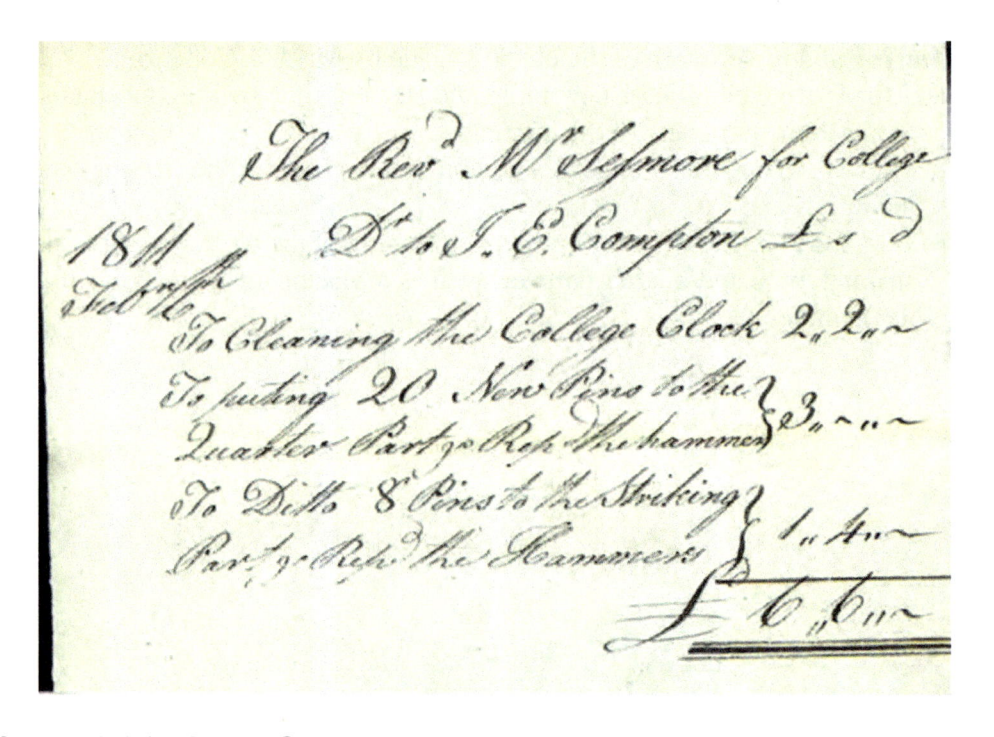

Figure 29: Winchester College Accounts 1811, Winchester College Archive.

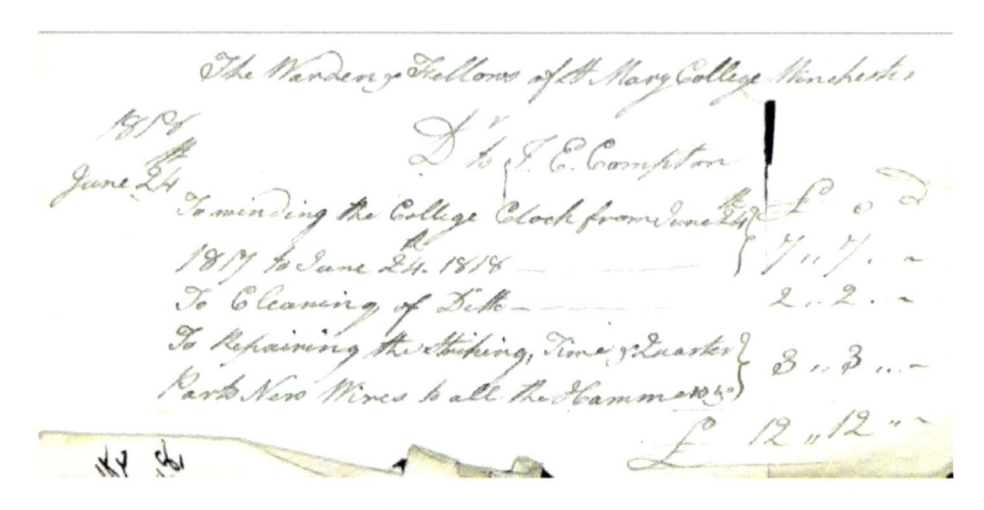

Figure 30: Winchester College Accounts 1818, Winchester College Archive.

1862-73 The impending failure of the Chapel Tower's foundation necessitated extensive work that was overseen by William Butterfield. This included the complete removal of the tower and its rebuilding with a concrete foundation and stone from Hartham Park, Bath, along with various other alterations and improvements. This work would have resulted in the reinstallation of the clock, bells, and chimes. The tower was hereafter known as the "Tower of the Two Wardens," in memory of Robert Speccott Barter (1790-1861), Warden of Winchester College and David Williams (1786-1860), Warden of New College, Oxford.

1879 *. . . The true explanation of the clock's irregularity in timekeeping is this. Besides the general debility which age and neglect have brought about, it has become, like many other antiquated institutions, clogged with the very oil intended to facilitate it's working. It requires a daily winding up, a daily correction of its tendency to lose time. On Sunday this takes place earlier than on weekdays, and, consequently, a good start must be given to the clock to enable it to last until winding time on Monday,* "The Wykehamist No. 136 - July 29, 1879, p. 292."

1927 The Chapel and Tower undergo extensive restoration and structural work. This work once again necessitating reinstallation of the clock, bells, and chimes.

1998 The clock is overhauled and modernized with electric motor driven winding mechanisms by Smith of Derby, a clockmaking firm founded in 1856.

The Bell Tower

Records summarized in the first part of this section show that the Chapel and Tower have been completely replaced twice, first between 1476 and 1481, and later between 1862 and 1873, as well as during a subsequent reconstruction begun in 1927.

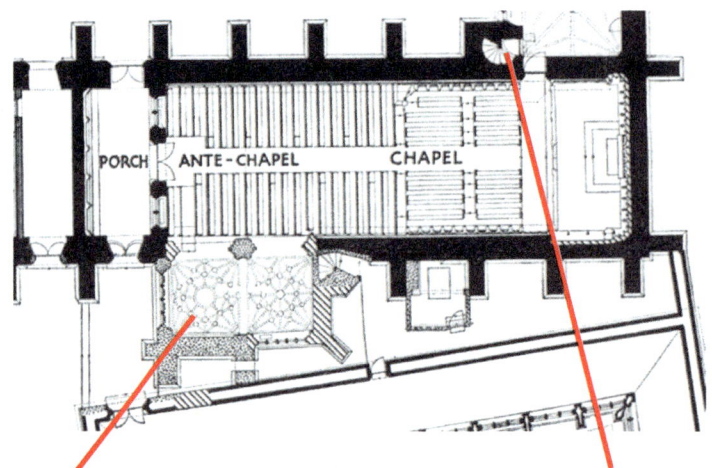

The Bell / Clock Tower above Thurburn's Chantry, the Muniment Tower and the Vestry.

Figure 31: Chapel from a 1954 plan of Winchester College by John H. Harvey and Donald W. Insall. (Satellite photograph of the Chapel, Google Earth, 2021)

The drawings presented as the following four figures are found in the 1926 publication: *Winchester College, its history buildings and customs* by the Winchester College Archaeological Society. They show the College as it appeared in 1404, 1675, 1838 and 1925, and clearly illustrate various changes to the exterior of the Chapel Tower over time.

Figure 32: Winchester College in 1404.

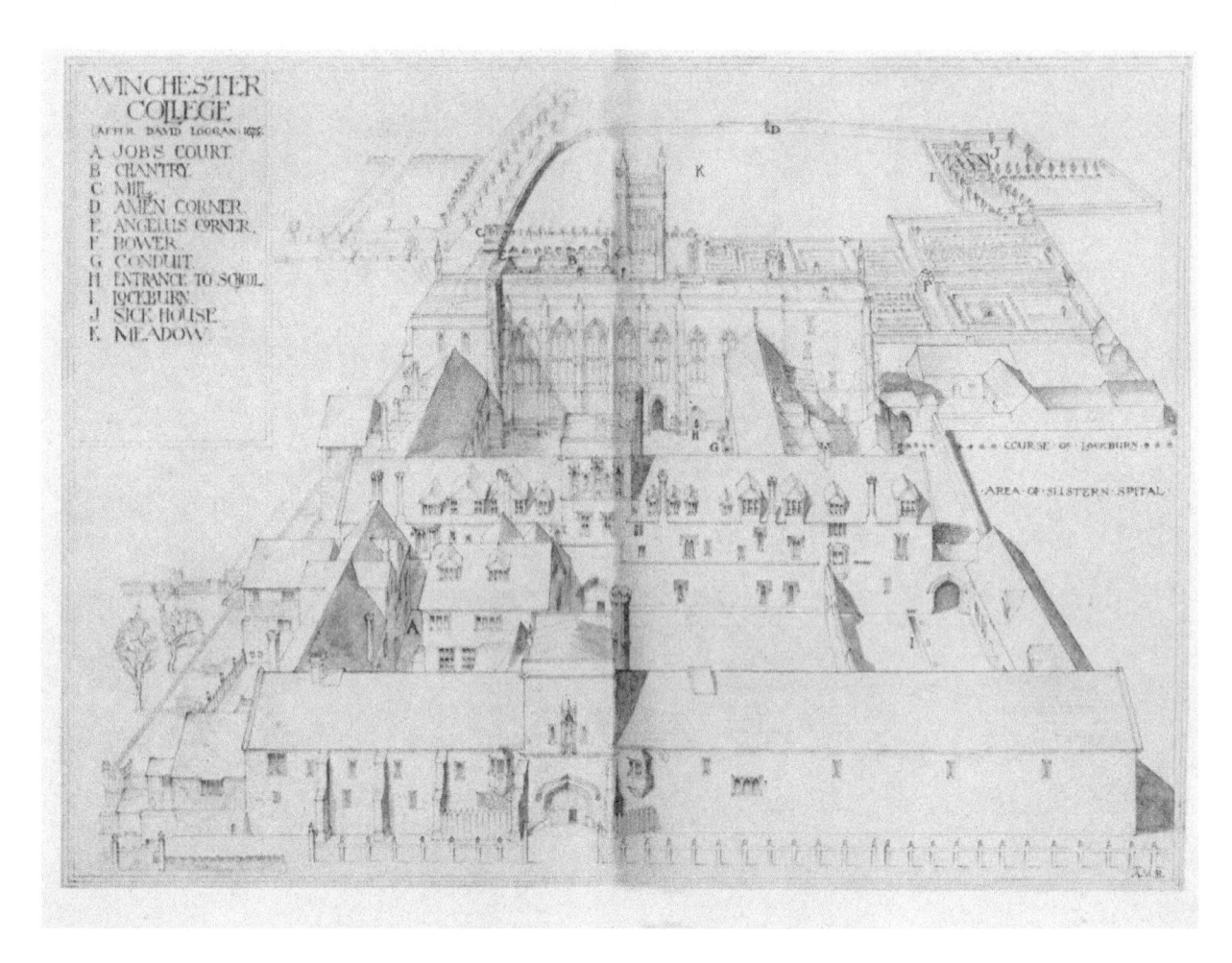

Figure 33: Winchester College in 1675.

Figure 34: Winchester College in 1838.

Figure 35: Winchester College in 1925.

A Description of the Turret Clock

The discussion which follows is the result of an inspection of the clock by a leading expert on British turret clocks, Mr. Chris McKay. His investigation revealed that the clock contains a mix of parts that were reused, and in some cases repurposed. Parts of the clock may well date to the sixteenth century, and there have been many repairs and improvements over the centuries. The result is a clock with a very complex history, reflecting well over 500 years of turret clock features and improvements.

The clock started life with a fairly large two train clock mechanism, with the trains placed end to end. It would have had a foliot with a verge escapement. A "train" is a grouping of interconnected gears serving a specific function, in this case striking bells or chimes, or regulating the hands of a clock.

The 1660 charge of £34 paid to a Mr. Davies, clockmaker is likely to have been for conversion of the clock from a two-train to a three-train movement. By comparison William Monk of Berwick St John supplied a three-train turret clock to Wimborne Minster, forty miles southeast of Winchester, in 1742, also at a cost of £42. Although 80 years later, inflation was small, so this remains a good comparison.

The name Davies may be a reference to a well-known clockmaking family of Windsor. There were three generations of Davis clockmakers, all with the given name John, while the senior John's father, William was the King's blacksmith at Windsor Castle. However, the Winchester College reference to Davies in the accounts of 1659-60 predates the earliest known Davis family clockmaker, John Davis (1650-1713), who is known to have been apprenticed to Daniel Quare in 1685 and was active in the clockmaking trade until 1709.

Keith Scobie-Youngs, Director of the Cumbria Clock Company, thought it more likely that conversion of the Winchester clock might be the work of Thwaites. Although Thwaites & Reed was not established until 1740, antecedents to the company date from 1610 based on records that have now been lost. Unfortunately, the College records shed no more light on the seventeenth century work on the turret clock, other than that Mr. Davies was paid for it. Perhaps he was an independent contractor.

The invention of the pendulum did not come to England until 1660, so it is unlikely that the new Winchester clock would have had a pendulum. But, if Davis was involved with Windsor Castle and hence the monarch, it is possible that the Winchester clock could have been a very early installation with a pendulum. Clocks before 1660 had a foliot as the time keeping element, a weighted horizontal arm driven by a verge escapement. [The "verge" (or crown wheel) "escapement" is the earliest known type of mechanical escapement, the mechanism in a mechanical clock that controls its rate by allowing the gear train to advance at regular intervals or 'ticks.']

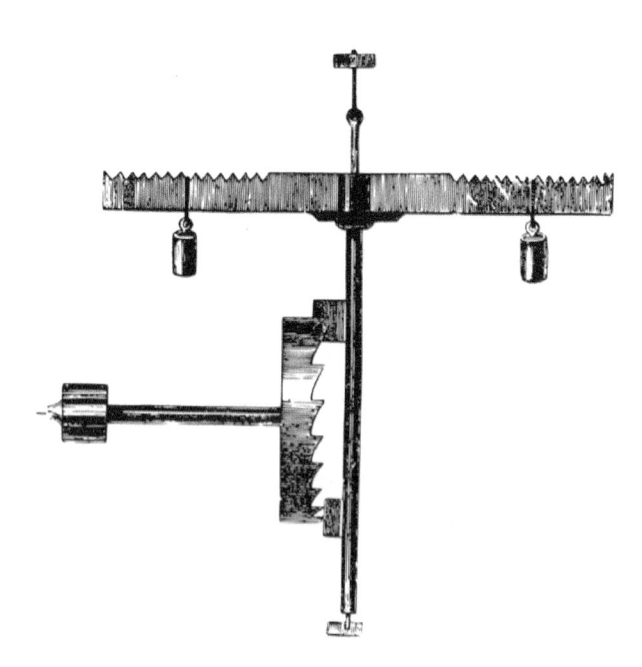

Figure 36: Verge and foliot escapement from the De Vick tower clock, built in Paris in 1379 by Henri de Vick. The Winchester would originally have had a similar regulating mechanism.

At some point in time, perhaps during the work in 1660, the Winchester clock was converted to a pendulum movement with an anchor escapement, a quarter train was added, and the frame re-built to accommodate three trains situated side-by-side. A date of 1720, as found by Smith of Derby in 1998, may reflect when these significant changes were made. In addition, there is no doubt that additional repairs and alterations were carried out in the late eighteenth and nineteenth centuries.

Figure 37: The Turret Clock in 2021, encased in a wooden case on a high balcony. Note the pendulum hanging below the balcony. Photographs by Suzanne Foster, March 2021.

The current clock is a three-train movement striking the hours and a ting-tang sound to denote the quarters on two bells. The frame is wrought iron and the trains are arranged side-by-side in the manner adopted by clockmaker William Clement (1638-1704) in his turret clock of 1671.

Figure 38: The Winchester College Turret Clock. Photographs by Suzanne Foster, March 2021.

The current escapement is a recoil anchor type, with the pallet nibs in the style developed by Thwaites, i.e. one is convex and the other is concave. Thwaites & Reed, is located 80 miles southeast of Winchester near Brighton have been making clocks since the founding of predecessor companies, perhaps as early as 1610, and are considered the oldest clock makers in the world.

Figure 39: Anchor/recoil escapement. Pallet nibs are the ends of the pallets that engage the gear teeth. Photograph by Chris McKay, May 2021.

There is no doubt that the Winchester clock is, to a great extent, a collection of recycled parts. The corner posts are very plain with a simple flat ball finial, with some unused holes indicating they have been reworked. The end cross bars have holes in their centres that indicate the movement would have started life as an end-to end movement, that would be pre-pendulum configuration, i.e. likely before 1660. In all the wheelwork is of mixed ages, with some wheels made of iron and some of brass from the period 1710-30. Brass wheels are on the going (i.e. main power mechanism) and hour strike mechanisms, while the iron wheels are on the quarter hour striking train.

Figure 40: l. Holes and notches in a side bar showing it has been reconfigured and r. rectangular slots in the end cross bars indicating a reconfiguration of the movement. The simple ball finials topping the corner posts are clearly visible, as is the top of the balcony railing at the left. The electric motors, installed in 1998 at the top of the frame allows for the clock to be wound automatically without having to use a hand crank. Photographs by Suzanne Foster, March 2021.

Notches on the main-movement/going-train mounting bar indicate there was once something else attached here, probably the potence, i.e. a support piece, for the verge. The brass wheel that is part of the hour strike mechanism was once a solid wheel without spokes, called a hoop wheel. All train mounting bars have unused holes. On the minutes setting dial, the engraving is in the style used in the 18th century. Unused holes in the going centre wheel are probably for a pin to operate an hour release lever.

Figure 41: The minutes setting dial and holes in the centre wheel. Photograph by Suzanne Foster, March 2021.

The clock was a 30-hour movement and would run for a day, hence the reason for adding automatic winders by Smith of Derby in 1998. Smiths reported a date of 1720 on the clock; however this has not been found but such a date could be on a part replaced at that date and in a place difficult to see. The automatic winders on the second wheels are not permitted by UK heritage bodies in 2021. When the winders need to be replaced, the drive should be changed to be on the barrels.

To completely unravel the history of this clock is difficult; although access is reasonable, viewing is very difficult as the gallery is so narrow and close to the clock case. A more complete survey would involve dismantling the clock, and possibly stripping off paint to see where ironwork had been modified. But that is a job for another day

Figure 42: The view from the clock balcony looking down at the bells and the spire on the roof. (Photographs by Suzanne Foster, March 2021)

8. Longcase Clocks

Much of the information pertaining to the Winchester Longcase Clocks comes from Mr. Lewis Walduck of The Clock Workshop, King's Worthy, Hampshire who services and maintains these clocks.

A Longcase clock, commonly referred to as a grandfather clock was, for nearly three hundred years, been an important accoutrement of an English home. Typically found in a residential setting, a mark of its importance is that it, along with the house and bed, is nearly always mentioned in a will. There are two exceptionally fine longcase clocks at Winchester College, both of which are gifts and that had originally been in residential settings. Only a brief overview of these clocks, to reflect their inclusion as part of the College's collection of horological instruments, will be presented here. The subject of longcase clocks is complicated with numerous variations in style and manufacture. Their popularity over the years has led to equally numerous collectors and specialists. An excellent survey of styles and types is found in Derek Robert's book *British Longcase Clocks,* Schiffer Publishing, Ltd., 1990.

The following is a brief overview of longcase clocks to place them in context with the other timekeeping devices discussed in this book. In all cases a longcase clock is a tall freestanding weight-driven pendulum clock. They are classified into two types: those measuring six foot, 3-inches and over being called grandfather clocks and those under six foot, 3-inches called grandmother clocks.

This type of clock owes its development to the invention of the anchor escapement claimed by British scientist Robert Hooke about 1657 and used by William Clement in his invention of the longcase clock about 1680. A more accurate variation of this escapement was invented in about 1675 by Richard Towneley, although it was not incorporated into longcase clocks until the early eighteenth century.

Longcase clocks typically have eight-day movements, a key factor in the development of the longcase clock, in that a longer fall from the movement drive weights allows for a longer period of operation. In addition, anchor escapement allows for a narrower clock since the arch of the pendulum was greatly reduced from 80°- 100° down to 4° to 6°.

The earliest clocks were made of oak and soft woods that facilitated marquetry as seen in the Winchester William II clock, while post-1750 clocks typically have mahogany cases.

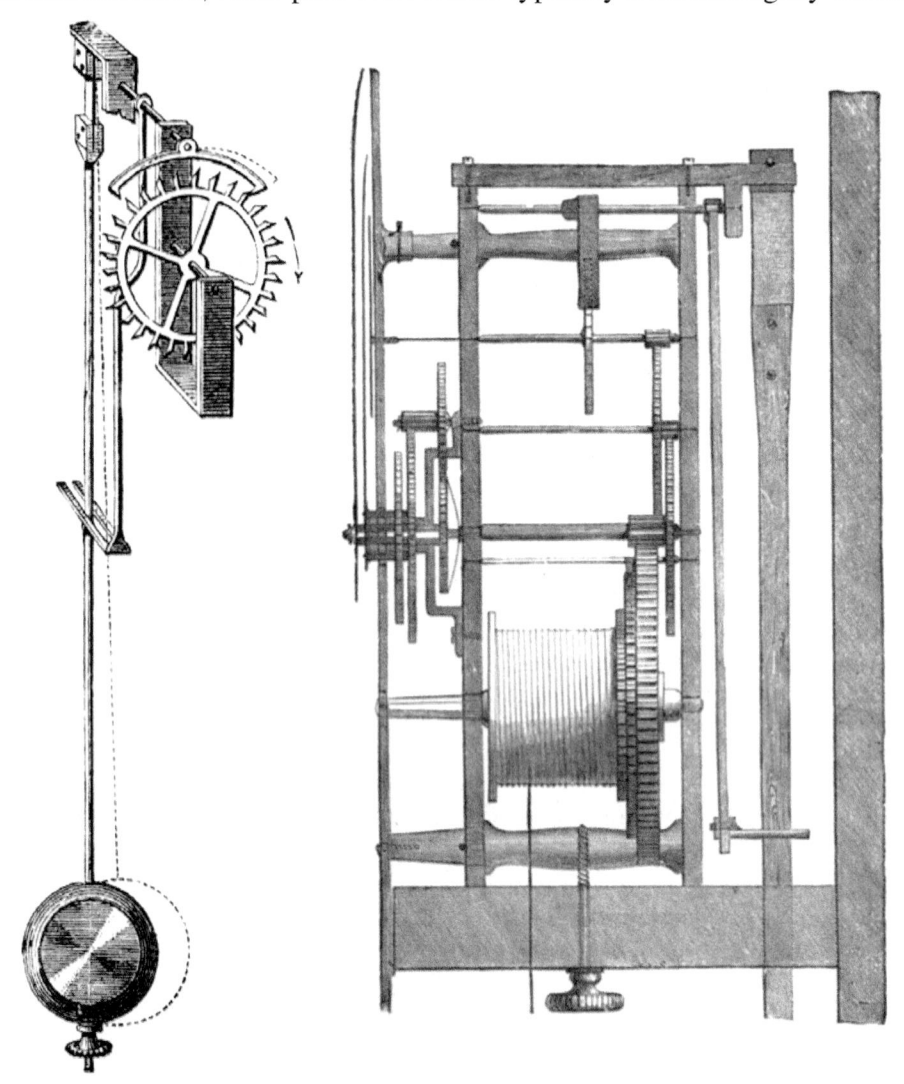

Figure 43: Long case clock anchor escapement, pendulum, and internal mechanism (*Watch and Clock Maker's Handbook* by F.J. Britten, E.F. Spoon, London 1896).

William III Longcase Clock - 1695

This clock is located in the entrance hall of the Warden's Lodgings and is dated and identified on the inside as having been made by William Carr, an obscure, lesser-known London clock maker. It is a fine example of an early clock of the "golden age."

The original escapement has been replaced and converted to a larger more standard size. This was due to wear and would have taken place in the early 19th century. With the exception of the escapement the rest of the movement is probably original.

The case is a great example of an early marquetry longcase, however the hood, i.e. the top part of the clock which houses the mechanism and dial, is not contemporary with the clock and has been taken off of another, probably later clock. A tell-tale sign of this is that the dial is a lot bigger than the hood and the marquetry is a different style and colour from the rest of the case.

The clock was donated to the College by Major Malcolm Robertson (1882-1956), a College don known as "The Bobber." He was first appointed to the College staff in 1905, and except for a period during WWI, taught there until 1946. He was also a housemaster from 1920-1943. He was especially interested in archaeology and natural history, as well as being a supporter and patron of music.

Figure 44: Major Malcolm Robertson "The Bobber" (1882-1956), c.1920. (Winchester College Archives)

Figure 45: William III longcase Clock - 1695. (photographs by Suzanne Foster, 2021)

This clock is located in the drawing room of the Warden's Lodgings. It was a gift from a former Warden (1904-1915), Lord Kenneth Muir Mackenzie (1845 - 1930). It is identified on its face as being made by Jean Gruchy (? - 1783) of Jersey, a well-known maker. The date is found on a label inside the clock. A number of Gruchy clocks survive, most with mahogany cases, typical of the period, as is the arched brass dials showing phases of the moon. All of his clocks date from between 1750 to 1780.

The Winchester Clock appears to be complete, and apparently has its original movement.

Figure 46: George II longcase Clock - c.1760. (photographs by Suzanne Foster, 2021)

9. Synchronome-Shortt Free Pendulum Clocks

Figure 47: The Synchronome-Shortt Free Pendulum Clock #61 at Winchester College, with its battery of *six* Leclanché Cells to the right. (Winchester College, 2021)

Figure 48: l. The main dial with hours, minutes, and seconds above, and the free pendulum dial subsidiary dial below; r. the pressure gage for the free pendulum vacuum chamber. (Winchester College, 2021)

Shortt Clock at the Science Museum [Nature Magazine - April 1935]
A SHORTT free pendulum clock has recently been installed at the Science Museum, South Kensington, London, and is now at work controlling the main public dials of the Museum. The Shortt clock was perfected by Mr. W.H. Shortt in 1921 as a result of a long period of experimental work in association with Mr. F. Hope-Jones and the Synchronome Company; the first clock was set up at the Edinburgh Royal Observatory in 1921, and Prof. R.A. Sampson's report on its first year's run aroused great interest among astronomers, as it had proved to have surpassed all previous clocks in its accuracy. A Shortt clock was adopted as the sidereal standard at Greenwich at the beginning of 1925, and has proved itself capable of measuring time to an accuracy of a few thousandths of a second per day, or better than 1 in 10^7 [The initial estimates showed the clock to be accurate to about one second per year, while measurements of a Short Clock in 1984 found it to be accurate within about one second in twelve years!] *The clock now exhibited in the Science Museum is identical with these observatory clocks except that the usual exhausted copper case for the free pendulum is replaced by a dust-tight glass cylinder: the clock is mounted on the wall of a public gallery with its slave* [i.e. subsidiary] *clock by its side. The delicate method of imparting an impulse to the free pendulum and the action of the hit-and-miss synchroniser can thus be studied in detail.*

Synchronome-Shortt Free Pendulum Clocks are extremely accurate timekeepers. Many sources refer to it as the most accurate pendulum clock ever made. However, there is an even more accurate regulator clock that was invented in 1952 in the Soviet Union by Feodosii Mikhailovich Fedchenko (1911-1989). The Fedchenko ACHF-3 clock, was a significant invention in and of its own right, and quite different than the Shortt clock, beyond having a pendulum in a tank. This phenomenally accurate and robust clock worked well in remote places, running on a small battery for many years, and was not subject to potential electromagnetic interference in the event of a nuclear attack.

The final advances in pendulum clock regulation were superseded by quartz crystal clocks in the 1940s, and even more accurate atomic clock in the 1950s, the exception being the Fedchenko ACHF-3. But from the 1920s until the early 1950s Shortt Clocks were the most accurate mechanical / pendulum time devices made. Only *one hundred and one of these clocks were made, all by the Synchronome Co., Ltd. of London. Suddenly the accuracy of time measurements was increased to about one millisecond a day, and it was not long before astronomical observatories all over the world made use of this system. The first one was installed in the Royal*

Observatory, Edinburgh in 1922, By 1926 time signals from Shortt No. 3, installed at the Greenwich Observatory, were adopted as the standard for sidereal time. Shortt clocks were key components for scientific research and were the principal clocks used for the national time dissemination services. It was the first clock to detect minute seasonal changes in the earth rotation rate, thus being a more accurate timekeeper than the earth itself.

The Shortt Clock at Winchester College is Number 61 and was made in 1923. The records maintained by H.E. Jones, the chief engineer responsible for the fabrication of the clocks, transcribed in R.H. Miles *Synchronome: Masters of Electrical Timekeeping* (AHS: London, 2011) show it was delivered in June 1937 to H. R. Fry in Chichester. This was his second Shortt clock, as he had obtained No 40 in 1931.

Henry Reginald Fry (1876-1950) was an accomplished amateur clock maker, cutting the gear wheels in his own workshop, as well as being elected a Fellow of the Royal Astronomical Society. He took a science degree at King's College, Cambridge and for thirty years was a partner and director of Barclay and Fry, Ltd., printers and box makers, a firm founded by his father in 1855.

H.E. Jones's records show that No. 61 was lent to Greenwich for use at the Magnetic Observatory, in Abinger, Surrey in 1940 and that it was returned to Fry in 1946. The facility at Abinger was originally established in 1924 because magnetic interference from local trains was anticipated to compromise scientific observations of magnetic fields and electro-magnetic instruments devices such as the Shortt Clock.

Just prior to World War II, Station "A" at Abinger was built to protect the national timing resources from the pending war. In addition to several Shortt Clocks, there was a celestial observatory with a 'transit instrument' to calibrate the clocks. All of the works were in temperature and vibration-controlled buildings. Following the London Blitz, Abinger became the source of the 'Greenwich' Time Signal. By the end of the War there were 12 even more accurate quartz clocks at Abinger, however the BBC time pips were still based on Shortt clocks until 1949, including the one now at Winchester College.

Shortly before his death H.R. Fry was admitted to the Worshipful Company of Clockmakers. He left his fine collection of precision clocks to his nephew, Mr. Cecil Fry of Bristol. Neither he, nor his nephew, seem to have had any direct connection with Winchester College and exactly when and why his Shortt clock came to be installed there is not known.

How the Shortt Clocks Work

Background information pertaining to this clock is included as Appendix A. This type of clock kept time with two pendulums: a primary pendulum swinging in a copper vacuum tank; and a secondary, called a subsidiary, pendulum in a separate clock, which was synchronized to the primary by an electric circuit and electromagnets. The subsidiary pendulum essentially did all the work, using a mechanism that both maintained its own operation but also that of the primary pendulum using an extraordinarily elegant system of impulsing, leaving the primary pendulum free of external disturbances. To prevent any possibility of coupling between the pendulums, the two units needed to be installed far apart in different rooms, or oriented so the planes of swing of the two pendulums were ninety degrees apart.

The subsidiary clock was a modified version of a standard Synchronome precision regulator clock. It was linked to the primary clock by wires which carried electric pulses that operated a hit-and-miss synchroniser each 30 seconds, thereby keeping the secondary pendulum locked to the frequency of the free pendulum. The secondary pendulum was rated to run slower than the free pendulum. For thirty seconds its rate would be behind that of the free pendulum. With the next synchronising pulse its rate would move ahead of the free pendulum, and then fall back over the next two cycles, before being synchronised again, hence hit-and-miss. The closeness of the rate of the two pendulums was sufficient that over short intervals the seconds impulses generated by the secondary clock could be used for observatory purposes.

Residual thermal expansion rates were compensated to zero with a bimetal insert. The vacuum tank with the primary pendulum was evacuated by a hand-operated pump; the vacuum being needed to prevent changes in atmospheric pressure affecting the rate of the pendulum, and also to greatly reduce aerodynamic drag on the pendulum.

Both pendulums are about one meter long, with a period of two seconds. The pendulums received a push once every thirty seconds to keep them swinging. The secondary clock has two clock dials on it, showing the time kept by each pendulum, to verify that they were synchronized. It also had electrical terminals which produced a timing signal. Wires could be attached to these to transmit the clock's ultra-accurate time signal to clocks in other cities or broadcast it by radio.

Power for the clock was provided by Leclanché Cells, a wet cell battery invented by French scientist Georges Leclanché in 1866. The battery consists of a conducting solution of ammonium chloride, a carbon positive terminal/cathode, an oxidizer of manganese dioxide, and a negative terminal/anode of zinc. These batteries proved useful for telegraphy, signaling and for electric bells. An individual cell was very low voltage, providing only about 1.4 volts, so a bank of six cells was necessary to provide the power boost to keep the Shortt clock pendulums operating and send time signals.

William Hamilton Shortt (1881 - 1971)

Shortt was a British railway engineer, noted horologist and director of the Synchronome Co Ltd. In 1921 he devised a system to keep two pendulums in precise synchronization (U.K. Patent No. 187814). This invention made possible the design of his synchronome free pendulum clock. His work on clocks derived from investigations on the safety of train travel and the accurate measurement of train speeds, following investigations into a fatal train derailment in 1906.

Shortt was born in Wimbledon, Surrey and worked for the London and South Western Railway (LSWR) from 1902, until 1916 when he joined the Army as a captain in the Royal Engineers in France. In 1919, he left the army and he returned to his experimental work, producing a series of clocks in which he continued to try new ways of delivering an impulse to the pendulum, while attempting to make the pendulum do as little work as possible. The theoretical ideal was a pendulum operating freely in a vacuum and doing no work.

Shortt was honoured for his work in horology and precision timekeeping with the Gold Medal from the British Horological Institute in 1931 and was inducted into its Fellowship in 1932. He was also awarded the John Price Wetherill Medal from the Franklin Institute of Philadelphia, Pennsylvania in 1935, and the Tompion Medal of the Worshipful Company of Clockmakers in 1954.

Frank Hope-Jones (1867–1950)

Hope-Jones was a British horologist who collaborated closely with Shortt beginning in 1910. He was born in Eastham, Wirral Peninsula, and became interested in electrical apparatus after assisting his elder brother Robert in the design and construction of electric organs. Frank moved into the field of electric clocks and was a founding member of the Synchronome Syndicate Company of London in 1897. Shortt joined the successor Synchronome Company at its incorporation in 1912.

Hope-Jones was also interested in timekeeping via radio signals. He was highly influential in the promulgation of wireless technology, urging the authorities to permit renewed wireless transmissions, following a wartime ban. He also suggested to the BBC that they should transmit a time signal and in 1924 the Greenwich pips were first broadcast.

Figure 49: l. William Hamilton Shortt; r. Frank Hope-Jones; courtesy of Dr. James Nye, Antiquarian Horological Society (AHS).

Figure 50: Advertisement for the Shortt Clock, from *The Horological Journal,* March 1928. (internet archives 2021)

10. Science School Magneta / Brillié Controlling Clock

In the Winchester College Science School is an electrically maintained pendulum controlling clock. The clock was obtained in September 1912, based on a note referring to the purchasing of clocks, bells and Leclanché wet cell batteries in William Bleaden Croft's scrapbook [no.8, p.64, Winchester Science School.] College records (Item No: A0823) identify the clock as having been made by the Martin Fischer, Zurich, Switzerland with the inscription *Magneta dictograph electric London* on the dial. This is a perfectly logical identification based on the inscriptions on the clock. However, as Dr. James Nye of the Antiquarian Horological Society (AHS), a historian of electrical horology and founder of the Clockworks Museum, London notes, the overt identification of this clock is completely misleading. *Magneta* is reflective of licensing and marketing agreements, while the clock was in fact made by *Brillié Master Clocks*, France. The identification of Martin Fischer, Zurich is probably due to the *Magneta* Company's early association with this inventor, however Fischer was not involved with the subject clock.

It has a half-second period pendulum made of Invar, a nickel-iron alloy with a very low thermal expansion. A horse-shoe shaped magnet functions as the bob, with one pole passing through an electromagnet, and with a brass sphere above, which is mounted on a threaded part of the rod and is used to regulate the clock. By becoming alternately magnetized and de-magnetized by a semi-rotation, it actuates an inductor, thus generating a momentary current, which passes into a circuit that is instantly sent down a wire to subsidiary clocks, thus giving them an impulse, which takes place synchronously with the movement of the inductor. In this way the time/bells of several subsidiary clocks around the building are all perfectly synchronized.

The clock mechanism is mounted on a marble slab for rigidity, as is typical of Brillié controlling clocks. Wires run in channels cut in the marble to protect and isolate them.

The mechanism is the invention of Lucien Brillié (1865-1911). The first Brillié clock of the type found at Winchester College appeared around 1908 and was made for the Paris Observatory (Observatoire de Paris). This clock was developed by Lucien and his brother Henri, along with Charles le Roy, based on a clock design by the French physicist Charles Féry. The shape of Féry's magnet was changed to provide a more uniform magnetic field and is found in later Brillié clocks.

Lucien Brillié, with his friend Charles Vigreux (1861-1908), founded the *Société en Nom Collectif (SNC) Charles Vigreux et Lucien Brillié* in Levallois, France in 1898. On the death of Vigreux,

Lucien, joined by his brother Henri, reorganized the company into the *Société anonyme des Ateliers (SNC) Brillié Frères*. When Lucien died in 1911, Henri continued, and the *Société Magneta* became a shareholder and distributed Brillié clocks in the Paris region, and in many French departments. The United Kingdom iterations of *Magneta*, however they were organized, rebranded *Brillié* clocks which were sold throughout the United Kingdom, as well as to countries around the world. In 1912/13 the French company's name changed to the *Société anonyme des Ateliers (SA) Brillié Frères*, the name that the company would maintain in France until the end of its existence in 1981.

The inscription *Magneta dictograph electric* is interesting. *Magneta* is a plural adjective simply meaning magnetic. *Dictograph* is a term trademarked in the United States in 1920 by Kelly Monroe Turner for his *Dictograph Products Company* which manufactured an audio transmission system, often confused with Edison's *Dictaphone*, a wax cylinder dictation machine. In this case, the term apparently refers just to the transmission of a signal sent down a wire. *Electric* is obvious but serves to differentiate this clock from controlling clocks operated by a purely mechanical system, i.e. a spring or weights, with only the subsidiary clocks activated by an electromagnet.

Unfortunately, none of the subsidiary clocks from Winchester College appear to have survived. But it is most fortunate that the controlling clock does still exist, as it is an especially early example of its type.

Figure 51: Lucien Brillié (1865-1911), http://www.janinetissot.fdaf.org/jt_brillié.htm.

Figure 52: Science School *Magneta/Brillié* Controlling Clock. (photograph by Suzanne Foster, April 2021)

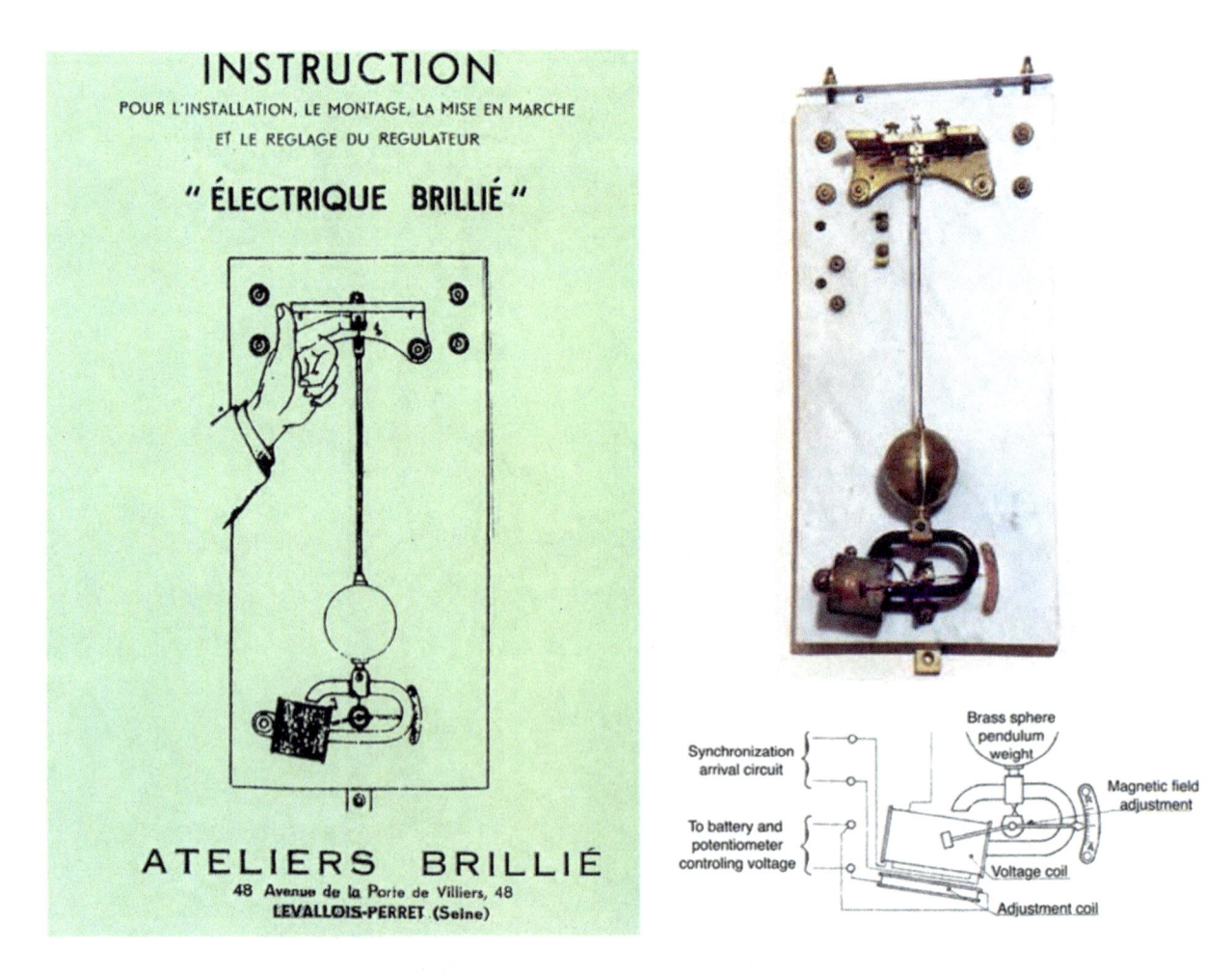

Figure 53: *Magneta/Brillié* instruction manual and description. (l. www.paulhageman.nl/brillie and r. www.mridout.force9.co.ik/ecw/brillie)

11. Sewills PendulumClock

A plaque at the base of this clock reads:

> *This regulator clock was commissioned*
> *to hang in Winchester College Science School in perpetuity*
> *to celebrate 69 years of Gregorian teaching.*
> *July 1999*

Martin Gregory taught physics from 1962 to 1999, and his wife, Jennifer, taught Biology from 1969 to 1999, when they both retired. In commemoration of their many years of service to Winchester College, a Sewills of Liverpool pendulum clock was permanently hung in the Science School.

The clock's enamel dial is inscribed "Sewills Liverpool," with medal prizes from the mid-nineteenth century, and is identified as an "Observatory Regulator Compensation Pendulum clock". It is a now rare eight-day wall clock, manufactured sometime in the late nineteenth or early-twentieth century and is one of the most accurate solely mechanical clocks ever produced. The clock has a precision striking mechanism, twin weight-driven eight-day movement, and a full regulator multi-dial showing seconds, minutes, and hours. It is in a mahogany frame case, with a thick beveled edge glass door, through which the dial, weights and pendulum can be seen working.

The mechanism makes use of a "dead-beat escapement" (i.e. a type that eliminates recoil of the escape wheel as it moves back and forth) , as well as having a compensated pendulum (i.e. a pendulum made of more than one type of metal that remains the exact same length regardless of changes of temperature.)

Joseph Sewill was a Liverpool clock and watchmaker. The business he founded flourished under his direct control from 1853 to 1856 and operated under the Sewill name well into the twentieth century. The company dominated production of precision marine instruments and chronometers for the British maritime industry.

Winchester College is fortunate to have such a beautiful high quality pendulum clock that fits neatly between the technology of their earlier seventeenth / eighteenth century longcase pendulum clocks and the extraordinarily accurate 1923 Shortt-Synchronome Clock.

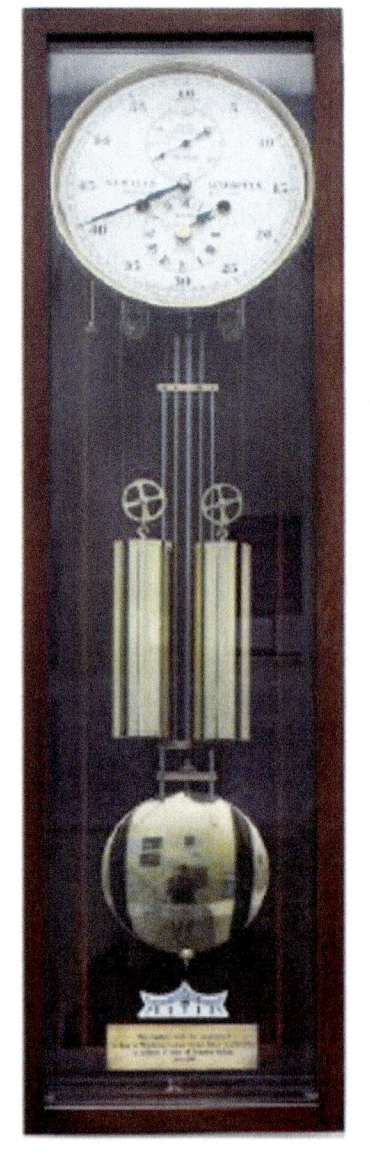

Figure 54: Sewills of Liverpool, Observatory Regulator Compensation Pendulum clock in the Winchester College Science School. (photograph by Suzanne Foster, 2021)

12. Empire Clock

Figure 55: The Empire Clock in the Winchester College Moberly Library. (photograph by Suzanne Foster, February 2021)

A large, dramatic clock, known as an 'Empire clock,' dominates the east wall of the Winchester College Moberly Library. The clock is a central decorative feature of a remodel designed by Sir Herbert Baker (1862-1946) of the then vacant old Brewery's conversion into the College's Library. Baker presented the clock to the College at an unveiling ceremony on March 21, 1936. He was a renowned British architect, who designed a large number of buildings throughout the Empire Commonwealth, including southern Africa, Kenya (known as British East Africa at the time) and

New Delhi. In addition, he also designed several important commissions in England, including the War Cloister at Winchester College, which may be the largest private war memorial in Europe.

Discussion for the expansion and relocation of the College main library began in 1926, with work started on the remodel of the old Brewery in late 1931. The renovation was completed in late 1933, and books transferred to the new location in December of 1933. The Moberly Library in the old Brewery officially opened in early 1934. A subsequent remodel in the mid-1970's added a second level which now allows for a close inspection of the clock, which was originally high above the ground floor.

In addition to Winchester College, others Empire clocks of Baker, all of which are incorporated into larger architectural schemes as part of their interiors, can be found at: the Bank of England, London (rebuilt by Baker between 1921 and 1939); two at South Africa House, also London (built 1931-33); London House, (installed in 1937) in what is now the Great Hall of Goodenough College, London; as well as in 1933 at Baker's ancestral home, Owletts, in Cobham, Kent which is now owned by the National Trust.

While Baker oversaw the design and installation of the half dozen Empire Clocks in the 1930s, most were strongly influenced by his son, Henry Edmeades Baker (1905-1994), Robert F. Stewart and others. A manuscript (MS P8/126) in the Winchester College Archive, states that:

> *The dials, hour and minute hands were set out by* (the sculptor) *Mr. Joseph Armitage (1880-1945) and made by* (the engraver) *G. T. (George Taylor) Friend (1881-1969) in London. . . . The sun and moon emblems were modelled by Sir Charles Wheeler, RA. (1892-1974) . . . Baker designed the symbols on the great dial and the surrounding stonework and presented the clock in 1936.*

An excerpt from Baker's memoirs, *Architecture and Personalities* (London: Country Life, 1944), includes the following:

> *Having two of my sons at the school* [Winchester College] *added greatly to my pleasure. In gratitude for what Winchester meant to us my son Henry and I gave an "Empire" clock, driven by electricity, set up in the old flint wall of the new Brewery Library. The outer twenty-four-hour dial, four feet in diameter, of the clock tells the standard times of the chief countries round the Empire. I designed the dials with the Empire symbols and Henry, with the help of Robert Stewart, a schoolmate, designed and made the whole of the works or "movement." Stainless steels of*

special grades were used, and some were so hard that they had to make their own cutting tools for the purpose. Inscribed on an old oak beam above it is a Greek hexameter, by (former Winchester College Headmaster) *Dr.* (Montague John) *Rendall* (1862-1950), *meaning, "My body was given by men, but by ether my spirit of life."*

The Winchester Empire Clock is a fairly early example of a synchronous clock utilizing the British National Electrical Grid. The National Grid was completed in 1933 and operated at a constant frequency. This allowed for an electrical motor to run at a constant speed, and thus for the widespread use of accurate electrical clocks throughout the Country.

A 1936 article from *The Wykehamist*, the College's student produced magazine, described the Empire Clock at the Moberly Library in the following words:

NEW CLOCK IN BREWERY [Winchester College Moberly Library]
Sir Herbert Baker has given to Brewery a new clock which has been placed in position upon the east wall. This clock, of which a full description is appended below, is the joint work of his son Henry (F, 1918-24) and R. F. Stewart (F, 1920-25). The clock was formally presented by Sir Herbert at a short ceremony in Brewery on Saturday, March 21st, and acknowledgement was made on behalf of the College by the Warden. The clock consists of an inner dial which is an ordinary twelve-hour clock with a second hand in stainless steel in addition to a gilt hour and minute hand. Round this is a dial which revolves once in twenty-four hours, the numerals of the hours being carved on the stone and gilt. On this outer dial are the symbols showing the time at Greenwich and the standard times or time-zones of the Dominions and some of the greater Dependencies. The saying that the sun never sets on the Empire is no mere boast but records the fact that the Dominions and principal Dependencies are on different longitudes; it is this fact that makes it possible to make a clock of this description. It would be impossible if, for instance, South Africa were on the same longitude as Greenwich or Australia on that of India. Thus there is no room on the dial to mark the time of Egypt and the East and West African Colonies as they are on or too near the longitudes of South Africa and of England. Thus too the West Indies are on those of Canada. The symbols and respective time-zones are as follows:

The Lion represents Greenwich time. The sun will have reached South Africa two hours earlier; therefore when it is noonday at Greenwich it is 2 o'clock in South Africa, which is symbolised by the Winged Springbok and the floral emblem of the Protea.

The Indian Ocean, symbolised by an early Arab ship, divides South Africa from India. India's standard time is five and a half hours ahead of Greenwich time and is represented by its symbol of the Great Star.

Burma comes one hour ahead of India and is shown by a symbol of a peacock feather from the arms of Burma, and the letter B.

Seven hours ahead of Greenwich time comes Singapore, which is shown by an anchor, a symbol of a naval port, and the initial S.

Then comes Australia which has three standard time-zones, eight, nine and a half, and ten hours from Greenwich. This is represented by the stars of the Southern Cross over wattle leaves.

Next is New Zealand, eleven and a half hours ahead of Greenwich, represented by the Southern Cross alone.

Then comes the Antipodes, or the dateline in the Pacific Ocean where the day changes, twelve hours from Greenwich, that is at midnight when Greenwich is at noon.

The Pacific Ocean is represented by a three-masted ship, there being no land on these three longitudes which would have a time of one, two and three hours in the morning when it was mid-day at Greenwich.

Then we arrive at Canada which has five time-zones, four, five, six, seven and eight o'clock. These are shown by maple leaves upon which, though they will hardly be seen, are symbols of the different nationalities, the leek for Wales, the shamrock for Ireland, the thistle for Scotland, the rose for England, and the fleur-de-lys for France.

At eight and a half hours a fish symbolises Newfoundland.

Finally the time-zones, nine, ten and eleven hours, where no land is in the Atlantic Ocean, are shown by the symbol of a two-masted ship of the early navigators.

The initial letters of the different lands and seas are placed above the symbols.

In the centre above twelve o'clock mid-day is shown Phoebus Apollo with the horses of the Sun shining in splendour ; below at twenty-four hours midnight is Selene asleep in her Crescent Moon.

The clock movement is driven by a small electric motor which runs at a constant speed of 120 revolutions a minute on the "time-controlled" frequency of the supply mains. A train of gears reduces the speed of the motor to each of the hands in turn, and finally to the large dial which revolves once in twenty-four hours.

Owing to the height of the clock face access to the back for setting the clock to time and for any other needs has been provided in the Bursar's office. A small "dummy" dial at the back carries a minute hand in the form of a handle, and a miniature hour hand, each following the hands of the main dial.

As most other countries do not change their times in the summer—and it would be impossible to record their changes if they did—the large dial remains always at the standard-zone sun time. To show the change to English summertime correctly on the twelve-hour ordinary clock, the hour hand can be put forward or back an hour by moving a lever from one position to the other without affecting the position of the other hands or the large twenty-four-hour dial. If the clock stops—as may happen on rare occasions when the main current fails—there are means provided for restarting it and resetting it by the use of the dummy dial.

All the spindles are carried on ball-bearings, of which there are thirteen in all, of a special design to prevent the 100 or more tiny balls falling out, if the movement is ever taken apart.

Almost the entire movement, the second hand and the framework of the large dial, are made from various qualities of stainless steel supplied by Messrs. Firth-Vickers. Some of the different kinds were new and their use experimental. Though these stainless steels are tougher to work than the brass and steel ordinarily used in clock making, they remain bright in handling and in use, and it is hoped that time will not affect them.

Except the gilded-brass symbols, hour and minute hands, the whole of the works have been designed and made by Henry Baker (F, 1918—1924) and Robert Stewart (F, 1920—1925) working together. Sir Herbert Baker designed the symbols on the great dial and the surrounding stonework. [THE WYKEHAMIST No. 814 - March 30th, 1936, pp. 186-187; author not identified.]

In addition to the following images of the Empire Cock, and its setting within the interior of the Moberly Library, Appendix B presents specifications, design details, and operating instructions, as well as photographs of various parts of the clock at the time of its fabrication.

Figure 56: The Empire Clock in the Moberly Library. The inscription translates as *My body was given by men, but by ether my spirit of life*. (Photograph by Suzanne Foster, 2021)

Figure 57: Concept drawing of the Empire Clock by Sir Herbert Baker. (Source: Winchester College Archives, 2021)

13. The Buckland and "Jacker" Clocks

A survey of the Winchester College clocks would not be complete without mention of two prominent commemorative clocks. Both are large electric exterior wall mounted clocks from the twentieth century.

The Buckland Clock - 1912

Edward Teddy Hastings Buckland (1864-1906) was a House Master at Winchester College, as well as a first-class cricketer whose career debut was at New College, Oxford. His memorial clock is located on the exterior of the rackets court near the Armoury/South Africa Gate. The inscription reads *Whatsoever his hand found to do he did it with his might*.

Figure 58: The Buckland Clock. (photograph by Suzanne Foster, 2021)

The "Jacker" Clock - 1972

This clock is located at the end of Flint Court and commemorates Horace Arthur "Jacker" Jackson (1884-1972), who served Winchester College as an instructor and house don over many years. He was twice wounded and taken prison during WWI. A favorite teaching technique was to comment during a lecture with the statement, *That is what I said, but that is not what really matters. What do you suppose that it led to?*

Figure 59: The "Jacker" Clock. (photograph by Suzanne Foster, 2021)

REFERENCES

The individuals and organizations listed in this book's Acknowledgements are the primary sources for much of the information presented in the book. Through numerous emails and references each contributed significantly to the final work.

GENERAL REFERENCES PERTAINING TO WINCHESTER COLLEGE:

Britten F.J.
1956 seventh edition - 1899 first edition   *Old clocks and Watches and Their makers: A Historical and Descriptive Account of the Different Styles of Clocks of the Past in England and Abroad: with a List of Nearly Fourteen Thousand Makers,* seventh edition, Bonanza Books, New York.

Firth, J. D'Ewes
1949   *Winchester College (The English Public Schools)* Winchester Publications Ltd., London.

Harvey, John H.
1982   "The Buildings of Winchester College", in *Winchester College: Sixth-Centenary Essays*, ed. Roger Custance, Oxford: Oxford University Press, pp 77–128.

Howgrave-Graham, Robert Pickersgill
1928   "Some Clocks and Jacks, with Notes on the History of Horology," *Archaeologia . . . Vol. 77,* pp257-312, The Society of Antiquarians of London.

Sabben-Clare, James
1981   *Winchester College After 606 Years, 1382-1988* P&G Wells, Winchester.

Winchester College Archaeological Society
1926   *Winchester College its history buildings and customs* P&G Wells Booksellers to Winchester College, Winchester, England.

THE WYKEHAMIST - The School Magazine

Sundials:
1946, June   School News, School Notes
1918, August   III. Meads from 1394 - 1780, Articles
1924, July   An Item of Our Debt - Articles

Clocks:

2017, November	The Porter's Lodge, Articles
1919, March	Correspondence
1923, February	Correspondence
1997, May	Obituary
1936, March	New Clock in Brewery, Correspondence
1933, November	Correspondence

PART I - THE SUNDIALS 1-6:

Brighton, John Trevor
1978 *The Enamel Glass-Painters of York: 1585-1795* (in Three Volumes) Thesis submitted for D. Phil. of the University of York, Department of History, York, UK.

British Sundial Society
2021 < https://sundialsoc.org.uk> for a comprehensive discussion and database of sundials throughout the United Kingdom.

Carmichael, John L. Jr.
2003 *Looking at: Stained Glass Sundials - Part I & II*. Sundial Sculptures, Tucson, Arizona USA.
2011 *Stained Glass Sundials* - Image Archive for the 16th and 17th centuries listing of all known such sundials. <http://www.advanceassociates.com/Sundials/Stained_Glass/sundials_Archive.html>

Corpus of Anglo-Saxon Stone Sculpture at Durham University
2021 *The Corpus of Anglo-Saxon Stone Sculpture: Catalogue* <http://www.ascorpus.ac.uk>

Cowham, Mike (ed)
2005 *Sundials of the British Isles: A Selection of Some of the Finest Sundials from Our Islands,* M.J. Cowham publisher, London.

Cramp, R. J.
1975 Anglo-Saxon Sculpture of the Reform Period, in Parsons, D. (ed), *Tenth-Century Studies,* Chichester, Phillimore &; Co. Ltd.

Daniel, Christopher
1987 "Shedding a Glorious Light - Stained-Glass-Window Sundials" *Country Life Magazine,* February 26, 1987, pp. 72-75.
1988 *Stained Glass Sundials in England and Wales* Clocks Magazine, April 1988.
2004a *Sundials,* London, Shire Publications.
2004b *Clocks Magazine* "The Sundial Page" Vol 27/6 p. 30.

Doubleday, H A (ed)
1900   *The Victoria County History of Hampshire*

Gatty, Mrs. Alfred
1900   *The Book of Sundials* Fourth Edition, George Bell and Sons, London

Green, A. R.
1928   "Anglo-Saxon Sundials", *Antiquity Journal* 8, pp. 489-516, Cambridge University Press, Cambridge.

Green, A R and Green, P. M.
1951   *Saxon Architecture and Sculpture in Hampshire,* Winchester, Warren and Son.

Hare, Michael
1980   "The Anglo-Saxon Church and Sundial at Hannington" *Proceedings of the Hants. Field Club Archaeological Society,* #36, 1980, 193-202.

Henslow, T. Geoffrey
1914   *Ye Sundial Book*, J.J. Keliher & Co. , Ltd. Craven House, Kingsway, W.C., p. 86.

Knowles, John A.
1923   *Henry Gyles, Glass Painter of York*. The Volume of the Walpole Society, Vol II (1922-1923), pp. 47-72, Published by: The Walpole Society, London.

Lane, Geoffrey
2005   "Glass Sundial Makers of 17th Century London" *Journal of Stained Glass*. Volume XXIX (2005), The British Society of Master Glass Painters, London. Reprinted in the British Sundial Society Bulletin 18(i).
2012   *The Tyttenhanger Sundial* Vidimus.org, issue 59.

Leadbetter, Charles
1769   *Mechanick Dialling or the New Art of Shadows* . . . London, printed for G. Pearch.

Le Conteur, J. D.
1920   *Ancient Glass in Winchester,* p. 116.

Woodford, Christopher
1954   *English Stained and Painter Glass*, Oxford at the Clarendon Press.

PART II - THE CLOCKS

7. The Turret Clock

Milham, Willis I.
1945   *Time and Timekeepers* MacMillan., p.188-194

Glasgow, David
1885   *Watch and Clock Making*. London: Cassel & Co.

Beeson, C F C.
1971   *English Church Clocks* London

McKay, Chris (Editor)
1993   *The Great Salisbury Clock Trial*, Antiquarian Horological Society turret clock Group,

8. Longcase Clocks

Barnett, Jo Ellen
1999   *Time's Pendulum: From Sundials to Atomic Clocks, the Fascinating History of   Timekeeping and how Our Discoveries Changed the World* Houghton Mifflin Harcourt   Publishing   Company,   Boston, Massachusetts.

Headrick, Michael
2002   "Origin and Evolution of the Anchor Clock Escapement" *Control Systems Magazine*.   Vol. 22   No. 2. Institute of Electrical and Electronic Engineers.

Nelthropp, Harry Leonard
1873   *A Treatise on Watch-Work, Past and Present*. London: E.& F.N. Spon, London / New   York.

Roberts, Derek
1990   *British Longcase Clocks* Schiffer Publishing, Ltd., West Chester, Pennsylvania

9. The Shortt Clock

Alvarez, Luis W.
1977   *Alfred Lee Loomis 1887-1975 : A Biographical Memoir* U.S. Energy Research and Development Administration, Washington, D.C.

Boucheron, Pierre H.
1985 "Just How Good Was the Shortt Clock?". *The Bulletin of the National Association of Watch and Clock Collectors. Columbia, PA: NAWCC. 27*

Milham, Willis I.
1945 *Time and Timekeepers.* MacMillan, New York.

Marrison, Warren
1948 "The Evolution of the Quartz Crystal Clock." *Bell System Technical Journal 27 (3): 510–588*, Washington, D.C.

Seidelmann, P. Kenneth; Dennis D. McCarthy
2009. *Time: From Earth Rotation to Atomic Physics.* Wiley Publishing, New York

Matthys, Robert J.
2004. *Accurate Clock Pendulums.* Oxford University Press, Oxford.

Riehle, Fritz (2004). *Frequency Standards: Basics and Applications.* Wiley Publishing, New York.

Usher, Abbot Payson
1988 *A History of Mechanical Inventions.* Courier Dover Publishing, New York

APPENDIX A: Background Data Pertaining to the Shortt Clock

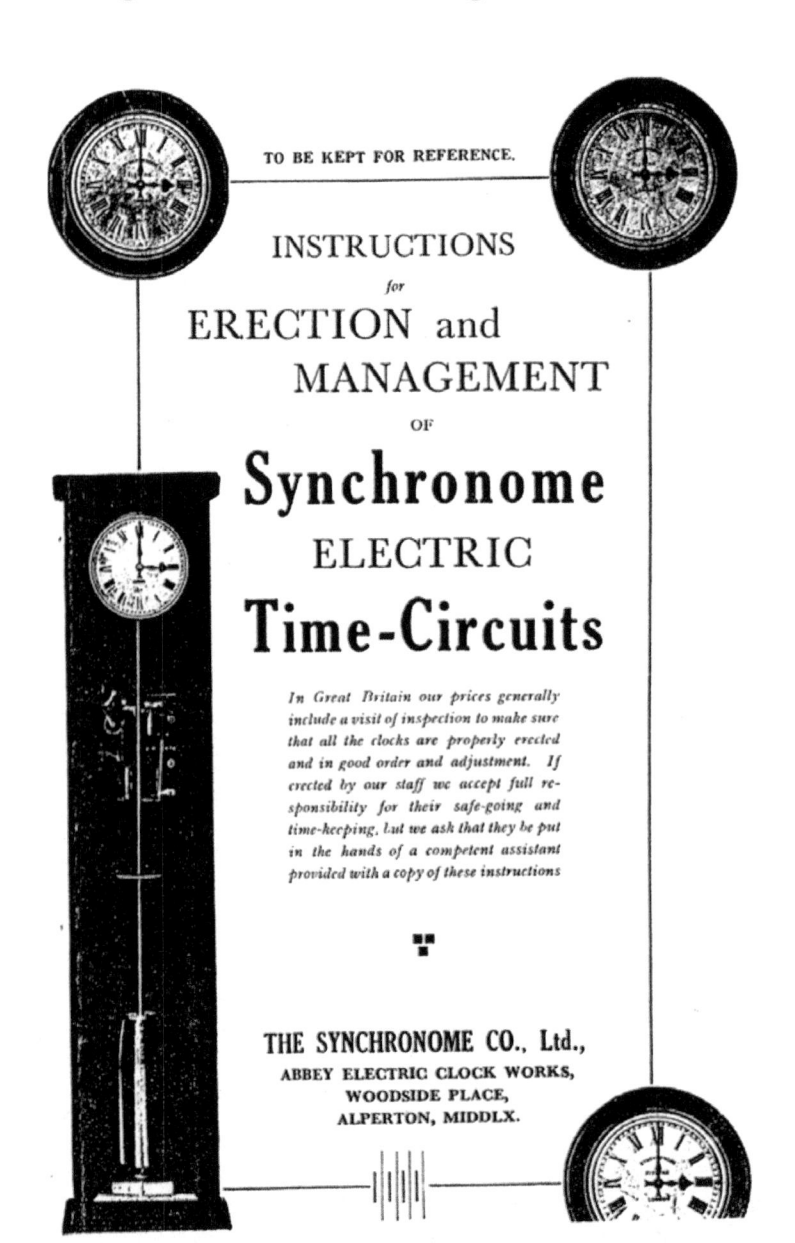

ERECTION

WIRING.—A single line to connect each dial to its nearest neighbour in simple series circuit, as shown in diagram on previous page. Electric light wire of 3/.036 (3/20) or 3/.029 (3/22) gauge is recommended on account of its mechanical strength.

BATTERY.—This may consist of any form of good primary cell, or accumulator battery trickle-charged from the mains can be used.

The consumption of current is negligible. Join up cells in series with clocks.

MASTER CLOCK.—Unpack carefully and hang **the pendulum case** on a substantial wall with its top no higher than 6 ft. 6 ins. from the floor.

It is important to hang the case vertically both with regard to in and out and side to side planes, and it should be fixed firmly by means of screws through the back, one on each side of the pendulum suspension and one behind the bob, into Rawlplugs or ordinary wood plugs in the wall. The brass plate at the top of the case is to assist you to hang it temporarily whilst " marking off " for the plugs and screws.

Take the nut and washer off the lower end of the pendulum rod, put the bob on and replace washer and nut, screwing the latter up to such a position that the filed notch in front of the rod is just in sight above the pendulum bob. This will give approximate regulation. Now slip the click B into position. It will be found in a small envelope with the beat plate and the key of the case, tied to the pendulum rod.

The pendulum being now complete, proceed to hang it in position in the following manner. Observe the position of the trunnion and suspension spring on the top of the cast iron bracket, slacken the wing nuts and swing the clamps to one side, thus releasing it. Take out the small metal screw in the split brass head of the pendulum rod and place the lower end of the suspension spring carefully in the slit and fix it by replacing the screw. The complete pendulum may now be hung, the pallet J and click B being on the left and the small set screw on the trunnion being in front; but before fixing it with the clamps and wing nuts it is necessary to see that the pendulum is in exactly the right position both with respect to in and out and side to side planes.

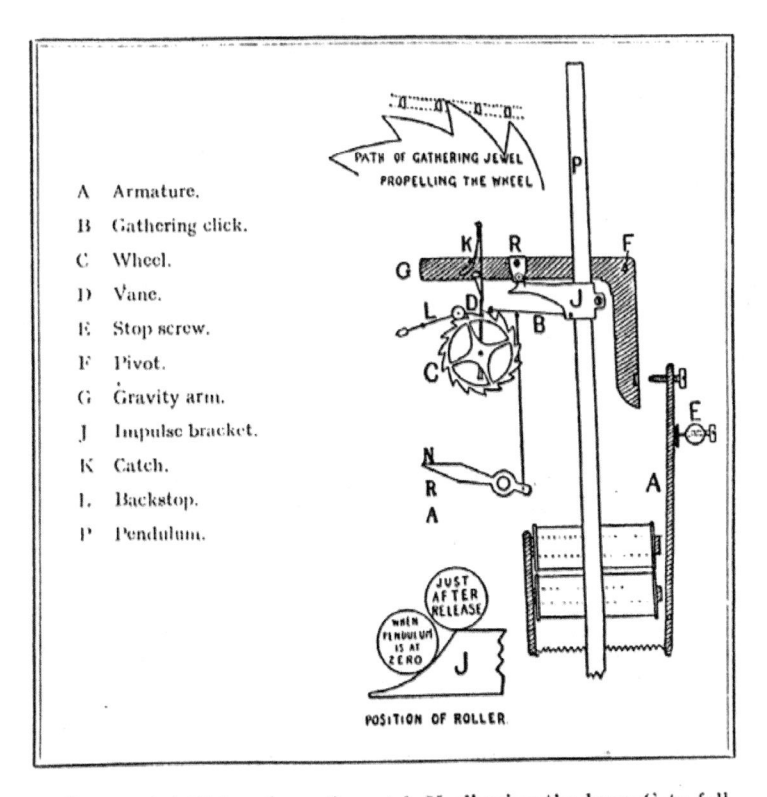

A   Armature.
B   Gathering click.
C   Wheel.
D   Vane.
E   Stop screw.
F   Pivot.
G   Gravity arm.
J   Impulse bracket.
K   Catch.
L   Backstop.
P   Pendulum.

To ascertain this, release the catch K allowing the lever G to fall. The steel roller R should then rest on the steepest part of the curve of the impulse pallet J. If not, the pendulum must be moved right or left along the trunnion and fixed by the set screw provided. The trunnion must be parallel with the back of the case and in such a position that the gathering jewel B lies squarely with its middle on the wheel C midway between the points of two teeth. This position can be adjusted by moving the trunnion inwards or outwards on the cast iron bracket, and when correct it should be clamped by the wing nuts.

The gathering jewel B should engage the wheel C with **just sufficient depth** to move one tooth at a time and no more. The steel wire which carries the jewel must not touch the N.R.A. wire when the indicator is at N (normal), and the upper surface of the pallet J should just not touch the roller R. Catch K being released the pendulum should be unable to reset lever G upon it when the current is off. The beat plate may now be placed in position and fixed if desired.

3

It is only when the pendulum is at or about zero and travelling (at its greatest speed) through a very small part of its excursion, that it is engaged in (1) turning the wheel, (2) releasing the gravity arm, and (3) receiving its impulse. Its entire freedom at all other times (particularly at the beginning and end of each swing when it is moving at its slowest) is the feature of overwhelming importance, and it is in this respect that it realises the ideal which horologists have been striving after for centuries.

THE DIALS may be hung like pictures on single screws or nails. The ends of the line wires must be carefully led into the back of the dial cases and securely gripped in the spring clip terminals.

THE BATTERY can be proved sufficient in the following manner. Having joined up the instruments in series circuit with all the cells and started the installation, reduce the battery one cell at a time until the magnet is incapable of resetting the gravity lever G without the assistance of the pendulum pushing roller R in its return excursion to the left. This is known as **battery warning**. Note the number of cells in circuit when this occurs and replace say 10% or 15% of that number.

MANAGEMENT

If a breakdown occurs you are earnestly requested to communicate at once with us, as the installation is guaranteed.

If the pendulum has stopped and it is desired to ascertain the cause, note whether **lever G is** supported **on** catch K or is **down**, resting against the pendulum. If the latter, start it swinging again gently with a sufficient arc to enable the contact surfaces to meet. If no current passes, then there is a disconnection at one of the terminals or a break in the line. On the other hand, if the magnet attempts to throw up the weighted lever but is unsuccessful, then either the current is insufficient, the automatic warning of impending failure having been neglected, or there is something preventing the spring catch K from holding the lever G.

If when the pendulum is stopped, lever G is found to be **resting on catch K** and the pendulum only requires to be restarted, the battery and wiring being all right, then the stoppage has been due to something impeding the motion of the pendulum, such as undue friction in the movement of the wheel or its releasing of the catch.

In the event of any one Dial stopping or dropping behind time, take it out of circuit, twist the wires together quickly between successive impulses, noting the precise instant of their occurrence by means of the seconds hand of your watch.

4

A Main wheel
B Electro-magnet
C Armature
D Armature lever
E Driving click
F Driving spring
G Backstop lever
H Momentum stop
I Stroke limit stop

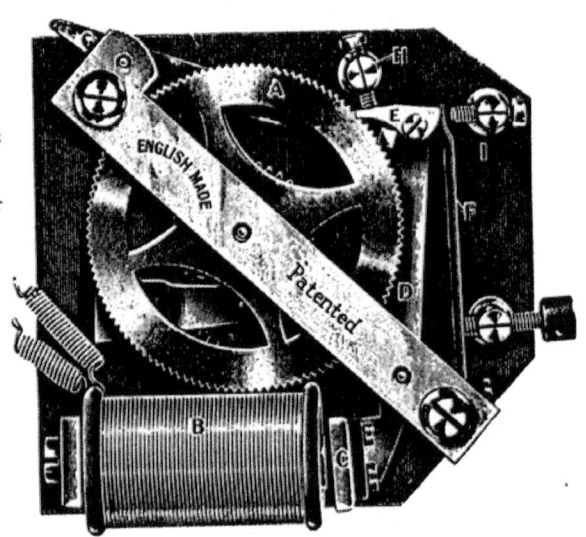

If it is desired to ascertain and correct the fault, open the back and lift the backstop lever G, which will hold the driving click E out of engagement with the wheel A, and spin the wheel A to find undue friction. If the wheel and hands revolve quite freely, there is only one thing more to look at, viz.: the flat steel spring F, which must be just strong enough to propel the hands, but not too strong for the electro-magnet B to pull it over. It may be easily adjusted by the capstan screw.

In the event of its being necessary to attend to any individual dial to turn the hands to time, **never touch the hands themselves,** but open the back and touch the armature with the finger, or lift the backstop lever and spin the wheel.

Notice to those who erect their own installations.

All adjustments are carefully made in these works before the instruments are sent out, and are securely locked. In order to prove that these adjustments have not been altered and to satisfy yourself and us that the Controlling Pendulum has been properly erected you are asked to fill in the following form by answering the questions. If this is done the Synchronome Co., Ltd., will accept it as a substitute for erection by their own staff, and will be responsible for the safe-going and time-keeping of the installation.

5

REGULATION

REGULATION.—Take hold of the pendulum rod firmly, just above the bob, in order to prevent its twisting and damaging the suspension spring or click B, and if the clock is slow, turn the rating nut so that the front edge moves from left to right, and the bob is raised : if fast, turn it in the opposite direction. **One complete revolution of the rating nut will make a difference of half-a-minute in 24 hours,** the figures 10, 20 and 30 on the rating nut representing **seconds** in 24 hours.

For accurate regulation, prove a small but definite losing rate by two or three observations, then turn the nut upwards accordingly, taking great care not to overshoot.

If an adjustable platform is provided at the middle of the pendulum rod, the addition of 0.6 gram weight will cause the clock to gain 1 second in 24 hours.

DIAL SETTING FROM MASTER CLOCK.

To set all the dials forward if slow :—

A Few Seconds.—After the release occurs, move the wheel forward, each tooth passed representing two seconds.

A Few Half-Minutes.—When the pendulum swings to the **left** release the catch K with your finger. **On no account must lever G be released unless the pallet J is underneath it to prevent its falling on to the armature contact, which might cause trouble.**

Longer Periods.—Depress the lever to A (accelerate). The switch will then work every two seconds instead of every half-minute. By this means the Summer Time advance of one hour will be accomplished in 4 minutes and 16 seconds.

To set all the dials back if fast :—

A Few Seconds.—Before the release takes place depress the tail of the backstop glass roller L and turn the wheel backwards, each tooth representing two seconds.

A Few Half-Minutes.—Hold a piece of paper between the contact surfaces before the gravity lever is released, and then reset it by hand.

Longer Periods.—Move the setting lever from N (normal) to R (retard) for as long as may be necessary. After one hour's stoppage to revert to G.M.T. in the Autumn, it will be necessary to start the pendulum again.

The Church Army Press, Cowley, Oxford, England.   14488

CONTROLLING PENDULUM ERECTOR'S CERTIFICATE.

Movement No...................erected by..
(See bottom of N.R.A. plate).

at... Date....................

address ....

What is the space between the poles of the magnet and armature? It should be one-hundredth of an inch. Insert a piece of thin notepaper and see that you cannot grip it.	....
What is stroke of the armature and gravity lever? It should be ¾ **travel in company** with ¼ **kick.**	....
What is the minimum arc of the pendulum on which the jewel will gather? It should be 1° + 1° or 20 m.m. + 20 m.m.	....
What is position of impulse roller when pendulum is at zero? Sketch the curve and the roller.	....
What is the minimum contacting arc? *i.e.*, minimum arc at which contact can be made and gravity lever reset.	....
What switch air gap results? *i.e.*, space between contacts when lever is on catch and armature is pushed against the poles of magnet.	....
Is the gathering click no deeper in engagement than sufficient to allow backstop roller to drop into next tooth?	....
Is N.R.A. adjusted? The lifting wire should be altogether clear of B when indicator is at N; should raise B clear of the wheel at R; and should raise the jewel to engage the accelerating arm of catch when the indicator is at A.	....
How many cells were taken off before battery warning?	....
How many cells were taken off further before dying kick? (battery too weak to replace lever).	....
How many cells were left operating the circuit?	....
In which room is battery situated?	....
Is pendulum case rigidly fixed to a substantial wall?	....
How many screws, and is wall plugged?	....
Who did the wiring?	....
Who keeps series order list, and/or wiring plan?	....

Fill in spare form and return to—
THE SYNCHRONOME CO., LTD.,

INSTRUCTIONS FOR THE ERECTION OF
FREE PENDULUM, MASTER AND SLAVE CLOCKS

Introduction. These clocks are operated from a common battery and arranged so that the half-minute impulses of the Master firmly hold the Slave in absolute synchronisation with the Master. The half-minute impulses of the Slave release the impulse mechanism of the Master and so relieve it of all work.

In order that the energy required to be supplied to the Master Pendulum to keep it moving may be as small as possible, the air pressure in the case is reduced to about 2 c.m.

The Master Clock, or Free Pendulum, is accordingly mounted in a cylindrical copper case closed at the top by a glass jar and at the bottom by a plate glass disc.

The ends of the cylinder are terminated by flanging the copper tube to form wide flat surfaces which enable grease joints to be made with the glasses. Each gunmetal ring is provided with a pair of lugs, or feet, which enable the case to be firmly bolted on the wall of the clock chamber or room.

For the best results, the Free Pendulum should be bolted to solid rock. In practice, it is rigidly fixed to a foundation wall in a clock chamber in a cellar.

Although every care is taken to make the temperature compensation as perfect as possible, it is undoubtedly desirable, if the very highest order of timekeeping is required, that the temperature of the clock chamber should be kept constant by means of an electric heater controlled by a thermostat. It is also desirable to instal a fan to operate when the heater is cut-out, in order to prevent stratification of the air.

If the Master Clock is mounted in a small cell, it is only necessary to control the temperature of this cell. A chamber of the following dimensions is sufficient:-

        4 ft. x 4 ft. x 8 ft. high

As the Slave Clock is controlled by the Master, there is no need to mount the former in the constant temperature cell: in fact, it is better to keep it outside, and it may be erected wherever its dial can be most conveniently seen.

The Erection of the Master Clock Case.
The clock case should be fixed on the wall of the clock room or chamber by four half-inch diameter steel bolts.

It is desirable to have a section of the wall 18 inches wide floated with cement from 12 inches up to 6 ft. above floor level, in order to ensure that it is quite flat and vertical.

The four half-inch steel bolts should be set into the wall and grouted up so as to project 2 inches from the face of the rendering, and they should be threaded half-inch Whitworth to within 1 inch of the wall.

The two bottom bolts should be set 10 inches apart centre to centre and 20 inches above floor level.

The two top bolts must be set vertically above the bottom bolts and at a distance of 36¼" from them, measuring from centre centre.

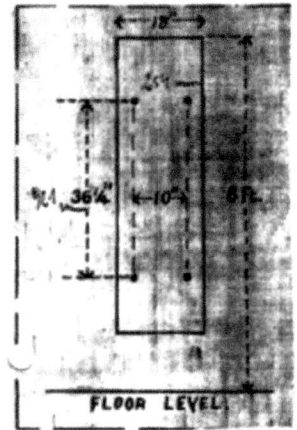

The marginal sketch indicates the positions also the cement rendering required.

The clock may be mounted at a greater height if desired, but this will put the movement more than 5 ft. above the floor.

When unpacking the cylindrical copper case, great care must be taken not to damage the surfaced ends.

It must be mounted so that the ring with the three projecting terminals is at the top. Proceed to fit up the case fittings as follows:-

Unpack the valve, remove the nut, steel washer and thick copper washer from the thread on the valve, leaving the thin copper washer on. See that the valve thread and seating, also the washers, are clean and free from dust. Put some of the special grease round the thread of the valve and the thin copper washer and insert thread into the hole provided for it on the left hand side of the bottom ring of the Free Pendulum case; having greased the remaining copper washer, place it in position on the projecting thread inside the case. Now place on the steel washer and nut and tighten up with the nozzle pointing downwards.

Unpack the glass base plate and bell jar, also the triangular frame and fixing screws necessary to hold it in place.

It will be found convenient to make the joint between the glass disc and the bottom of the case before fixing the case to the wall; for this purpose, the case should be inverted (a soft pad being placed on the ground to protect the surfaced end) and the bottom surfaced end carefully cleaned and rubbed over with a uniform layer of the special jointing grease, a tin of which is supplied.

The plate glass disc, after being cleaned, should then be carefully placed in position and gently squeezed, with a slight rotary motion, into contact with the copper flange, seeing that glass is correctly centred, and the joint free of air bubbles.

A fillet of grease should finally be formed round the glass disc where it joins the copper flange by rubbing the junction round with the special grease with the aid of the finger.

If the triangle casting is fitted with a mirror, bowline, etc., these should now be assembled as shown on Drawing 24124. When a microscope is supplied, this is already in position on the triangle as shown on Drawing 18138.

Place the triangle in position over the glass, fix it in position with the three fixing screws, after which the three padded screws in the corners of the triangle may be gently turned until they press firmly upon the glass and prevent any possibility of it moving.

The cylinder is now ready to be bolted to the wall. This should be done as follows:-

Remove the nuts from the bolts built into the wall, lift the cylinder into position, sliding the feet of the two end castings over the bolts. Place a flat washer on each of the two top bolts and spring washers on the two bottom bolts. Replace the nuts and tighten up the two top ones. If the wall is not absolutely flat, there will be a space between one of the bottom lugs and the wall.

Erection of Master Movement and Pendulum.

The erection of the movement and pendulum can now be proceeded with.

The first thing required is the pendulum. The pendulum rod has a hook formed at its top end and when mounted up this hook will face the front, a little lower down is a cross pin called the safety pin, used in conjunction with the safety plate on the head-casting (see Drawing No.14124). Near the bottom will be seen the brass compensating collar; remove the steel pin holding the compensator and slide it off the rod.

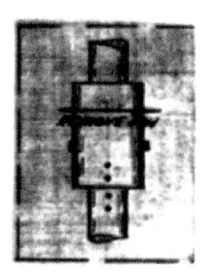

Insert the end of the pendulum rod through the small hole in the top of the bob.

After making sure that the seating, at the point where the large hole joins it which will rest on the top of the compensator, is quite clean, slide on the compensator and replace the steel pin, seeing that the compensator is not reversed; the double dot (:) on it and the rod indicate the correct way.

Then put the beat plate on at the bottom of the rod making sure that it is parallel to the plane of swing.

Then slide the ring magnet on to the rod and temporarily fix it by tightening it's screw at about two inches from the bottom of the pendulum rod.

Next put the beat plate on to the bottom of the rod as far as it will go. The beat plate should then be pinned to the rod by first lining up the dot on the collar of the beat plate holder with a corresponding dot on the front of the rod, and then inserting the pin, from the right, through the hole provided for it.

Adjusting screws A.A., Drawing No.10720, are fitted to the beat plate holder to enable the scale to be swivelled round, one way or the other, should the scale not be travelling straight when the pendulum is suspended and in motion. This adjustment cannot be made until the pendulum is fitted in position, set in motion and observed through the microscope.

It will be necessary for the plate glass circle to be removed whilst this operation is being tested and dealt with.

Having fitted the beat scale, lower the magnet on to it until it is resting on it and fasten the ring magnet by means of the screw in the collar; this screw should be facing the front.

NOTE. Great care must be taken not to touch or rub the stainless steel scale as the diamond engraving is very finely cut and may easily be damaged and affect its reflecting properties adversely.

The pendulum may now be lifted and carefully placed in the cylindrical case, the beat plate resting on the plate glass bottom.

Erection of Head Casting and other Fittings at top of case.

The three specially bent connecting wires should be connected to the inner ends of the three terminals passing through the top ring casting of the case.

Slacken the hexagonal nuts and hook the appropriately labelled ends of the wires into the corresponding terminals, behind the washers and re-tighten the nuts, taking care that the rising portions of the wires are vertical.

Now screw the small L shaped brass bracket to the right hand side of the top ring where a hole is provided, with the countersunk headed screw, the upwards pointing arm being towards the pendulum. Fit the spark condenser at the back of the top ring.

Unpack the four-legged casting, clean it and place it in position on the top ring of the case, so that the two legs which carry the projections are on the right hand side. The Print No. 14124 will be helpful.

It will be found that the pendulum rod is just too long to enable the top of it to be inserted in the elongated hole in the safety plate attached to the underside of the body of the head casting; therefore lift the casting carefully to a sufficient height to enable this to be done and then lower it again into position, rotating the pendulum so as to get the safety pin through the slot in the safety plate.

The head casting may now be screwed down with the aid of the four cheese headed brass screws to the top ring of the case, the four holes in the finished surface for the reception of these screws will have already been noticed.

Finally adjust the milled screw holding the left hand end of the safety plate until this plate is level, place the fingers underneath the weight tray and lift the pendulum until the safety pin is just clear of the safety plate, rotate the pendulum rod through about 90° so as to bring the safety pin squarely across the elongated hole in the plate and then lower gently until the safety pin rests on the safety plate and the latter takes the whole weight of the pendulum.

Pendulum Suspension.

The next thing to be done is to carefully unpack the pendulum suspension from its small box. The greatest care must be taken in unpacking this piece of apparatus to ensure that the special spring is not damaged in any way.

The cross pin attached to the lower end of the suspension is provided to take hooks at the top of the pendulum rod and before placing the suspension in position, care should be taken to see that the hooks on the pendulum are facing the front and the rod is central in the round hole.

When the position of the pendulum has been satisfactorily adjusted, the suspension may be carefully lowered into position between the six adjusting screws, which must be withdrawn sufficiently to allow the cylindrical portions to set down on the top of the steel blocks.

The cross pin should pass in front of the hooks on the pendulum and if these hooks are not high enough to enable the cross pin afterwards to pass under it into its proper position, the milled screw supporting the left hand side of the safety plate should be turned and the plate and pendulum raised until the suspension cross pin will pass under the hooks.

When this has been done, the safety plate may be gently lowered until the suspension cross pin takes the whole weight of the pendulum and it swings freely.

It is again necessary to emphasise that every care must be taken to prevent tortional vibration of the pendulum and the buckling of the spring.

The safety plate should not be lowered clear of the safety pin more than is sufficient to ensure that there is no possible danger of their touching one another.

Assembling and Erection of Movement.

The movement itself may now be carefully unpacked from the box containing it. In order to ensure that it should not be damaged in any way during transit, the heavy re-setting lever, marked X on the accompanying Drawing No. 181229 of the movement, has been removed and also the light impulse lever marked Y.

Before replacing these levers in the movement, it should be tried in position on the right hand side of the head casting, so as to make sure that it can be readily inserted and removed subsequently, also that the connecting wires come in their right position etc.

This having been done, the insertion of the heavy re-setting lever may be proceeded with. For this purpose, remove the screws indicated by the letters A.B.C. and D. on Drawing No. 181229 and lift off the inverted 'T' shaped front plate of the movement. See that the pivots of the heavy lever are quite clean and carefully insert the proper pivot into the jewelled hole in the back plate of the movement and, whilst holding the lever in its proper position carefully place the jewelled hole in the front 'T' shaped plate of the movement over the other pivot of the heavy lever and replace the fixing screws A.B. and C. The utmost care must be taken in this operation that the jewels in the holes are not in any way damaged or strained by the pivots.

The screw D may now be replaced through the centre of the continuity hairspring and the electrical connection from terminal B to the contact screws at the end of the contact arm of the heavy lever completed.

It will be noticed that there are two cylindrical weights in the box with the impulse lever, the heavier one is for use in normal air pressure and the smaller weight for the reduced air pressure. Fit the heavier weight on the impulse lever exactly midway between the impulse corner of the jewel and the pivot.

When this has been done the insertion of the impulse lever may be dealt with on similar lines. Remove the cock piece by taking out the screw E, place the impulse lever into position with its lower pivot in its pivot hole, then replace the cock piece and screw, being careful to gently guide the top pivot into its bearing hole, great care must be taken not to damage the pivots or the jewels.

The movement may now be placed in its proper position on the head casting and the connecting wires fixed to terminals on the movement. The flex from the movement to be connected to the spark condenser.

Fitting of Impulse Wheel Carriage.

The next stage in the erection of the Master clock may now be completed by unpacking the impulse wheel carriage. This carriage carries the small impulse wheel at its lower end and only requires to be hung in position on the pendulum. The two pointed steel screws go into the two holes already mentioned in the brass block fixed to the pendulum just below the safety plate.

When hung in position, the impulse wheel should only just clear the underside of the 'D' shaped impulse jewel and unless the adjustments of the various parts have altered in transit, this should be found to be the case when the pendulum suspension has been placed with the aid of the six adjusting screws so that the pendulum hangs in the centre of the case.

The plane of the impulse wheel when the pendulum is swinging to and fro should pass through the centre of the 'D' shaped portion of the impulse jewel.

The position of this jewel relative to the position of the impulse wheel when the pendulum is at rest is defined on the accompanying enlarged print No.2423D of the impulse wheel and lever. From this print it will be seen that the left-hand edge of the impulse jewel should be exactly 1½ millimetres on the right-hand side of a vertical line passing through the pivot of the impulse wheel.

The necessary adjustment to effect this may be made in two ways: one by shifting the pendulum bodily to the right or left by means of the two adjusting screws at the top of the head casting, or by adjusting the milled screw at the bottom right-hand corner of the movement plate, which rests against the small bracket attached to the top of the case.

Measurement of Arc.

It only remains to adjust the bowline at the outside of the bottom of the case to enable the arc of vibration to be measured from time to time.

The bowline should be carefully adjusted to coincide with the zero of the beat plate scale, but this, of course, must be done after the pendulum has been finally adjusted for position.

The normal total arc of vibration should be 110 minutes approx. The minimum arc on which the clock will work is 60 minutes, which is represented by a movement of the beat plate of 20 mm: or from 1cm. to 1cm. on the beat plate scale which is divided into millimetres.

If a microscope is provided with your Free Pendulum, the reference to the working arc above mentioned does not apply, and a memorandum will be found attached, illustrating the scale on the special beat plate and the method of reading it.

The Free Pendulum may now be left for the moment, with the bell jar placed in position to protect the movement from dust or damage.

Erection of Slave Clock & Wiring of Circuit.

The slave clock should be unpacked and erected and the electrical wiring and battery arranged.

As already explained, the position of the slave clock does not require the same care in selection as that of the Master, but a good wall and sound fixing are essential.

The accompanying print shows the electrical wiring required and as the terminals of both the slave and Master are lettered S.B.F. respectively, there should be no difficulty in correctly starting them up.

As the Master movement has not yet been set going, connect together temporarily the two terminals on the Master's case marked S and B so that the slave may be started going, without the Free Pendulum.

INSTRUCTIONS FOR THE ERECTION OF THE SLAVE CLOCK.

Unpack the clock and its parts contained in the small boxes, the case keys will be found in one of the boxes, open the case and remove the tissue paper, unpack the pendulum rod and bob.

It is necessary to fix the clock on a substantial wall free from vibration if the best results in timekeeping are to be obtained.

The clock should be erected so that the top of the case is about 6 ft. above the floor level, this will bring the clock movement to a convenient height for fitting up now and attention in the future.

A hanging plate will be noticed on the back of the clock case. Plug the wall and fix screw in plug so that the clock may be hung by its hanging plate on the wall at the recommended height.

A set of wood screws will be found in one of the small boxes, one screw 1½" long to hang the clock on and four 2½" screws for fixing the clock firmly to the wall.

As the clock is hanging on its one screw, open the door and hang a plumb line from the top of the case and down the left hand side of the clock, bring the clock to an upright position and mark off wall through the 4 - ¼" diameter holes in the back board of the case. Remove the clock and plug the wall in the four marked off positions.

Replace clock and screw back through the 4 holes firmly to the wall using the 2½" screws for this purpose.

Ascertain with the plumb line that the clock is not leaning out or inwards i.e. that the face of the wall is upright. If the clock is not upright in this respect, the fixing screws should be slackened off and hard wood packing of the right thickness placed behind the top or bottom batten to make it so, and the screws tightened up again.

Having got the clock firmly fixed to the wall, remove the wire ties from the seconds switch lever and the half minute gravity lever.

Proceed now to complete the assembly of the pendulum. Drawing No.20638 should be referred to.

Fit the top chops in which is fitted the suspension spring and cross bar or trunnion, remove screw from the suspension spring chop at the top end of the pendulum rod and insert spring into the slot until the holes in the spring and chop line up taking care to see that the clamping screws in both chops will be the same way round. Replace screw in the pendulum chop and tighten up until the spring is gripped firmly but not dead tight.

The bob should now be fitted having the rounded brass collar at the top and the flat shouldered collar let in at the bottom. Screw the rating nut on until the top of the rounded collar at the top of the bob is level with the line marked on the pendulum rod.

If the clock has a magnetic corrector fit the ring magnet on the plain part of the rod below the rating thread having the grub screw at the front, fit the beat ring at the bottom of the rod so that the black beat line is at the front - Drawing No. 20638 shows this.

Fit the jewelled click B into the special slotted screw at the back of the pallet so that the arm of the click comes to rest at the bottom of the circular slot.

Hang the pendulum in position and check for the right to left position whilst the pendulum is hanging stationary. Sketch 5 on Drawing No. 20638 shows the correct position with the gravity lever off its catch and the roller R resting on the pallet J.

If the clock is mounted upright the pendulum should be correct for position. If a slight adjustment is required use the trunnion traverse screws. (See Drawing No.9542).

When the pendulum is settled for position check the adjustments of the toggle, pallet and synchronising spring and re-adjust if necessary.

First adjust the seconds switch toggle for correct height on the rod which should be so that the rocking toggle piece just lifts the steel catch lever supporting the heavy switch lever just sufficient to release it, plus ¼ millimetre to spare as the pendulum is swinging from left to right and vice-versa.

Now adjust pallet J for position relative to roller 12 on gravity lever G. The top corner of the impulse curve of the pallet should swing under roller R with 1/100 inch clearance when gravity lever G is supported on its catch K. The pallet should also be adjusted so that its length is parallel to the plane of swing or to the back of the clock

The jewelled click B should now be in the correct position for gathering one tooth only of the fifteen toothed wheel for each complete swing of the pendulum however large the arc. The clock was sent out with this adjustment correct but should it need further adjustment the click wire may be slightly bent.

Next come the synchroniser fittings. Adjust the wire support ring so that the spring support wire is ⅜" below the lip of the synchroniser blade and adjust the synchroniser block holding the spring so that the top hook end of the spring is free to pass under the tip of the synchroniser blade with 1/100 inch to spare, see also that the spring is resting against its support wire and that the block and support wire are in a parallel plane to the swing of the pendulum. The position of the synchroniser fittings are shown on Drawing No. 191229.

Finally see that the weight tray is about ⅜" below the synchroniser block.

Magnetic Corrector. (See memorandum attached)

The battery may now be wired up to the clocks as shown on Drawing No. 11252, but as stated before, terminals S and B on the Free Pendulum should be temporarily connected together so that the slave may be started going. 6 volts is sufficient for all purposes.

Start the pendulum on a small arc, just large enough to ensure the 15 toothed wheel being rotated and the electrical beating of the seconds switch operating.

After about 1 hour the arc should have increased to 4 plus 4 centimetres on the beat scale.

On the right hand side of the case will be seen a panel with two adjustable resistances, one for the F.P. and the other for the slave. Providing the wiring resistance is negligible the F.P. resistance should be set at 7 ohms when the Atmosphere test is in progress i.e. when the heavy weight is being used on the F.P. gravity lever, and at 9 ohms when the F.P. is working at the reduced pressure of 20 millimetres of air i.e., when the light weight is being used. The slave resistance should be set at 7 ohms. In the latter case of the Free Pendulum and in the case of the slave clock these adjustments allow for the current flow to be 1/3 amp which is correct working value.

When the heavy weight is being used on the Free Pendulum gravity lever more current is required to operate the switch, adjusting the resistance to 7 ohms ensures this.

On the left hand side of the case are a similar pair of resistances mounted on a calibrated panel which, as will be seen by Drawing No. 11252, are for use in the seconds circuits. The top resistance is in series with the seconds switch and regulator dial coil and should be adjusted to 15 ohms to ensure a working current of 75 milliamps. The lower resistance provides a further seconds beat electrical circuit if required and the dotted line wiring on Drawing No. 11452 shows how this may be used. It is advisable not to pass more than .25 amp through this circuit which may be used for operating relays or chronograph pen or additional dials of seconds beat.

The Seconds Beat Regulator Dial.

The propelling of the dial wheel work is by means of a reciprocating brass lever having an armature plate at its top end which is attracted at each impulse by the magnet, and at the bottom end

As the armature is attracted the click steps back and down one tooth of the wheel and the spring resting on the heel of the click drives the armature brass lever forward on cessation of the impulse. Whilst this operation is taking place the wheel is held steady by a backstop i.e., a brass lever terminating in a steel square which fits into the teeth of the wheel.

To set this dial to time the minute hand must be turned in a forward direction by means of the set button on the back end of its arbor, the hour hand will follow the minute hand.

The seconds hand may be set by pressing on the left hand end of the back stop lever i.e., that part which overhangs its pivot, the wheel is then free to be revolved forwards to the correct second. If the seconds hand is some seconds slow the armature may be tapped on in between impulses.

The F.P. and Slave Dials.
The action of these movements is similar to the seconds beat dial excepting that they only move half-minute at each impulse.

To Set to Time.
Depress left hand end of backstop lever which will free the wheel work of the click and backstop and turn large wheel until the correct time is indicated. If a little slow these movements can also be tapped on in between impulses.

The above Slave Clock's normal rate when uncontrolled must be a losing one of six seconds per day, relative to the time to be measured (Sidereal or Mean as the case may be) and the rating of the Slave should be attended to before bringing it under the control of the Free Pendulum.

Starting up and Rating of Master Clock.
Two sets of regulating weights will be found among the accessories and the position of the weight tray and the weight of the pendulum bob have been so arranged that the placing of a one gramme weight on the tray will accelerate the pendulum by one second per day. The tray should be 5.5/16" below the safety pin, which will be found to be about ¼" below the surface on which the bell jar rests.

The compensator supporting the bob has been pinned to the pendulum in such a position that the clock will lose a few seconds per day on sidereal time at destination in vacuum, so that if a 10 gramme weight is placed on the weight tray, the rate should be found to approximate closely to sidereal time, during the preliminary rating at ordinary atmospheric pressure.

The time has come to start up both the Free Pendulum and Slave, but before doing this replace the appropriate wires on the S and B terminals on the Free Pendulum case which were connected together during the trial run and rating of the Slave clock, also stop the slave pendulum.

Now start up the Free Pendulum taking care that it swings in a true plane and not with a circular motion, work it up gently until the arc is about 18 mm. plus 18 mm. on the ivory beat plate or 100 minutes on the diamond engraved beat plate. Replace the bell jar whilst attention is now given to the Slave clock. Start the slave pendulum in motion to a little under its normal arc. It will be found that when its switch action occurs, the release magnet on the Master will operate, i.e., every half-minute.

The operation of the releasing magnet will allow the impulse lever to drop, and when this lever reaches the limit of its movement, it will release the catch holding the re-setting lever which, in its turn, will gently re-set the impulse lever upon its catch and finally close the Master remontoire circuit by means of the screw mounted on the contact arm. This energises the re-setting magnet and causes its armature to throw the re-setting lever back on its catch once more.

The closing of the Master remontoire circuit causes an impulse to return to the synchroniser on the Slave clock.

The action of the synchroniser should occur just as the slave pendulum is passing through zero on its excursion from right to left but owing to both pendulums most likely not being in a relative phase on starting up, the phase of the Slave pendulum should be gently retarded or quickened, whichever is nearer to synchronisation, by hand until a synchroniser HIT occurs i.e., when the spring on the pendulum is caught and bent back by the synchroniser blade.

The synchroniser action can be tried more frequently than its normal half-minute spaces by waiting until the Slave pendulum is over to the extreme left when catch K can be pushed aside by the finger thus releasing the gravity lever. Each time this is done the cycle of operations will be repeated.

Having got the Slave clock into a position where it is being synchronised it now remains to leave the clocks to work normally and watch the action of the synchroniser.

Owing to the slowing rate of the Slave of approximately six (6) seconds per day relative to the Master, the interval between the release of the impulse lever and the operation of its remontoire will gradually decrease, until the time arrives when the synchronising spring on the Slave just fails to get under the end of the synchronising magnet armature before this armature moves, that is to say, the armature will come down before the spring reaches it, with the result that the spring will engage with the end of the armature and be deflected as the pendulum continues its swing to the left.

This engagement and flexing of the spring naturally results in a shortening of the time of the particular swing of the slave pendulum by an amount dependent on the strength of the spring. The spring has been adjusted so that each time it is flexed that particular period of the slave is decreased by 1/240th of a second. As 6 seconds per day equal 1/480th of a second per half-minute, it follows that the slave will only drop back this amount between successive contacts and that it will not have dropped back sufficient for engagement to take place at the next contact and a miss will occur. At the end of another half-minute, however, it will drop back where it was before, and an engagement should take place. Thus engagements and misses should follow one another alternatively for an indefinite period, if the rate of the clocks does not change.

If the engagements and misses do not occur alternatively, or approximately so, the rating of the slave should be altered by adding or removing weights from its weight tray in order to bring this about. If more misses occur than engagements, the slave is obviously going too fast and weights should be removed from the tray. On the other hand, if the engagements preponderate, the clock is going too slow and weights should be added to the tray.

As soon as the synchronising of the slave is in satisfactory operation, the rate of the Master Clock can be determined. When the rate is definitely known to 1/10th of a second per day, arrangements for sealing the case and pumping out the air may be made. Before doing so, it is necessary to remove 12.25 grammes from the weight tray of the Master Clock, in addition it will be necessary to lighten the impulse lever by removing the weight and substituting it with a smaller weight. In ordinary air pressure the current rate is somewhat more than normal, owing to the use of the heavy cylindrical weight which, when being replaced by the lighter weight will bring the current to normal. Therefore it will be necessary to re-adjust the Free Pendulum resistance in order to obtain the standard current rate of .33 amp.

These alterations should not be made while the movement is in place. It should be removed from the case for this purpose. When the lever has been lightened the movement can be replaced.

Next, the mercury and oil gauge should be unpacked and set up on the top ring of the case on the left hand side. The fixing screws will be found with the gauge. Take care to see that the mercury is to the top of the tube side of the gauge with the scale reading. Now remove the oil gauge bulb with its opal scale and put into its container pump oil to the depth of about 10 millimetres, then replace the bulb so that the end of its tube is immersed almost the complete depth of the oil. The object of the oil gauge is to give a pressure reading of about ten times greater than the mercury gauge.

It must be remembered that the impulses are now insufficient to maintain the arc of the pendulum under ordinary air pressure. It is therefore necessary to gently increase the arc by hand at least 50% above its normal amount and to proceed with the sealing and exhaustion of the case immediately, otherwise it may be found that by the time the case has been exhausted, the arc of the pendulum has got below the minimum value at which the mechanism will operate.

Now clean the bell jar, and carefully grease the ground edge with the special grease. Clean the surface of the top ring of the case, place the bell jar in position and gently squeeze it into close contact with the copper with a slightly rotary motion.

The pump should now be prepared. Cut the rubber tube into two convenient lengths, attach one piece to the valve inlet of the Free Pendulum case, and its other end to one side of the glass drying tube. Fit the other piece of rubber tube to the remaining end of the drying tube and its other end to the pump. Now put about one third of the bottle of drying salts, supplied for the purpose, into the drying tube. The clock case is now ready to be pumped out.

Open the valve by withdrawing the screw plunger about two turns and start pumping. Pumping should be continued until the mercury gauge shows 1.8 c.m. from a vacuum. Now let sufficient air into the case to send the oil up the tube and until the mercury reaches 2 centimetres.

When this value has been reached, close the valve by screwing the plunger home and note the position of the mercury and oil. After allowing the case to remain undisturbed for an hour or so, again carefully note the position of the mercury and oil, repeat two or three times at intervals of twelve hours. The oil will probably move a little for the first two or three observations owing to the settling down of the temperature, in fact, the oil will continue to fluctuate if the clock is not kept in a constant temperature.

If the oil and mercury has remained steady, the test may be considered satisfactory. On the other hand, should a movement be disclosed a leak is indicated and all joints and connections must be carefully examined. The order of probable leakage is as follows:-

1. Joint between bell jar and copper flange.
2. Joint between glass disc and bottom flange.
3. Joint between valve and socket and bottom casting.
4. Joints between terminals and top casting.

The whole case was carefully tested as above before despatch and proved to be able to hold 74 cm. of vacuum indefinitely.

If it should happen that while pumping out the air, the arc of the pendulum has got below the minimum value at which the mechanism will operate, shut the valve up and remove the rubber tube. Now place a finger over the valve inlet and unscrew the valve plunger about two turns, watch the pendulum and as it commences to swing away from the valve, let a spurt of air in for a duration of about half a second. Repeat this until the pendulum has regained a reasonable arc. These air impulses will rapidly restore the pendulum to the required arc. The valve may now be closed, the rubber tube replaced and pumping re-commenced when the valve is opened again.

Assuming that the case has been satisfactorily sealed, the pressure should be reduced until the mercury gauge reads 2 cm. or thereabouts, and the rate of the clock under this pressure can then be accurately determined.

As the effect of the reduction of the air pressure is not known to within 1/10th of a second per day, it is probable that the rate of the clock when exhausted may be so far from time it cannot be corrected by increasing or further reducing the air pressure. Under these circumstances, there will be no alternative but to open the case and adjust the regulating weights on the weight tray accordingly, in the proportion of 1 gramme to one second per day. This alteration should not, of course, be made until the rate of the clock is known to the nearest 1/100th of a second.

The amount of the arc is a valuable indication of the satisfactory going of the clock and once this arc has settled down it should remain absolutely constant, so long as the density of the air within the case is unchanged.

DR'G No 10552

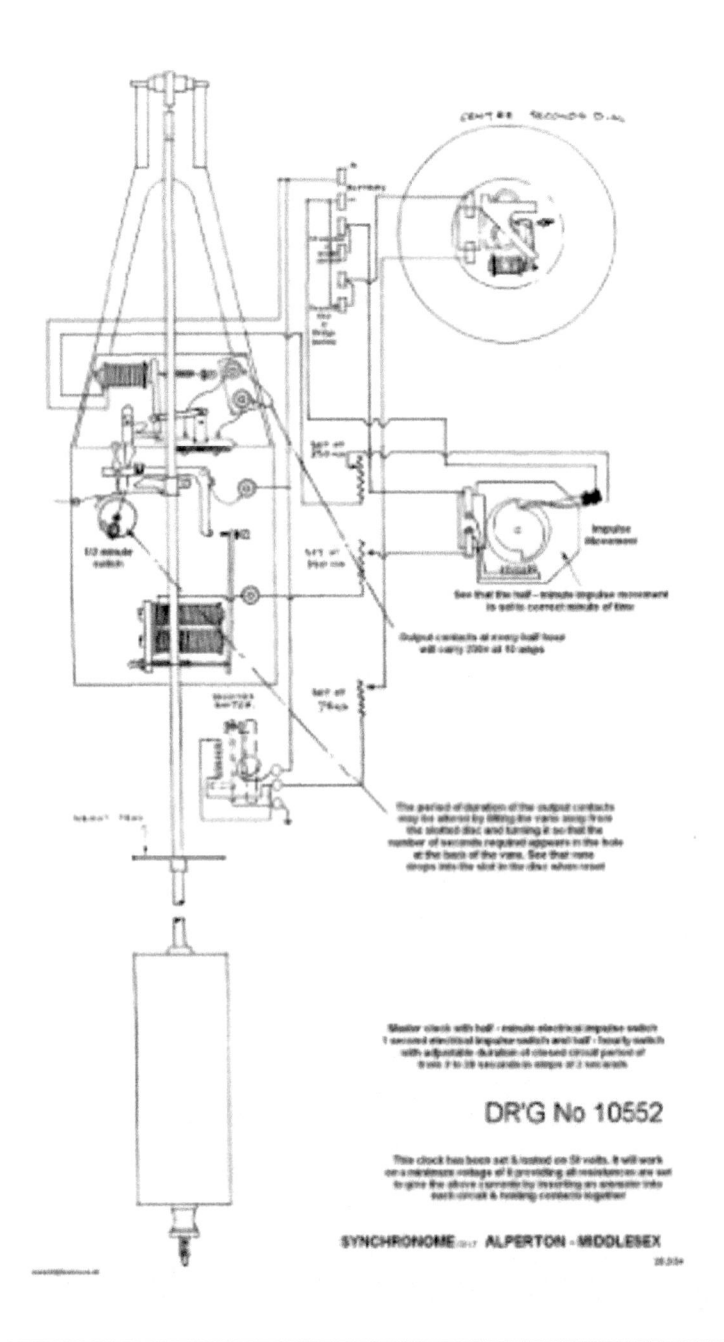

SYNCHRONOME — ALPERTON - MIDDLESEX

SIDEREAL INSTALLATION

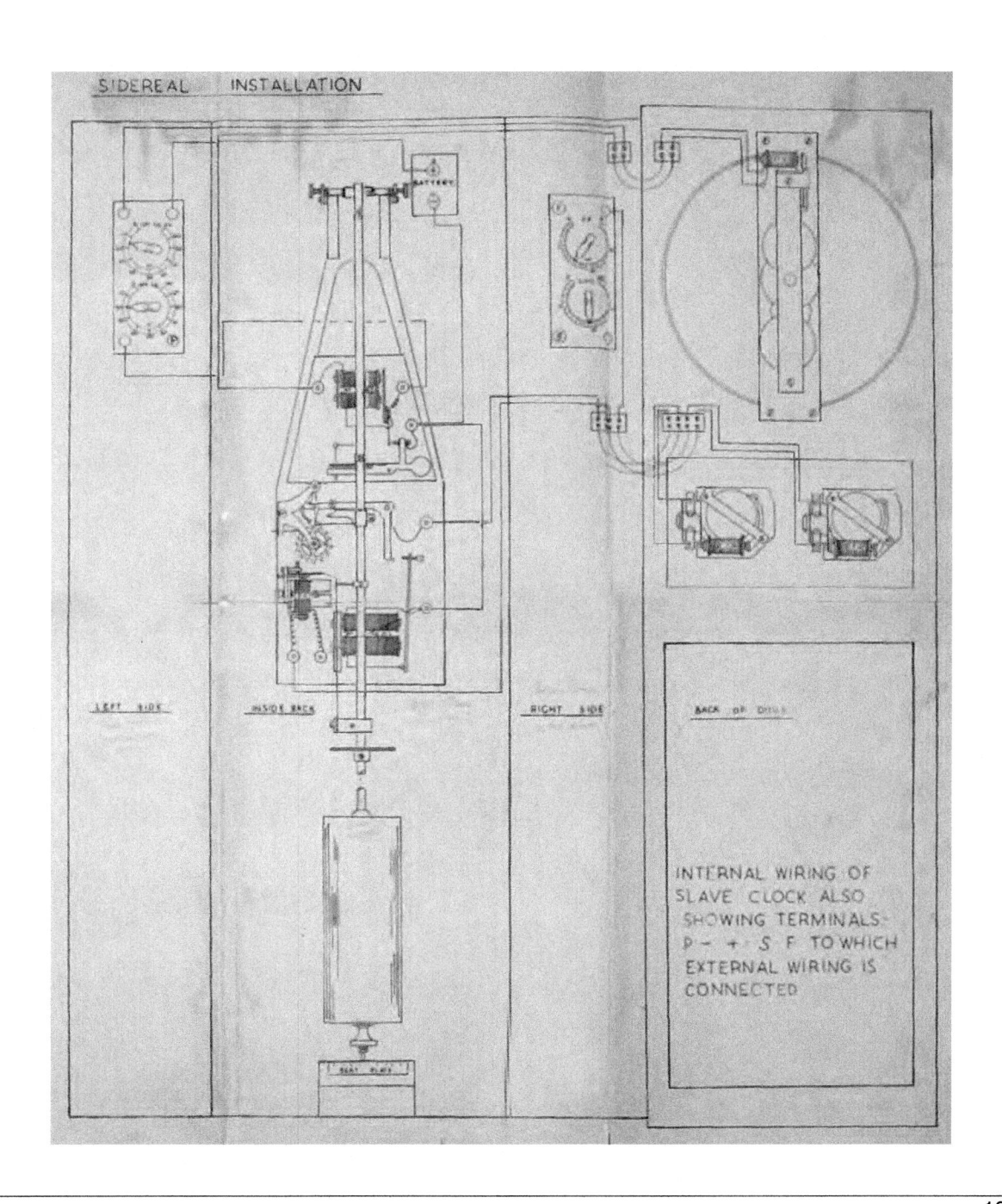

LEFT SIDE

INSIDE BACK

RIGHT SIDE

BACK OF DIAL

INTERNAL WIRING OF SLAVE CLOCK ALSO SHOWING TERMINALS P – + S F TO WHICH EXTERNAL WIRING IS CONNECTED

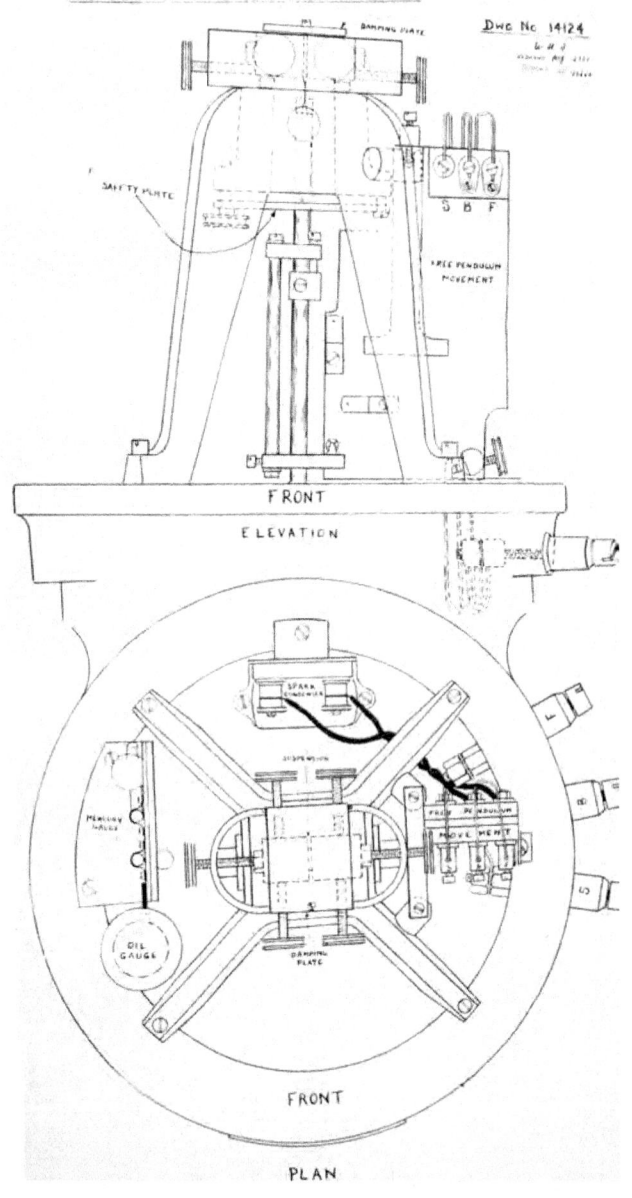

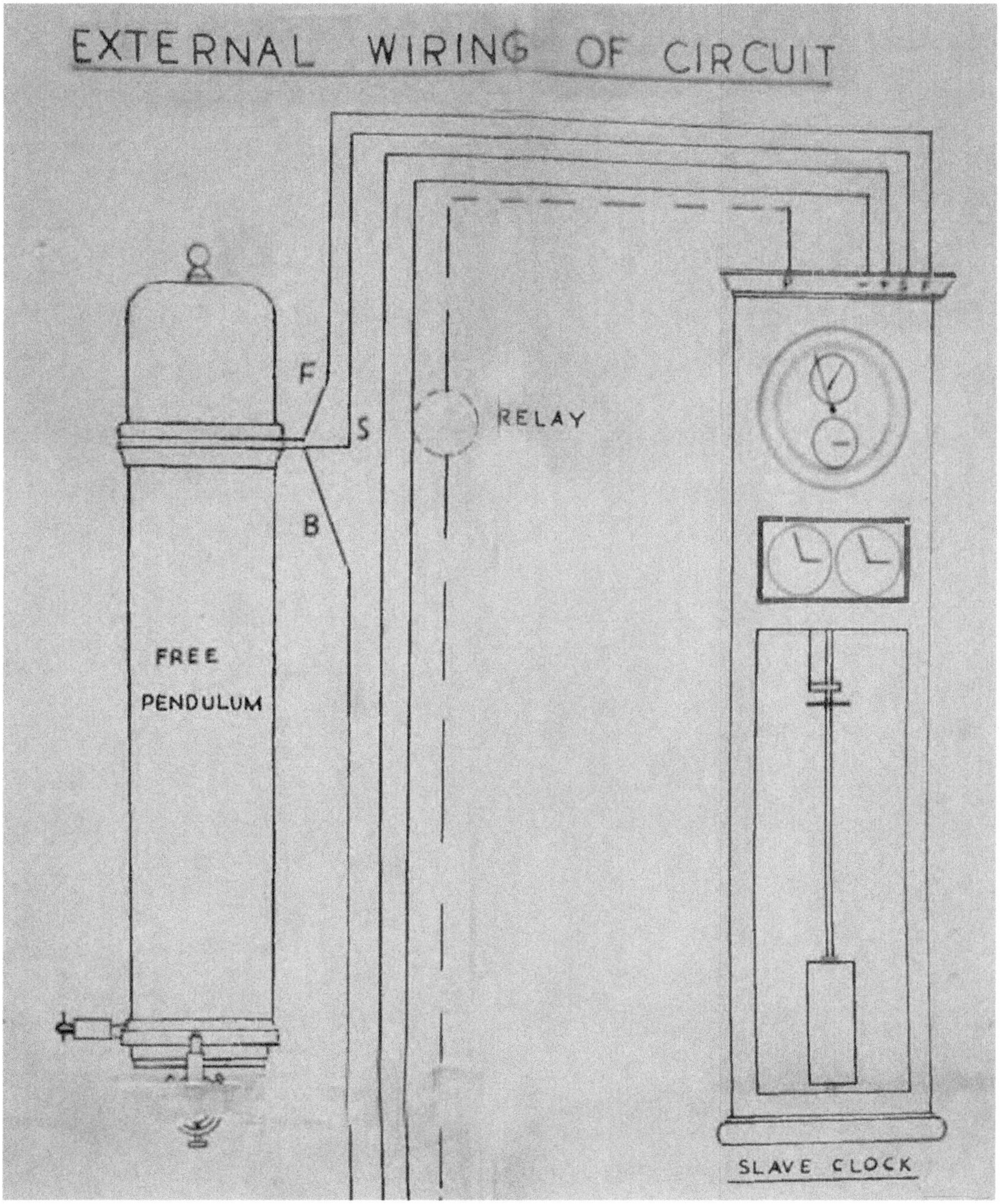
EXTERNAL WIRING OF CIRCUIT
F
S
B
RELAY
FREE
PENDULUM
SLAVE CLOCK

SYNCHRONOME Cº Ltd. Woodside Place Alperton
Bottom of Free Pendulum case with its fittings showing
microscope and its traverse and lower end of pendulum.
SCALE ½ FULL SIZE

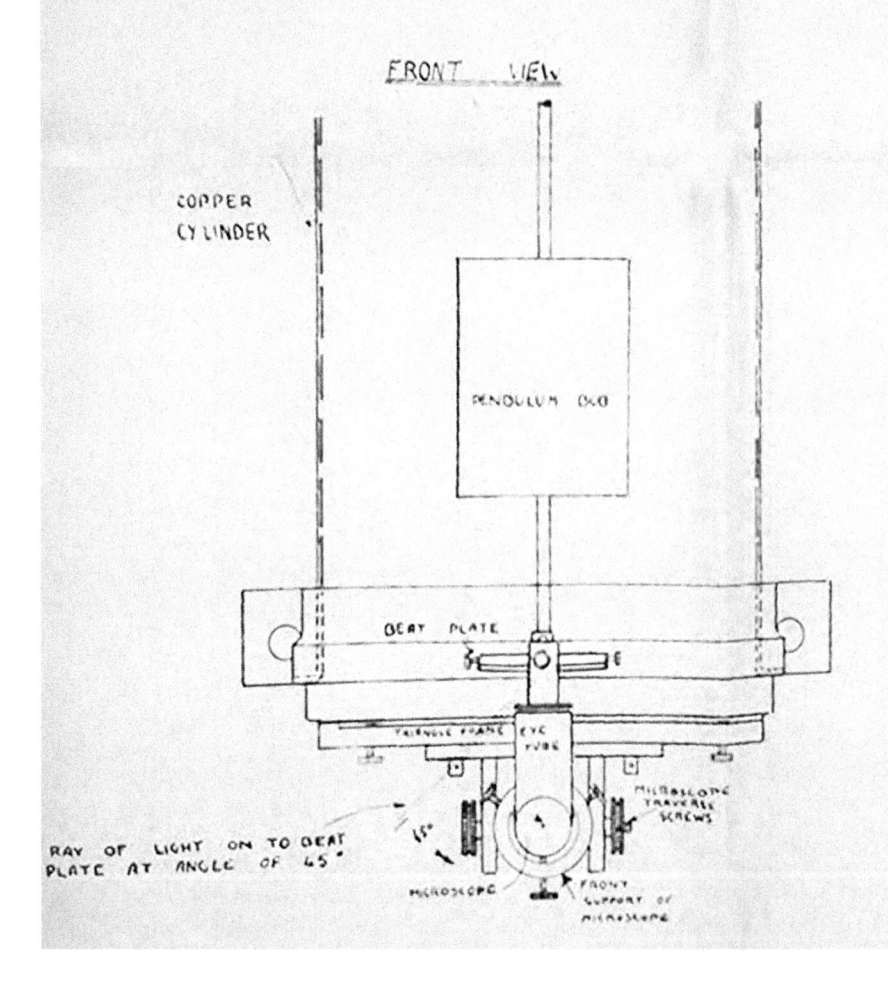

FRONT VIEW

COPPER CYLINDER

PENDULUM BOB

BEAT PLATE

TRIANGLE FRAME   EYE TUBE

RAY OF LIGHT ON TO BEAT
PLATE AT ANGLE OF 45°

MICROSCOPE   FRONT SUPPORT OF MICROSCOPE   MICROSCOPE TRAVERSE SCREWS

DRG 18138

113

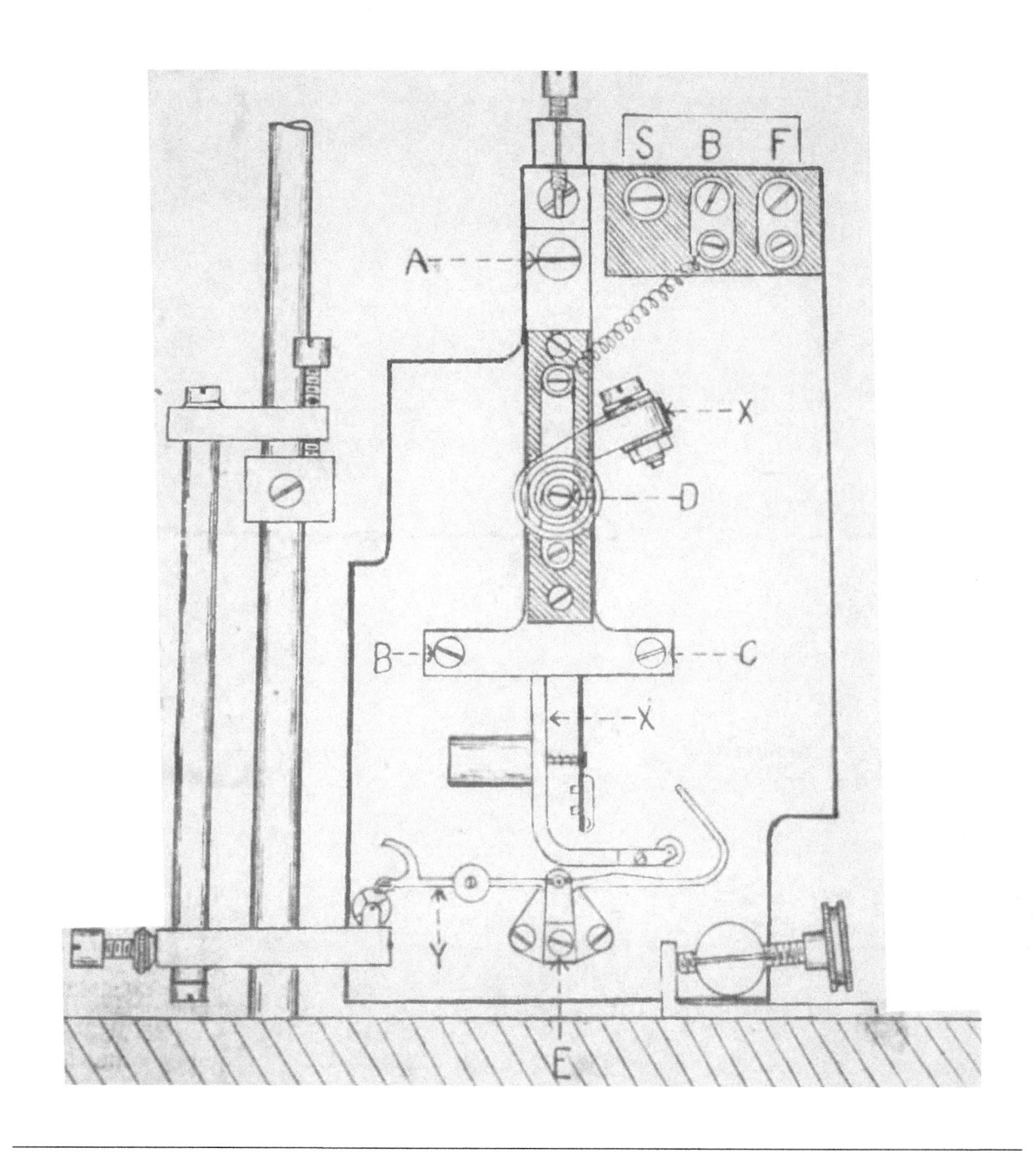

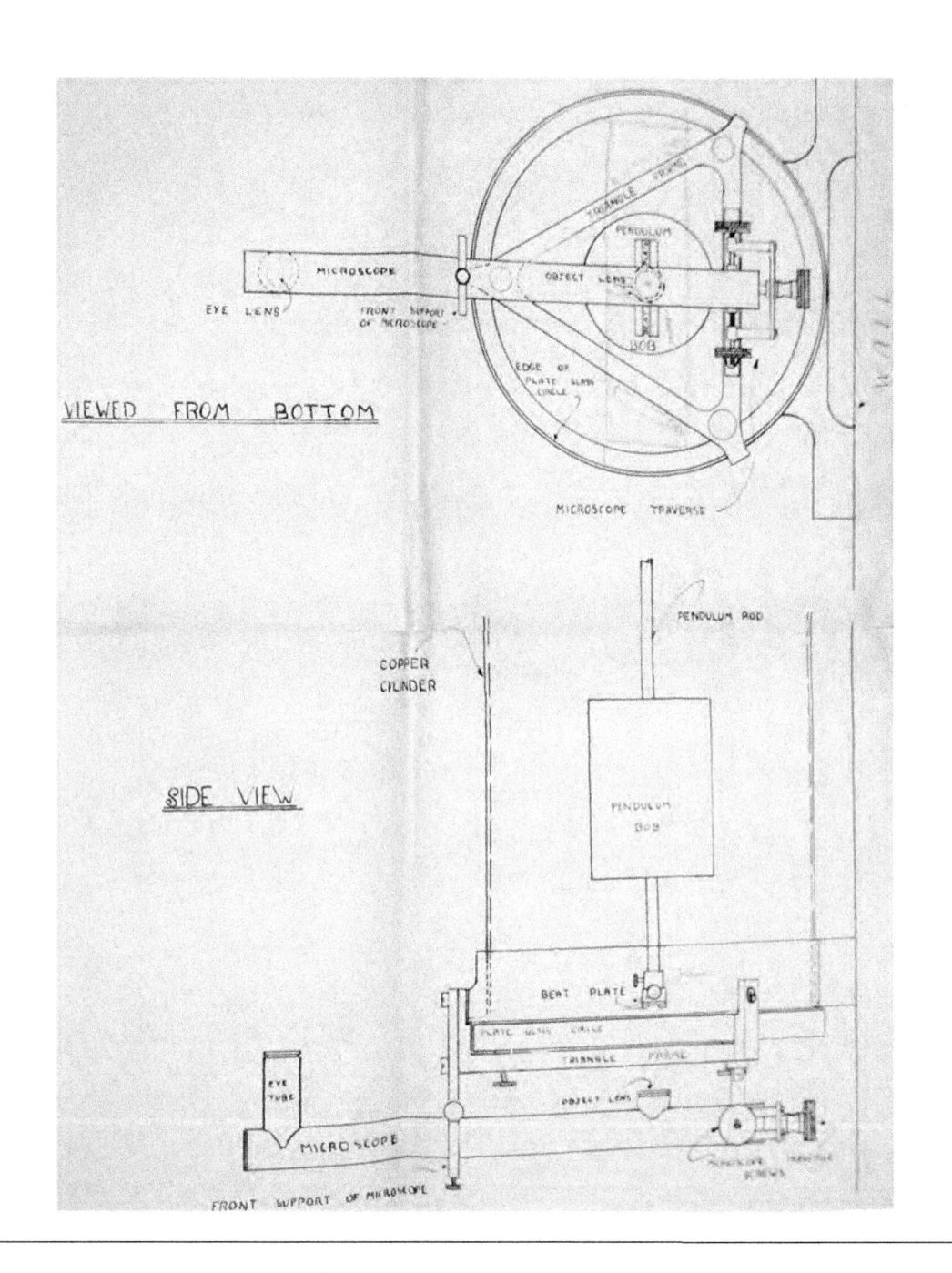

Appendix B: Winchester College Empire Clock - Documentation from the Winchester College Archives, April 2021

23rd October, 1976.

The Bursar,
Winchester College.

Rec'd by hand 23/10/76

Dear Sir,

Empire Clock in Moberly Library

I have pleasure in handing you two copies of the History of the Clock since it was given to the College in 1936 by Sir Herbert Baker, Mr. R.F. Stewart and myself.

Bound in with this is a revised instructions for setting the clock to time with particular reference to getting the 24 h dial correctly set and 'Summer Time'.

Also in the file are the instructions for overhauling the movement and a set of the drawings needed for doing the work.

I have been happy to look after it all these years and hope to continue to do so, or that my heirs will follow on. They should be given the opportunity before the work is handed to anyone else.

Yours sincerely,

H.E. Baker.

24th September, 1976.

WINCHESTER COLLEGE - 'EMPIRE' CLOCK   No. 3

For account of opening ceremony see the 'Times' of 31st March, 1936.

For design and materials of clock and copies of drawings and photographs, see account written by R.F.S. in 1936. Copy in Moberly Library.

Instructions for starting and setting to time are framed on access door at the back.

Explanation of dials see draft of 'rased version by Bursar in Reading Room.

History of running and maintenance, see following pages:

HISTORY

Summary of Overhauls

		Intervals (Years)
Erected	March, 1936	
Examined	August, 1936	
Examined, Checked & adjusted	1936 and 1937	1
Cleaned by R.F.S.	1939	2
Examined and Cleaned	July, 1945	6
Removed for overhaul	April, 1947	2
Removed for overhaul	March, 1953	6
Dismantled and cleaned	August, 1962	9
Dismantled and cleaned	June, 1976	14

Details of Overhauls

March, 1936	Erected in Moberly Library
21st April, 1936	Unveiled
22nd August, 1936	Examined. 12 h Dial altered to small circular polish. Bearings washed and refilled with oil/vaseline mixture. Wear slight, oil discoloured. Refixed by H.E.B. and R.F.S.

....cont.   - 2 -
                    WINCHESTER COLLEGE - 'EMPIRE' CLOCK

28th August, 1937   Examined and cleaned.
                       Ball bearings showed wear on outer races greatest
                       on motor and generally on one side of race –
                       presumably on underside of shaft.
                       Wear in sleeves slight on seconds, negligible on
                       hour and minute.
                       Oil sticky and slightly discoloured. Cleaned and
                       refilled with clock oil only on all but motion
                       shaft bearings.

1939   Cleaned by R.F.S. Some ball bearings dirty.

War   Running throughout, except when supply failed.

14th July, 1945   Dismantled, cleaned and replaced by R.F.S. and H.E.B.
                       Oiled with clock oil and vaseline.
                       Left running quietly.
                       Dust moderate and not affecting running.
                       Black oil in some bearings due to running on cages:
                       others including motor and intermediate, in good
                       condition.
                       Seconds parallel bearing shaft worn into a groove.
                       Parallel races not examined, but oiled liberally.
                       Motor pinion – very slight wear. Sleeves good –
                       plenty of oil and only slight discoloration.
                       Motor flywheel bush clean and free.
                       Gilding bright – slight marks or scratches.

12th April, 1947   Removed Movement to Owletts.
                       Slight discoloration of oil as in 1945.

                       Motor – dismantled and cleaned – good order.

                       Intermediate – parallel bearings good – shaft races
                       polished.

                       Seconds Shaft – parallel bearing good – just tight
                       on shaft to keep balls in worn groove.

                       Sleeves – good. Washed only. Spider spring on
                       minute tightened.

                       Counter shaft. – Shaft race at back grooved –
                       replaced.

                       Minute – setting shaft. Shaft races polished.

                       Lay shaft – Shaft races polished.

                       Hour hand – Catch made with new boss for DST.
                       (Spring rather too light).

                                                           contd.....

...contd.

WINCHESTER COLLEGE - 'EMPIRE' CLOCK

                   Minute hand - boss grub screws replaced by stainless steel.

                   24 h Dial - screw heads turned down .02" to clear hub.

                   12 h Dial - Sand-blasted and reblacked by G.T. Friend. Matt finish gives better visability.

                   All cleaned with petrol - re-oiled with vaseline and Windles' Clock Oil.

3rd May, 1947   Refixed and left working.

14th March, 1953 Removed for inspection to 13, Hereford Square and Owletts.

                   Motor - free - slight discoloration of back bearing probably due to dust from seconds wheel. Both bearings washed and cleaned.

                   Intermediate - 'ditto'. Bearings cleaned and tightened slightly.

                   Seconds Shaft - Back bearing 'ditto'. Sleeves nearly dry but O.K. Wheel rubbing on hub of counter shaft. Dust falling onto bearings below. Thought to be sole cause of sticking. Bad adjustment of position last time. B. bearing O.K. - cleaned.

                   Counter shaft - O.K.

                   Sleeves - O.K. - not quite dry.

                   Hub - Screws of last wheel were loose - rubbing plate. Bearings cleaned and packed with grease.

                   Motion shaft - O.K.

                   Hand setting shaft - O.K.

                   Remainder of bearings topped up with vaseline and clock oil.

                   Wheels and bearings adjusted - just tight.

2nd May, 1953   Re-assembled

                   Motor coil appears O.K. Electrician said it was faulty - low insulation resistance.

17th October, 1959 Clock inspected.

...cont.

WINCHESTER COLLEGE - 'EMPIRE' CLOCK

                      Time of dial wrong due to resetting from summer time of minute hand only. Corrected and advised under-porter.
Red powder in double helical gears. Running quietly.

22nd October, 1960   Inspected. Running O.K.

15th August, 1962   Taken down completely except motion work. Cleaned,
(HEB, HB, MHB &   oiled and refixed except hands to be gilded.
RHB)

Found to be running well with only slight rusty powder between teeth of first wheel and motor pinion. Some discoloration of motor bearings and oil in flywheel bush: all dismantled, cleaned and refilled with Clock oil and Vaseline.
Some difficulty in re-assembling spring drive of flywheel - rotor. One ball in back Intermediate bearings replaced and all 7 in front bearing.
Slight wear on teeth of motor pinions and intermediate pinion.

Seconds shaft - worn to groove in parallel bearing. One ball of front motion shaft bearing fell out on dismantling - replaced. This bearing is liable to damage by a jerk on 24 h dial. A standard parallel bearing would have been better than the conical special ones used on the other shafts.

Rest of clock in very good condition. External dust slight. Sleeves clean, and would have run for several years. Bearings, other than motor, not dismantled, but oiled; Vaseline put in shaft ends. All sleeves oiled only - clock oil and MOS_2 - note: MOS_2 is black and disguises wear in sleeves. No bearings adjusted endways.

20th September,   Hands replaced after re-gilding by Messrs. Morris,
1962   Singer, Basingstoke. Left running O.K.
(HEB & RHB)

August, 1966   Description sent to Bursar for printing and exhibition in Moberly Library.

22nd November, 1969   In summer motor bearings were noisy and loose.
(HEB & Richard B)   Visit to check: motor removed by 2 - 4 BA screws to front plate.
Some play in bearings and oil dry and discoloured, otherwise no defect seen. Some wear of outer race. Washed and replaced with Vaseline and clock oil. Flywheel not removed, but oiled under collar.
Rest of movement ran freely and was not treated in any way.
1 - 4 BA screw dropped between wall and dial as

                                                          contd...

....cont.

WINCHESTER COLLEGE - 'EMPIRE' CLOCK

they were very difficult to hold in place while fitting motor.
Left running: 1 screw only. Captive screws or screws with a short lead are required.
Flex was stiff and replaced by a piece available - new 3-core with E. required.

21st March, 1970 2 - 4 BA screws with 3/16" turned down fitted without stopping motor.
Clock changed to 'summer time' and left running smoothly.

June, 1973)
March, 1974) Clock incorrectly set; advised Bursar.
Spot light required.

June, 1975 G.C.W. Dicker in office behind would tackle Bursar to get competent person on it and fit the spot light. M. Zvegintzoff suggested 'Prefect of Clock'.

7th June, 1976. Clock reported stopping at 25 mins to hour. Assisted by Golding and College electrician I removed it entirely, dismantled and cleaned between 11 a.m. and 6 p.m. (-1½ hr. for lunch with G.D.)
Dials and hands washed by Golding.
Too much play in first pair (motor-inter) allowed Intermediate shaft to slide off balls in bearing and jam. Motion shaft and hub were stiff so I decided to take it all apart.

Motor - bearings were discoloured - cleaned and replaced with Vaseline and clock oil. Rotor sleeve oiled.

Intermediate - bearings dismantled and cleaned. Assembled with Vaseline and clock oil. Front bearing retaining ring tightened slightly.

Seconds shaft - Good only rather dry in sleeve.

Counter shaft -)
) Good - PTFE .005" washers between
Minute shaft -) hand on front only.

Motion shaft - Differential pinions nearly seized with black grease - dismantled and re-assembled with clock oil and Vaseline. These had not been dismantled before as they appeared good. Resetting mesh of pinions needs care.

Hour Sleeve - Good.

Hand Setting - good-lay-shaft bearings oiled only.

contd...

...cont.

- 6 -

WINCHESTER COLLEGE - 'EMPIRE' CLOCK

<u>Hub</u> - 2 - 1" ball bearings sticky with dried grease - removed and washed with paraffin and replaced with grease.

<u>Refixed and left running</u>

Condition was similar in previous overhaul of all parts then cleaned or re-lubricated. Clock oil Merchants in Hatton Garden or Clerkenwell Road should be able to supply best quality oil. Otherwise sewing machine oil could be used. Motor needs Earth wire - electrician will run one and clamp under one of the nuts.

H.E. Baker.

WINCHESTER COLLEGE 'EMPIRE' CLOCK   No. 3.

Schedule of Drawings

No.		Date	Medium	Signature
3/1	Assembly of Movement Full size	12.5.35	Ink Tracing	H.E.B.
3/2	Motor Shaft Assembly 4 x F.S.	5.5.35	Ink Tracing	H.E.B.
3/3	Coil for Motor F.S.	25.10.35	Blue Print	R.F.S.
3/4	Ball Bearing ⅛" 10 x F.S.	5.5.35	Ink Tracing	H.E.B.
3/5	Ball Bearing 3/16" 10 x F.S.	24.12.35	Ink Tracing	H.E.B.
3/6	Ball Bearing Parallel ⅛" 8 x F.S.	18.10.35	Ink Tracing	R.F.S.
3/7	Tooth Forms	14.6.36	Ink Tracing	R.F.S.
3/8	Dials Details of Construction	7.10.35 rev. 15.10.35	Ink Tracing	H.E.B.
3/9	Frame Built in	9.1.36	Pencil Tracing	H.E.B.
3/10	Spider spring for minute shaft	24.11.35	Ink Tracing	H.E.B.

Note: Nos. 3/1, 2, 4, 5 & 6 Prints in Instructions for Maintenance.
Above and Nos. 3/7 Print in Description by R.F.S. 1936
No. 3/3 Print (only copy) in description at Owletts.
Originals and other drawings of the construction and dials at Owletts. See lists in drawings cabinet.

H.E. Baker
18th October, 1976.

WINCHESTER COLLEGE 'EMPIRE' CLOCK   No. 3

Instructions for Setting Clock

The 'Crowned Lion' on the big dial should show always GMT so that the other symbols show their own time. To achieve this proceed as follows at the back of the clock.

1. **Summer Time**

    Move lever on left of movement up or down to 'Summer Time 1 hour fast' or 'Winter Time'. See that it clicks home at end of track.

2. **Local Time**

    Turn Minute hand on pilot dial to bring Hour hand to time of day 'Morning' on the left or 'Afternoon' on the right. Then set the time on this dial.

3. **Motor**

    Start motor by turning knurled knob anti-clockwise, see arrow, until it runs "in step".

    Motor can run backwards and might reverse as the result of a momentary power failure.

Note: a) If 'Double Summer Time' is introduced again, the main hour hand on front of clock has a spring catch on its boss allowing it to be moved forward 1 hour without altering world time on the 24 hour dial. It should be moved back the hour before the lever on back of clock is altered.

b) British Standard Time was fixed by law as 1 hour fast of Greenwich Mean Time. The clock should remain set at 'Summer Time: 1 h fast'.

c) This Act was repealed and the country reverted to changing time twice a year.

H.E. Baker
18th October, 1976.

24th September, 1976.

WINCHESTER COLLEGE 'EMPIRE' CLOCK   No. 3.

Instructions for Dismantling and Lubricating

Assembly drawing no. 3/1

1. Second-hand – Pull off.

2. Minute-hand – Two grub screws 8 B.A.

3. Hour-hand – Two grub-screws 6 B.A.

4. 12-hour dial – Undo flat nut: two holes for round-nosed pliers and lift off.

5. 24-hour dial – Take out 6 – 2 B.A. screws. Lift off. Heavy; ease off gently. Take care not to jerk gears which may damage front bearing of motion shaft. Note marks for reassembly.

   NOTE: Pointers on rim of dial. Stand dial on sector which has none – "Pacific Ocean".

   NOTE: ABOVE ITEMS IN FRONT FROM A FIRM LADDER. FOLLOWING ITEMS FROM THE ACCESS DOOR AT THE BACK.

6. Unplug lead to motor. This should be done FIRST. Motor may be removed before taking movement from wall.

7. Remove 4 – 5/16" bolts between main plate and frame in wall. Hexagons smaller than standard. Lift out movement, take care to retain packing washers.

8. Bolt plate to loose stand upside down – motor at top.

MOST OF MOVEMENT CAN BE OVERHAULED IN THIS POSITION.

9. Motor – 2 – 4 B.A. screws with extended ends. NOTE: dowel pins not fitted. Meshing of Motor pinion 1 and Wheel 2 must be close but not tight in any position. Teeth should be cleaned with petrol and brush.

9.1. Undo starting knob by 10 B.A. thread on shaft after loosening recessed lock nut by screw-driver.

9.2. Remove back plate by 2 – 2 B.A. nuts.

9.3. Lift out motor shaft.   Drawing No. 3/2

9.4. Remove flywheel – 10 B.A. grub screw in collar and driving springs on pins may be removed by small bent-nosed pliers. It requires patience to hook the four loops over the four pins.

9.5. Coil and magnet plates should not be removed. For specification of coil see RFS's drawing 25 x '35 in correspondence.

10. Pilot dial. Minute hand – 8 B.A. grub screw engaged with recess in shaft. Retain spacing sleeve.

contd...

.cont.

WINCHESTER COLLEGE 'EMPIRE' CLOCK

Instructions for Dismantling and Lubricating

10.1. Dial - 2 - 2 B.A. nuts. Remove dial and hour wheel together. "Lay" shaft will be loose but cannot fall out.
Note: Pinion 20 runs on lower pillar.

11. Main back plate - 4 - 5/16" B.S.F. nuts. Prise off gently.

11.1. Remove all wheels in turn. Some are interleaved. Take care none fall out, particularly the 'intermediate'.

11.2. Minute shaft has slipping clutch for setting to time. Wheel 8 is held on by shaft nut with recessed-head locking screw. Spider spring is driven by key in shaft, which also drives pinion 11.

11.3. Motion shaft is held by arm and track of differential - 2-4 B.A. screws and dowels. Knob held onto Arm by 2 - 4 B.A. screws. It contains a 3/16" ball and spring.

11.4. Differential assembly on motion shaft is attached to Motion Wheel 12 which is held on by shaft nut and key. Two planet pinions 13 and 14 are on excentric bushes on motion Wheel. They engage with each other and 13 engages with 15 which is on a sleeve fixed by 2 - 8 B.A. grub screws to the Arm. Pinion 14 engages with pinion 16 which drives Wheel 17 - the Hour Hand. Moving the Arm through 120° moves the hour hand through one hour - 30° and Pinion 22 driving the Dial is held on 1 - 8 B.A. grub screw.

In reassembling make sure (a) pinions 13, 14, and 15 are correctly meshed by turning and locking the screws and excentric bushes. (b) Arm is the right way round. NOTE: rubbing marks on Arm from curved track and grub screws enter recesses in sleeve of pinion 15. (c) Pinion 22 is right way round and grub screw enters recess in shaft.

12. 24-hour Hub. 2 - 1" dia. ball bearings are easy press-fit on stub shaft.

NOTE: Dust cover plates at each end. Stub screwed into front plates and can be removed by through bolt (3/8" or 1/2") tightened and turned. Put soft washers under bolt head and nut.

13. Conical ball bearings should be dismantled by lifting the retaining ring on top of the balls with tweezers or bent-nosed pliers. This ring is snapped into a groove in the hardened steel outer race. The balls are also retained by a screw (4 B.A. or 3/16" x 60) from the back which can be used for oiling from outside. Wash out with petrol if dirty; replace balls 1/16" if worn or discoloured. There should be no appreciable wear or discoloration of the lubricant over many years of running, particularly on the slower shafts.

Drawing Nos 3/4,5.

cont......

...cont.

WINCHESTER COLLEGE - 'EMPIRE' CLOCK

Instructions for Dismantling and Lubricating

3.1. To replace, fill groove with vaseline and lay in balls (7 in small-bearings, 8 in parallel and 18 in hand-setting bearing) and snap in cover ring. Add a few drops of clock oil.

3.2. Parallel bearings for intermediate shaft and back of second-hand are intended to allow the shafts to move endways. They have cylindrical inner and outer races, the balls being retained by sleeves screwed in as shown on drawing by R.F.S.
                  Drawing no. 3/6

3.3. There are a few spare bearings for the conical ball races. The outer race is part of $\frac{1}{2}$" dia. sphere, the inner race a 60° cone. Thread in plate is $\frac{1}{4}$" d x 40 t.p.i.

3.4. Polish races by fine emery and finish with 'diamentine' (alumina) on soft wood stick, turned to a ball end for the outer spherical races.

3.5. If bearings have to be taken out or replaced ensure that they are locked with no end-play, i.e. just tight. Ensure that clearances between the wheels and shafts are not disturbed. Note. Shafts and pillars are of same steel (S80).

4. Parts NOT TO BE UNDONE EXCEPT FOR REPAIRS:-

 All pillars in plates.

 Motor front plate and magnet and coil.

 Motion shaft front plate.

 Bearings and lock nuts.

5. Lubrication of hand sleeves was first done by clock oil and vaseline and proved good for several years provided a good reserve was left in the space around the middle length of each sleeve. Later experiments at R.C.S. were made with coloidal MOS^2 coating and mixed in thin oil. FLUON (P.T.F.E.) washers .005" between inner shoulders and bosses of hands. There is no room at Winchester for these washers except in front between hands.

5.1. Spider spring and differential parts may be lubricated with MOS^2 and oil.

5.2. Dial ball races: Wash out if necessary and refill with ball-bearing grease.

6. REASSEMBLY

 Proceed in reverse. One person each side is needed for setting hands and dials.

                     contd....

...cont.

- 4 -

WINCHESTER COLLEGE 'EMPIRE' CLOCK

Instructions for Dismantling and Lubricating cont.

16.1. Teeth may have to be slipped to get 24-hour dial and minute setting hand together on the hour. Release back-plate slightly and take care nothing falls out!

16.2. Push pilot hour-hand round to time on Dial.

16.3. Catch on boss of hour-hand should be set at '1' unless "double summer time" is in force.

16.4. Set hands on sleeves so that there is end clearance.

16.5. Run hands round 24 hours to ensure all clearances are correct.

16.6. Ensure that all nuts and screws are tight.

Tools Required for Overhaul

Spanners:	Open	5/16" downwards adjustable.
		2 BA.
	Box	5/16".
		2 BA.
	'C'	Special for bearing lock nuts 9/16" d.
Screwdrivers:		For screws 2, 4, 6 & 8 BA.
		Long stem for hands grub screws.
Pliers:		Small straight.
		Small round nosed.
		Small bent nosed for springs, and balls in bearings.
Tweezers:		For balls, caps & C.
Pin Chuck		For wire or small rods (long screwdriver).
Lubricants:		Clock oil.
		MoS_2 in oil - thinned.
		Vaseline.
Washers:		Fluon .005" thick.
Balls:		1/16" bearing quality.
Cleaners:		Petrol or lighter fuel.
		Paint brush and toothbrush.
		Small pot for bearings.
		Saucer for other parts.
		Rags, pipe cleaners.

H.E. Baker

Section on ℄ of balls.

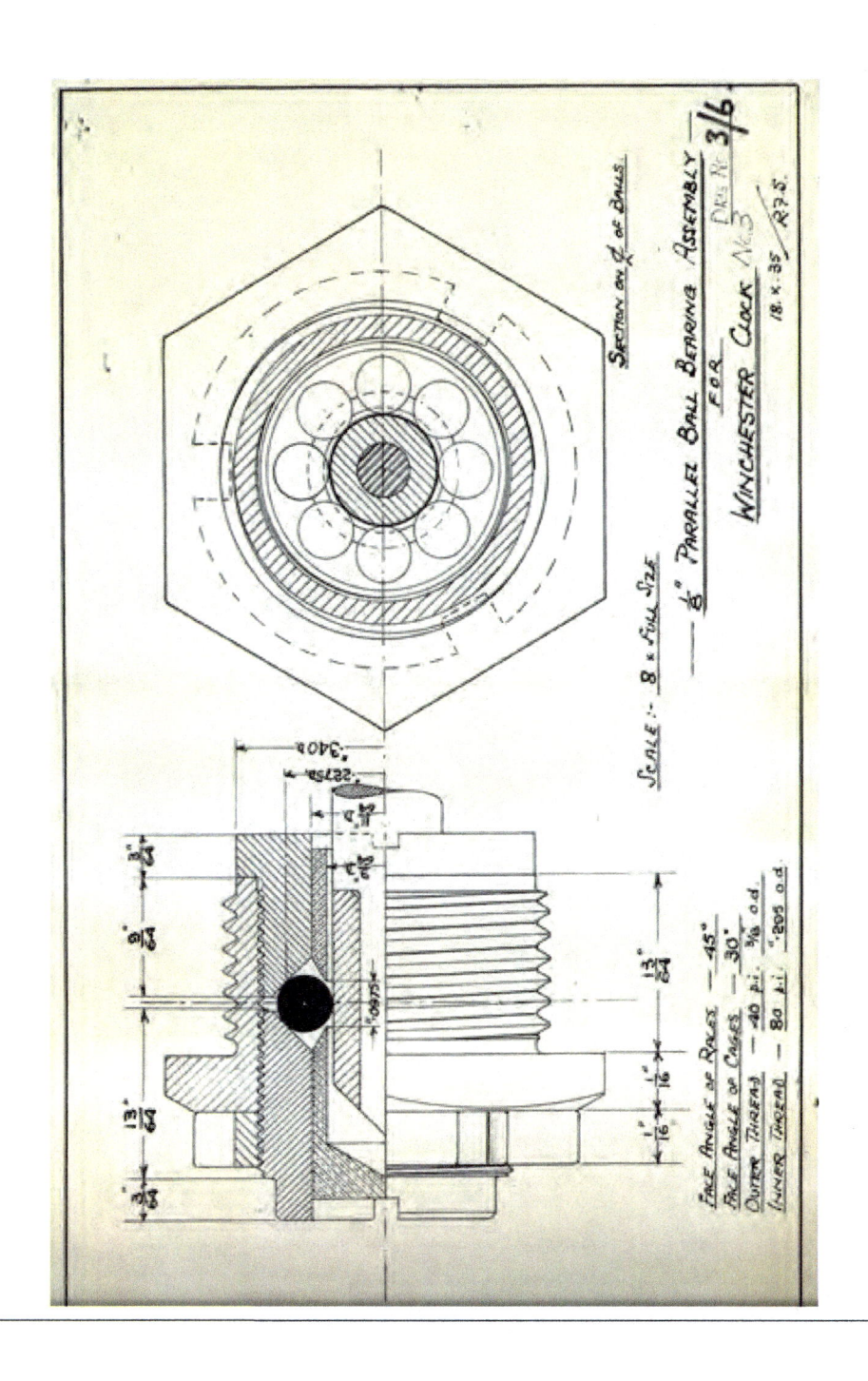

Scale :- 8 × Full Size

6" Parallel Ball Bearing Assembly
for
Winchester Clock No 3

Drg No 3/6
18.x.35 R.J.S.

Face Angle of Races — 45°
Face Angle of Cages — 30°
Outer Thread — 40 p.i. ³⁄₁₆ o.d.
Inner Thread — 80 p.i. .205 o.d.

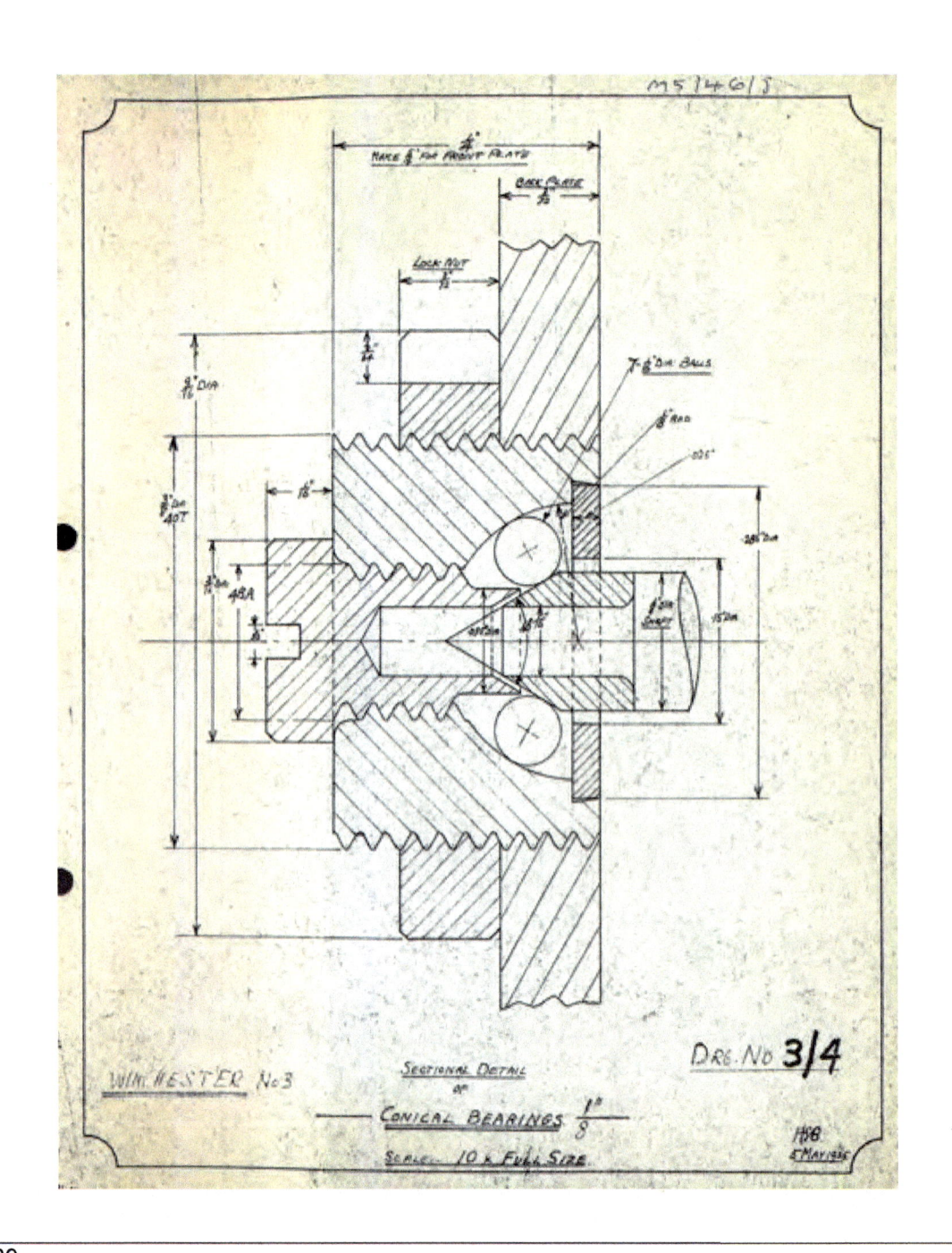

WINCHESTER No 3

SECTIONAL DETAIL
of
CONICAL BEARINGS $\frac{1"}{8}$

SCALE: 10 x FULL SIZE

DRG. No 3/4

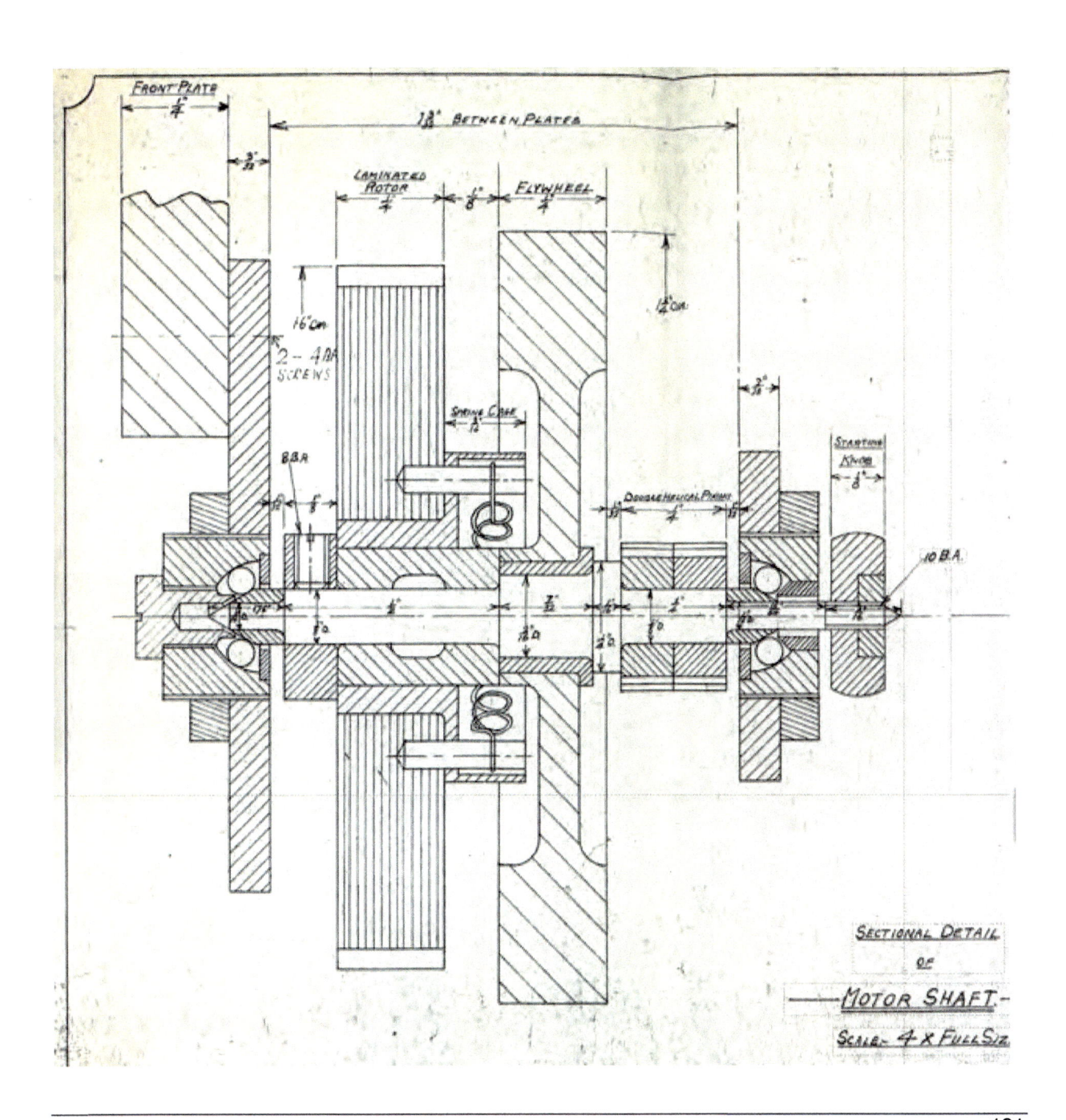

SECTIONAL DETAIL
OF
MOTOR SHAFT
SCALE: 4 × FULL SIZE

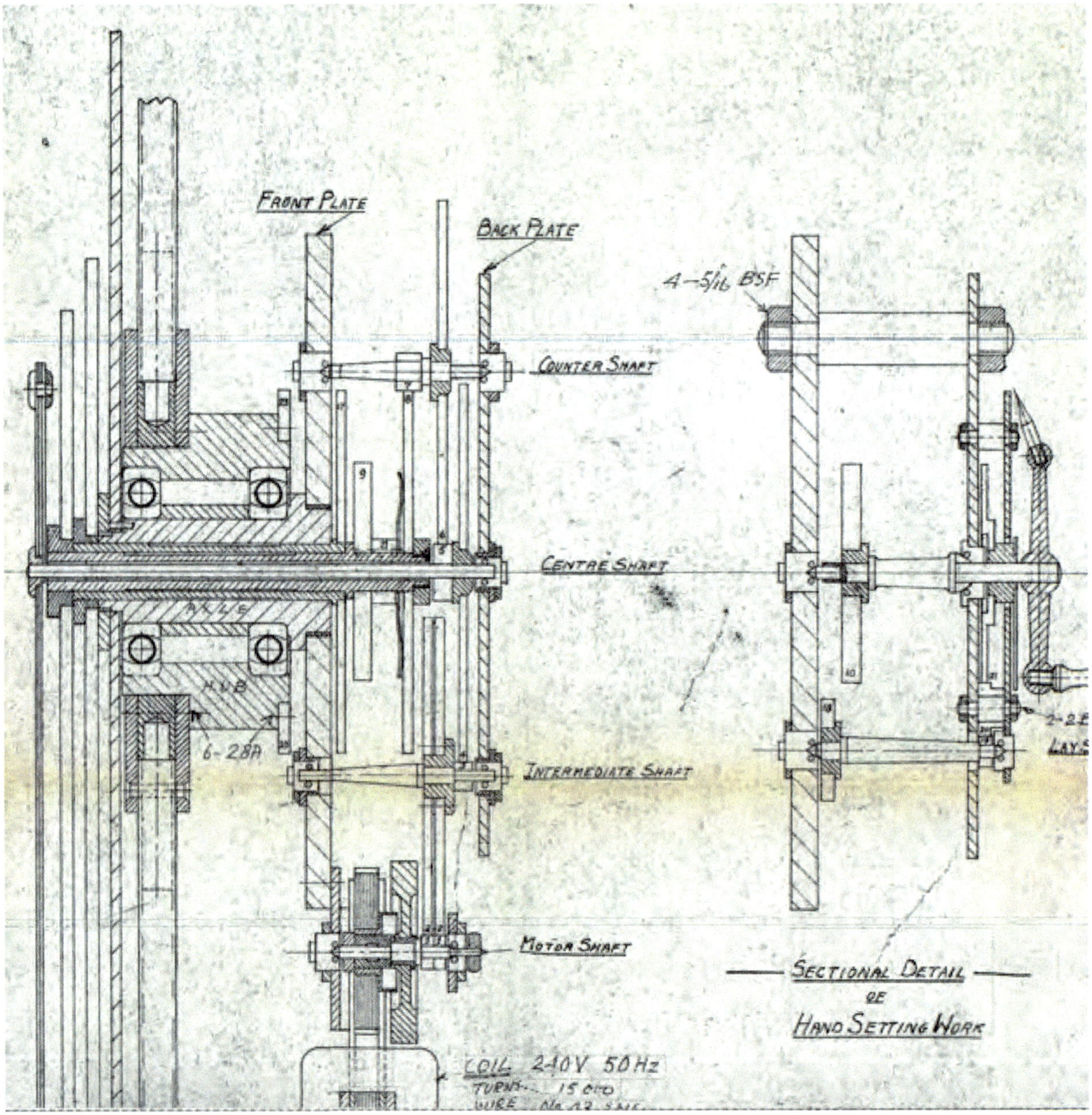
FRONT PLATE
BACK PLATE
4-5/16 BSF
COUNTER SHAFT
CENTRE SHAFT
INTERMEDIATE SHAFT
6-28A
MOTOR SHAFT
SECTIONAL DETAIL
OF
HAND SETTING WORK
COIL 240V 50Hz

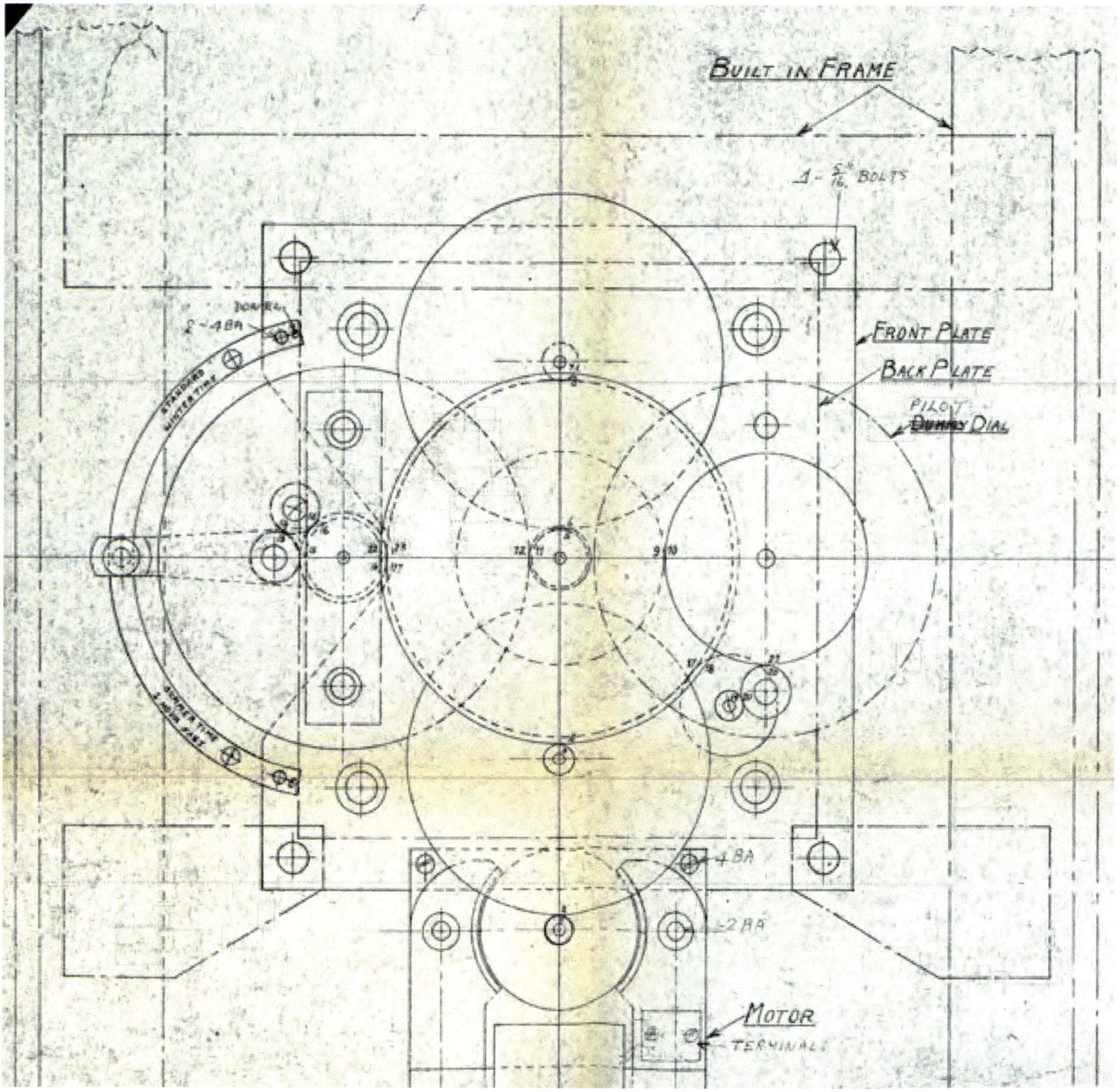
BUILT IN FRAME
FRONT PLATE
BACK PLATE
DIAL
MOTOR
TERMINAL
2-BA
4 BA
2-4BA
STANDARD WINTER TIME
SUMMER TIME

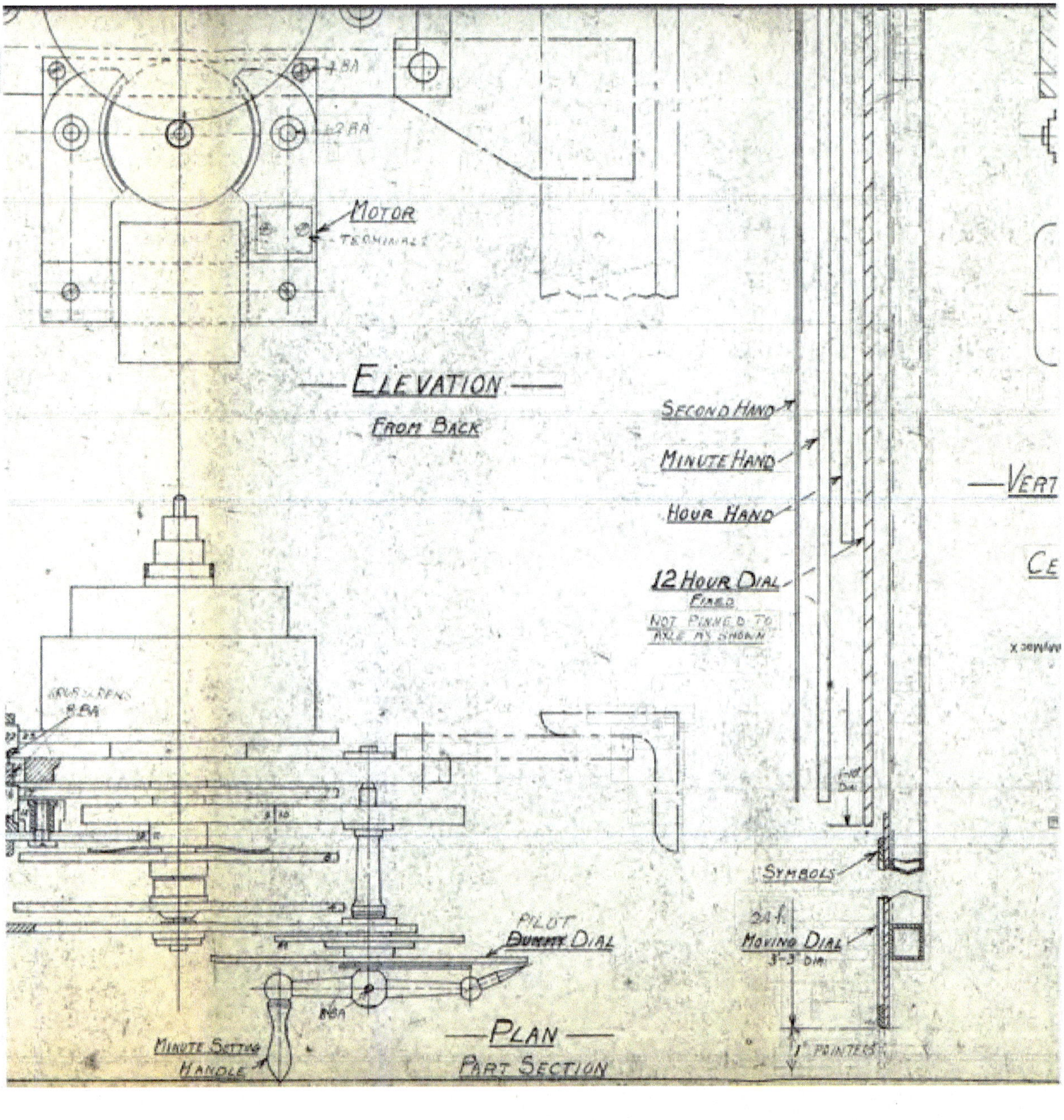

MOTOR
TERMINALS
ELEVATION
FROM BACK
SECOND HAND
MINUTE HAND
HOUR HAND
12 HOUR DIAL
FIXED
NOT PINNED TO AXLE AS SHOWN
SYMBOLS
MOVING DIAL
PILOT
DIAL
PLAN
PART SECTION
MINUTE SETTING HANDLE
1" POINTERS

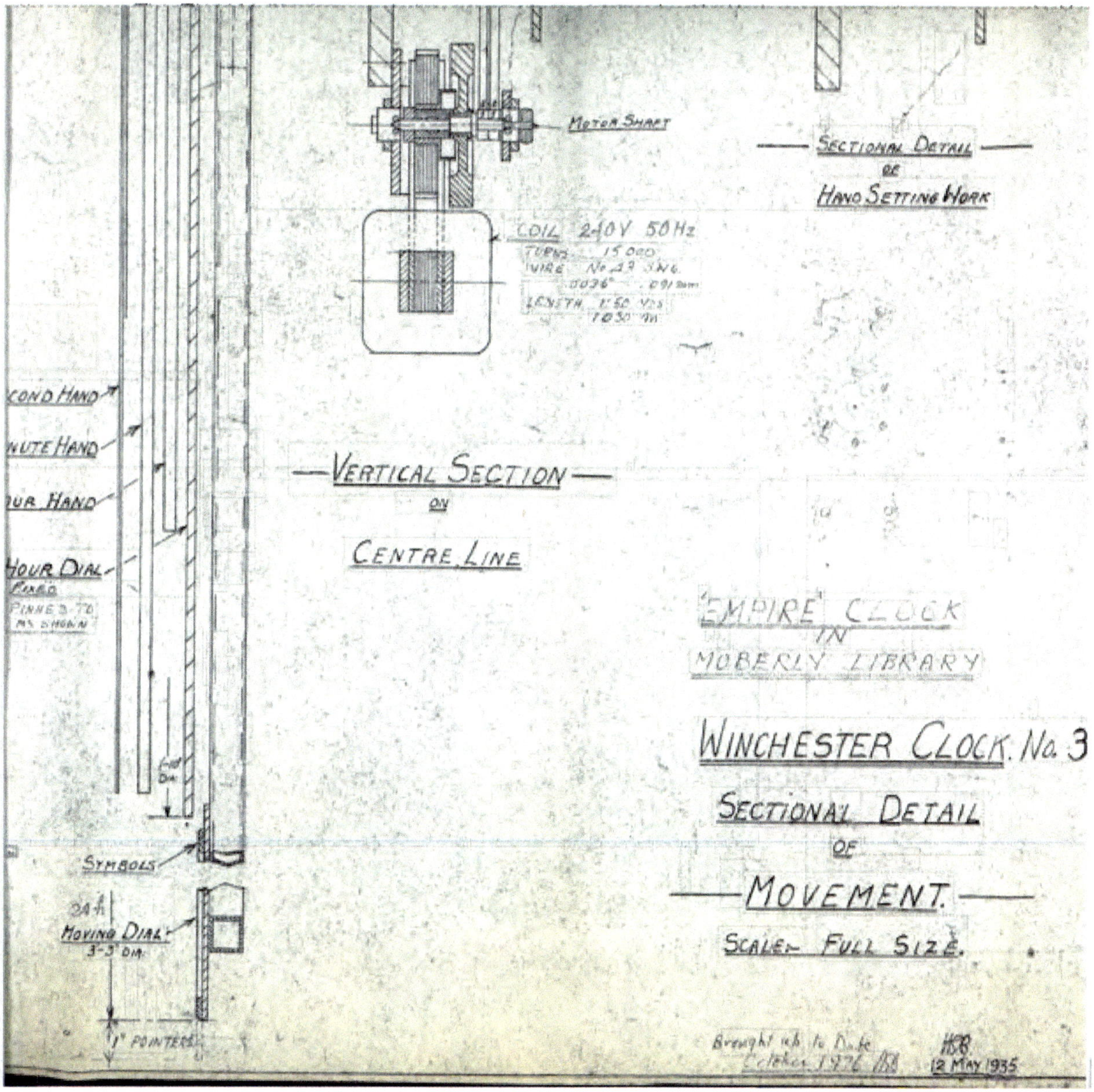
MOTOR SHAFT
SECTIONAL DETAIL OF HAND SETTING WORK
COIL 240V 50Hz
COND HAND
NUTE HAND
UR HAND
HOUR DIAL FIXED
PINNED TO AS SHOWN
VERTICAL SECTION ON CENTRE LINE
'EMPIRE' CLOCK IN MOBERLY LIBRARY
WINCHESTER CLOCK No 3
SECTIONAL DETAIL OF MOVEMENT.
SCALE:- FULL SIZE.
SYMBOLS
24 h
MOVING DIAL 3-3" DIA
1" POINTERS
12 MAY 1935

DESCRIPTION OF EMPIRE CLOCK IN THE NEW LIBRARY AT WINCHESTER COLLEGE.

When the old Brewery at Winchester College was being converted into a library by Sir Herbert Baker it was thought that a clock would look well on the end wall. This clock is of rather unusual design, having an ordinary clock dial 23" in diameter with centre-seconds-hand, and outside this rotating dial 40" in diameter carrying various symbols representing the major parts of the British Empire in their correct time zones. Abbreviations for the names of each country are placed outside the symbols, and ships of various designs show where the oceans occur. It is remarkable that "the Empire encircles the globe" and only a few minor possessions have been omitted where they fall on the same time zones as major countries. The dial carrying the symbols rotates once in 24-hours against a ring of 24 numerals carved in the surrounding stonework, so that each symbol always points to the correct local time at that place. A photograph of the clock in position is shown in figure (1).

The symbols were designed by Sir Herbert Baker, while the movement was designed and made by Mr. Henry Baker and Mr. Robert Stewart. The dials were made by Mr. J. Armitage and the plaques were modelled by Mr. Charles Wheeler.

It was decided that this movement should be made as far as possible of alloy steels of the "stainless" range, and this has been carried out with success very nearly throughout the movement. A general arrangement of the movement is shown in figure (2).

The clock is run from the Corporation electricity mains on a 230-volt 50-cycle system. The motor is of the multipolar non-starting type with a plain slotted soft-iron rotor rotating between slotted pole-pieces energised from a coil connected across the mains. Starting is effected by spinning the rotor shaft by hand, the rotor falling into step very easily at 120 r.p.m. The rotor and stator poles are made of laminated soft iron and dull chromium plated.

All shafts, with the exception of the hand sleeves, are carried on ball bearings of two special designs which will be described later. The wheels were cut by a hobbing attachment built specially for the purpose and fitted to a lathe.

The clock is built into a wall at a height of 15 ft. and access to the movement and to the controls is obtained from a first-floor room behind this wall. For setting the hands to time, an auxiliary dial having minute and hour hands is provided on the movement, the minute hand being in the form of a handle for turning the clock.

In order to advance the hour-hand one hour for Summer time without moving the 24-hour dial, since Summer time is only adopted in a few parts of the Empire, a differential device has been incorporated so that the movement of a lever through an arc of 120° moves the hour-hand one hour

-2-

without disturbing any other parts of the clock. This can, of course, be done while the clock is going, and without losing the time setting.

Various preliminary tests were made to find the best steels for each purpose and with the help and courtesy of Messrs. Firth Vickers a very good range was selected. This includes five different alloys.

1). <u>Staybrite Sheet FST</u>.
  Main plates.
  Seconds-hand.
  Spider boss for 24-hour dial.
  24-hour dial on which are mounted the gilded symbols.
  Auxiliary setting dial.
  Auxiliary dial hour hand.
  Summer time lever and quadrant.
  Motor plates.
  Motor flywheel.
  Minute hand friction drive spider spring and nut.

  <u>Staybrite Tube FST</u>.
  24-hour dial spider.

  <u>Staybrite Rod FST</u>.
  Auxiliary dial setting handle.
  Summer time handle.
  All bolts, nuts and screws.

2). <u>S 80 Sheet</u>.
  All wheels.

  <u>S 80 Rod</u>.
  24-hour dial hub.
  All spindles except seconds-hand.
  Main plate pillars.
  Motor plate pillars.
  Minute and hour-hand sleeves.
  24-hour dial stub axle.
  Auxiliary dial pillar.
  Motor starting knob.

3). <u>Hardening Quality FH</u>.
  All pinions and differential pinion journals.
  Auxiliary pillar carrying pinion.

4). <u>Ball Bearing Quality</u>.
  All outer races of spindle bearings.

5). **Stainless Iron FI.**
     Wheel collets.
     Main 12-hour dial (engraved).

The auxiliary dial was etched with the recommended acid solution with fair success. It is difficult to get rid of bubbles and prevent polarization and consequent uneven etching.

The only parts of the movement in which other metals were used are:-

Seconds-hand spindle, made of $\frac{1}{4}$" silver steel.
Inner races of bearings, of silver steel.
Motor flywheel bush of phosphor bronze.
Seconds-hand bearing bushes, of phosphor bronze.
Bearing balls, 1/16" standard Hoffmann Balls.
24-hour dial bearings, standard 1" light-type Hoffmann ball-races.
Motor core and poles, of soft sheet iron.

As regards the working of these various alloy steels, neither of us had had any previous experience to speak of in machining stainless steel.

The lathes used were a $3\frac{1}{2}$" Drummond, a small watchmakers' lathe and a 4" round-bed Drummond on which all the wheels were made.

The turning tools used were ordinary High-speed steel cutter bits ground to the recommended angles.

Drills were all "Speedicut" high speed.

The wheel-cutting hobs were machined from hammered blanks of E.S.C. STYR 22% tungsten steel. The profile of the teeth was worked out to give a nice-looking tooth shape together with one which would not produce undue under-cutting on the pinions. An enlarged drawing of this is shown in figure (3). The cutters for forming this tooth shape were made by means of a pantograph tool-rest shown in figure (4) and 20 x full-size template which was used to turn a disc of tool steel to the correct profile. This disc was then cut in half and hardened and used as a form tool for a second disc-cutter which then became the hob-tooth profile cutter. To obtain the maximum hardness these tool steel discs were case-hardened with Kasenit and then cut, on the whole, very well.

The hob was first cut as a single thread and slotted with 12 flutes. The profile cutter was then mounted on a special backing-off attachment, figure (4), and the cutting edges relieved. The hobs were sent to the Manchester works of the English Steel Corporation for hardening, the flutes being ground on their return. It is interesting to note that they cut the whole range of wheels, shown in figure (5), in S 80 and hardening steel as well as a few sample wheels in staybrite without any resharpening and with no apparent deterioration of the cutting edge.

The pitches used were 100 d.p. for the first reduction from the motor shaft to the first wheel, this pair of gears being of a double helical form to give silent running, and 40 d.p. for all the remaining movement. Many designs were made to find wheel and pinion ratios all of the same pitch which would fit in in a neat manner.

The hobbing gear is shown in figures (6), (7) and (8). No trouble of any sort was found in machining the teeth in S 80 or the hardening quality steel, though the staybrite samples were not as good owing to lack of rigidity in the lathe. The accuracy of the pitch diameter of all wheels when in mesh is within ".0005.

The spokes were drilled to jig, cut out with an ordinary metal piercing fretsaw and filed to shape. This process was laborious, but no difficulty was found in doing it, one saw lasting for one to one-and-a-half inches of cut.

Very little trouble was found in this steel from internal stresses. The double helical wheel, made in two halves, had to be flattened to a small extent after roughing out the spokes, but this was the only one on which it was noticeable.

The pinions were hardened in an open air-coal-gas blow pipe and polished. Only in one case was there any noticeable distortion. Great care had, however, to be used in pressing the smallest pinions on to their shafts. An interference fit of ".0005 was first attempted on a $\frac{1}{8}$" shaft, but in three cases the pinions split and an interference of ".00025 was finally used. The S 80 shaft tends to "pick-up" slightly as the pinion is pressed on. With this fit, they seem to be perfectly tight on the shaft.

Such precision of fit was, of course, not necessary when pressing the S 80 wheels on to their collets of stainless iron. The collets were finally spun over a little and skimmed up. This steel spins over quite easily.

A "depthing tool", shown in figure (4) was made to check the mesh and running of the wheels, and a drilling jig, working on much the same principle, was made for drilling the main plates for the bearings.

The shafts were turned in the watchmakers' lathe and fitted with glass-hard silver steel bearing cones $\frac{1}{8}$" in diameter at the larger end. This S 80 turns beautifully at high speed with light cuts and polishes up very well indeed, no difficulty being found in obtaining a high degree of accuracy of diameter where required. The set of shafts is shown in figure (9A).

No attempt was made to harden or temper the S 80 steel for the shafts, though this might be preferable in finer work.

The staybrite setting lever (9b) and the Summer time lever and handle (9c) and (9d) presented no particular machining difficulties, though it is not easy to turn staybrite to very fine limits owing to its ductility and tendency to blunt the tool. It takes a very high polish, however, and is ideal for parts which are to be handled. The .028" staybrite cold rolled sheet is sufficiently springy for the friction drive spider, (9e), to the minute-hand.

The machining of the plates caused a good deal of trouble. These are made from ¼" and 3/32" staybrite sheet. The sheet was flattened by light hammering and then turned up on a faceplate, care being taken to avoid distortion in bolting. The internal stresses in this steel are, however, very troublesome and as soon as the surface is removed considerable distortion occurs. Lapping with emery was finally resorted to in order to get a flat surface, and the heat generated by this treatment was another source of distortion. It was decided that staybrite was not really a suitable material on which to attempt to get a plane polished surface of this sort and we regretted not having used S 80 for this part of the movement. The material is also too soft and ductile and is easily bent out of shape.

The drilling of the plates presented no difficulty, but tapping them was troublesome. The bearing housings are tapped ⅜" x 40 T.P.I., and three taps of silver steel were made to get these threads finally to size. Lubrication with light oil undoubtedly assists tapping, but is not recommended for drilling and certainly not for turning. The ordinary small B.A. tap sold for general workshop use is quite useless on staybrite. Taps made from silver steel are, however, very successful in these small sizes, 4, 6 and 8 B.A., and ground taps also cut well. They must be left as hard as possible.

Drilling small holes in staybrite is an acquired knack. Exact grinding of the drill point is necessary and a light steady pressure. Once the drill point has gone it must be sharpened immediately. A light lever drilling machine was found to be a good deal easier to handle than a screw feed.

Staybrite rivets very well and easily and we were surprised to find no trouble from work-hardening of the rivet heads, subsequent machining being quite possible. The radial spokes of the 24-hour dial spider were riveted to the boss. This spider was made of ⅜" square welded 20-gauge staybrite tube, the six spokes being some 18" long and acetylene welded to a hexagonal ring of the same tube. After some practice the welding was successfully accomplished, though in thin sections such as this it is not an easy process. This, however, is clearly a matter of practice.

One of the most interesting features of this clock are the ball bearings. These are of two types, a plain self aligning type with spherical outer races, used for most of the shafts, and a different type where end-play is required, as in the case of the double helical wheels which must be allowed to centre themselves, and for the back end of the seconds-hand shaft.

The first type consists of an outer race of ball bearing stainless steel bored to ¼" diameter sphere and lapped with a boxwood ball and emery. These were hardened and polished. The design is shown in figure (10) and (12). The seven 1/16" balls are held from falling out by a cage formed by a thin outer disc snapped into the front of the race and a small sleeve screwed into the end of the race. They are perfectly self-aligning over a reasonable angle and may be handled without fear of the balls falling out.

The second type, figure (11), is designed to allow free end-play for the shaft. It is adjustable, the balls are again caged, and the race is to all intents and purposes self-aligning over small angles of displacement. It will be seen that both of these types required very careful machining and a considerable degree of accuracy. No difficulty was found, however, in working this steel to the highest limits. The inner thread of the second type is about 9/32" diameter and 80 threads to the inch, and was screw-cut and chased with a die without any difficulty or tendency to strip.

Some anxiety has been felt as to whether these races will be hard enough as we were not able to get a very high degree of hardness in this steel. Several tests were made in order to get the correct temperature for quenching, an oxy-coal-gas flame being used with greatest success. It was found that the steel was still just machinable with a sharp tool after hardening. An inspection of these bearings after a few weeks running will be of interest.

Our conclusions on the question of these alloy steels for precision work of this kind may be summed up as follows.

We were delighted with the S 80 in every way. It turned magnificently, though, as one would expect from its tensile strength, rather slower than ordinary steels. It requires no special tool angles though high speed tools are practically essential for good work. Lubrication was found to be necessary for finishing. It finishes well from the tool and polishes nearly as well as staybrite. It appears to have high non-corrosive properties.

The Staybrite, we thought, had a much more limited use. It is fairly easy to turn but requires frequent tool grinding, and precision on small parts is not easy to obtain. We did not attempt any form of precision grinding. The sheet suffers to a troublesome extent from internal stresses and a high coefficient of expansion and is in any case too ductile for most precision work. It is unquestionably the least corrosive of the alloys and is excellent for the more ornamental work. Its non-magnetic properties are of great value in electrical work.

The stainless iron is a good soft material for such parts as collets, but does not turn nicely and is not easy to machine to fine limits.

The hardening qualities machine well, second only to the S 80 and seem to be perfectly suitable for pinions and hardened bushes. Time alone will show whether their hardness is sufficient for the bearings, but this is the only point on which we have been anxious. The pinions and wheels running together should have a long life.

We had difficulty in obtaining staybrite bolts, nuts and screws of anything approaching instrument-work standard. All the nuts had to be re-tapped and re-machined all over as the faces were not square with the threads and the threads were not true with the hexagons. Many of the screws had to be rethreaded and the heads polished up as the slots were often ragged. There would seem to be an opening here for some firm to specialize in producing better work in this direction. We found no difficulty in making certain special screws ourselves.

We should like to express our thanks to Messrs. Firth Vickers for their assistance in the first part of our work over the question of deciding upon suitable steels and for supplying us with the materials we finally selected.

If our many hours of careful work on this clock movement have served in any way to introduce a more wide use of these alloy steels into the realms of instrument work, we shall feel gratified. There is no doubt that this material gives a finish which is most attractive to the eye and which should wear well and last for many years.

WINCHESTER CLOCK.
TABLE OF WHEELS AND PINIONS.

No.	Drive	Teeth	D.P.	P.D.	Centres	O.D.	Material.
1	Motor pinion	29	100	.315	) 1.722	.346	St.St.H.
2	Intermediate wheel	288	100	3.129	)	3.159	S 80.
3	Intermediate pinion	12	40	.3	) 1.9625	.368	St.St.H.
4	Seconds wheel	145	40	3.625	)	3.693	S 80.
5	Seconds pinion	22	40	.55	) 1.925	.618	St.St.H.
6	Countershaft wheel	132	40	3.3	)	3.368	S 80.
7	Countershaft pinion	14	40	.35	) 1.925	.418	St.St.H.
8	Minute wheel	140	40	3.5	)	3.568	S 80.
9	Minute setting pin	84	40	2.1	) 2.1	2.168	S 80.
10	Minute pinion	84	40	2.1	)	2.168	S 80.
11	Minute pinion	25	40	.625	) 2.1875	.693	St.St.H.
12	Motion wheel	150	40	3.75	)	3.813	S 80.
13	Inner diff. pinion	20	40	.5	) .5	.568	St.St.H.
14	Outer diff. pinion	20	40	.5	) .6875	.568	St.St.H.
15	Fixed pinion	35	40	.875	)	.943	St.St.H.
16	Hour pinion	35	40	.875	) 2.1875	.943	St.St.H.
17	Hour wheel	140	40	3.5	) 2.25	3.568	S 80.
18	Layshaft wheel	40	40	1.0	)	1.068	S 80.
19	Layshaft pinion	12	40	.3	) .4	.368	St.St.H.
20	Idle wheel	20	40	.5	) 1.3	.568	St.St.H.
21	Hour setting wheel	84	40	2.1	)	2.168	S 80.
22	Dial pinion	35	40	.875	) 2.1875	.943	St.St.H.
23	Dial wheel	140	40	3.5	)	3.568	S 80.

FIG. (3)

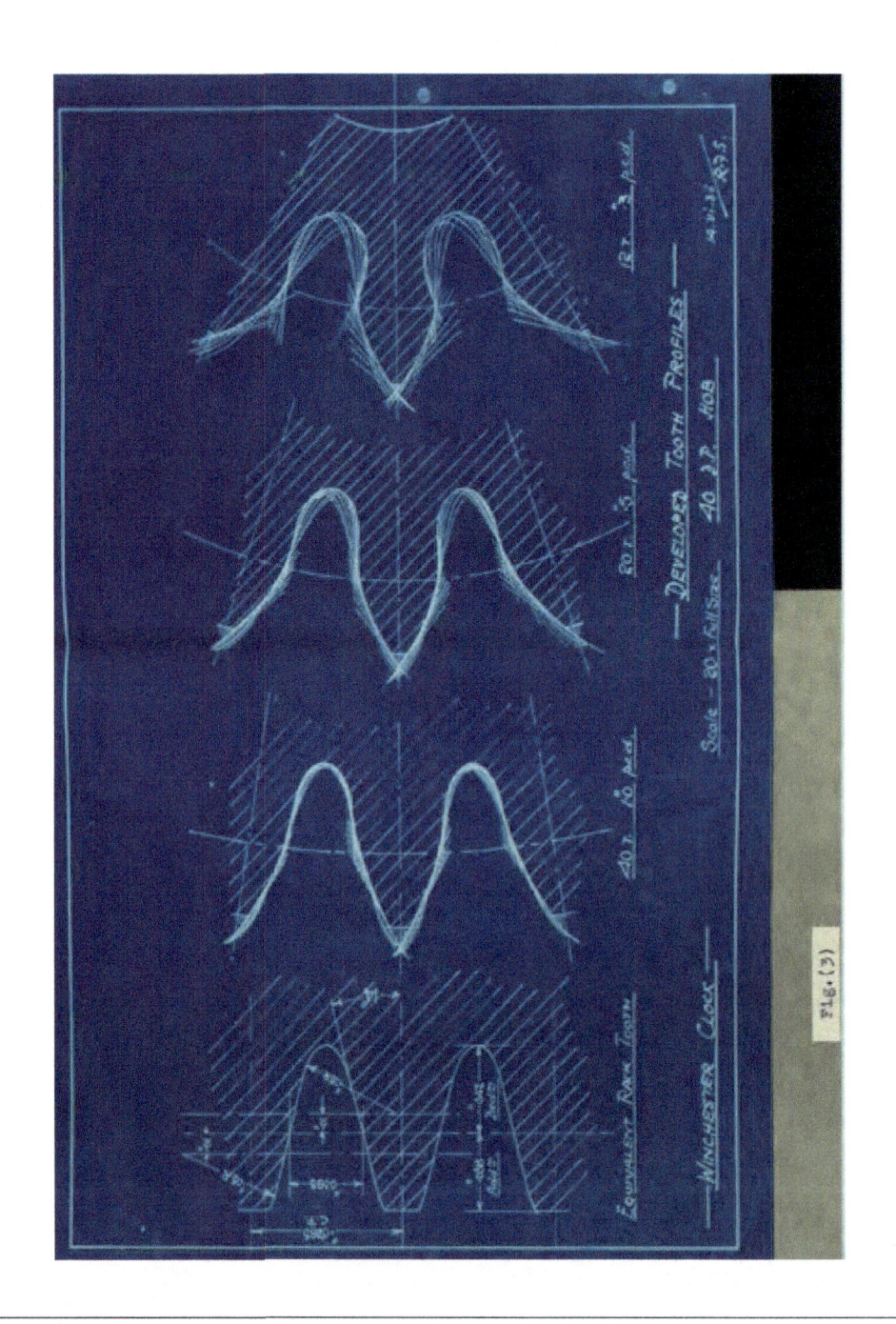

Depthing Tool.   Pantograph Tool Holder.
Eaching-off Attachment.
Fig.(4)

Fig.(5)

Fig.(6)

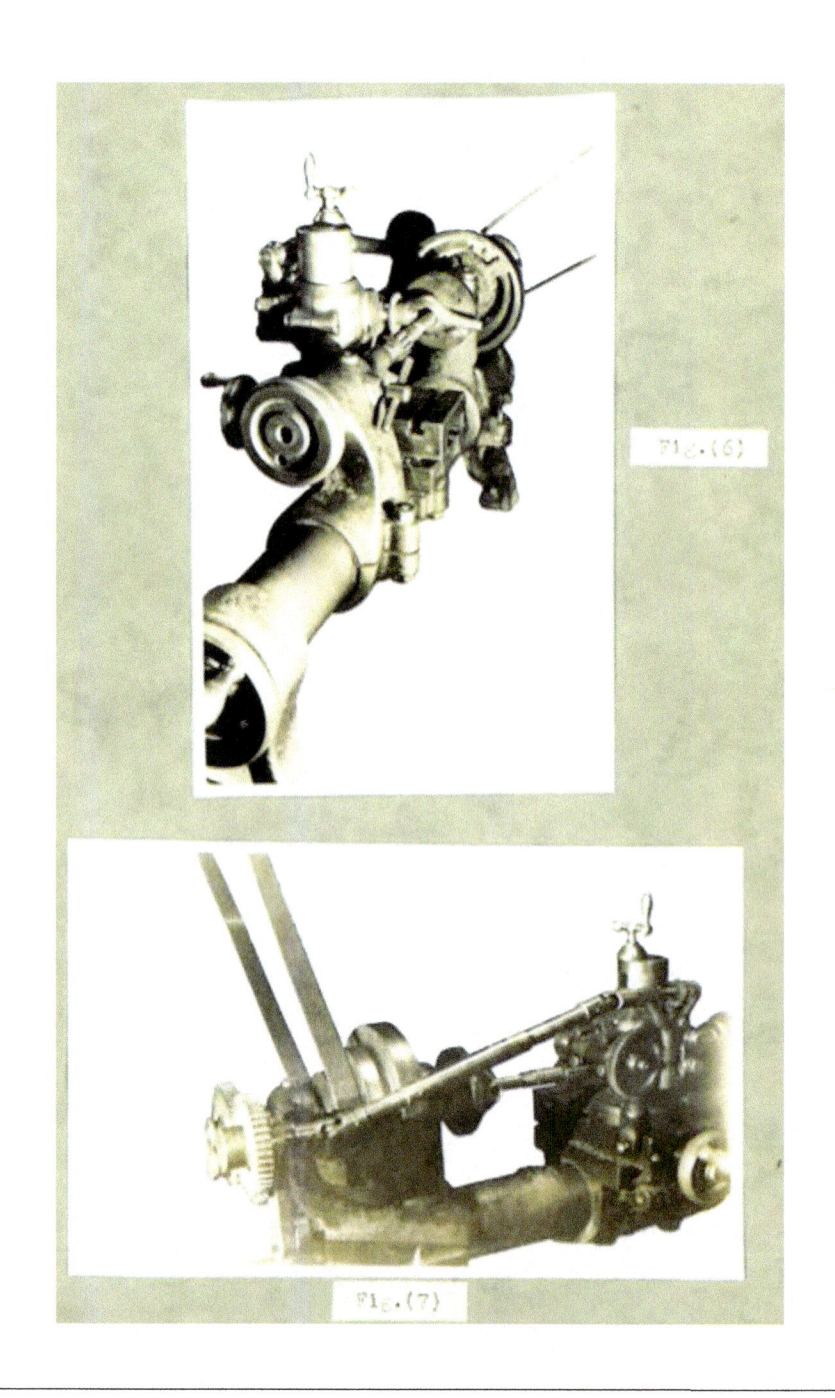

Fig.(7)

Fig.(8)

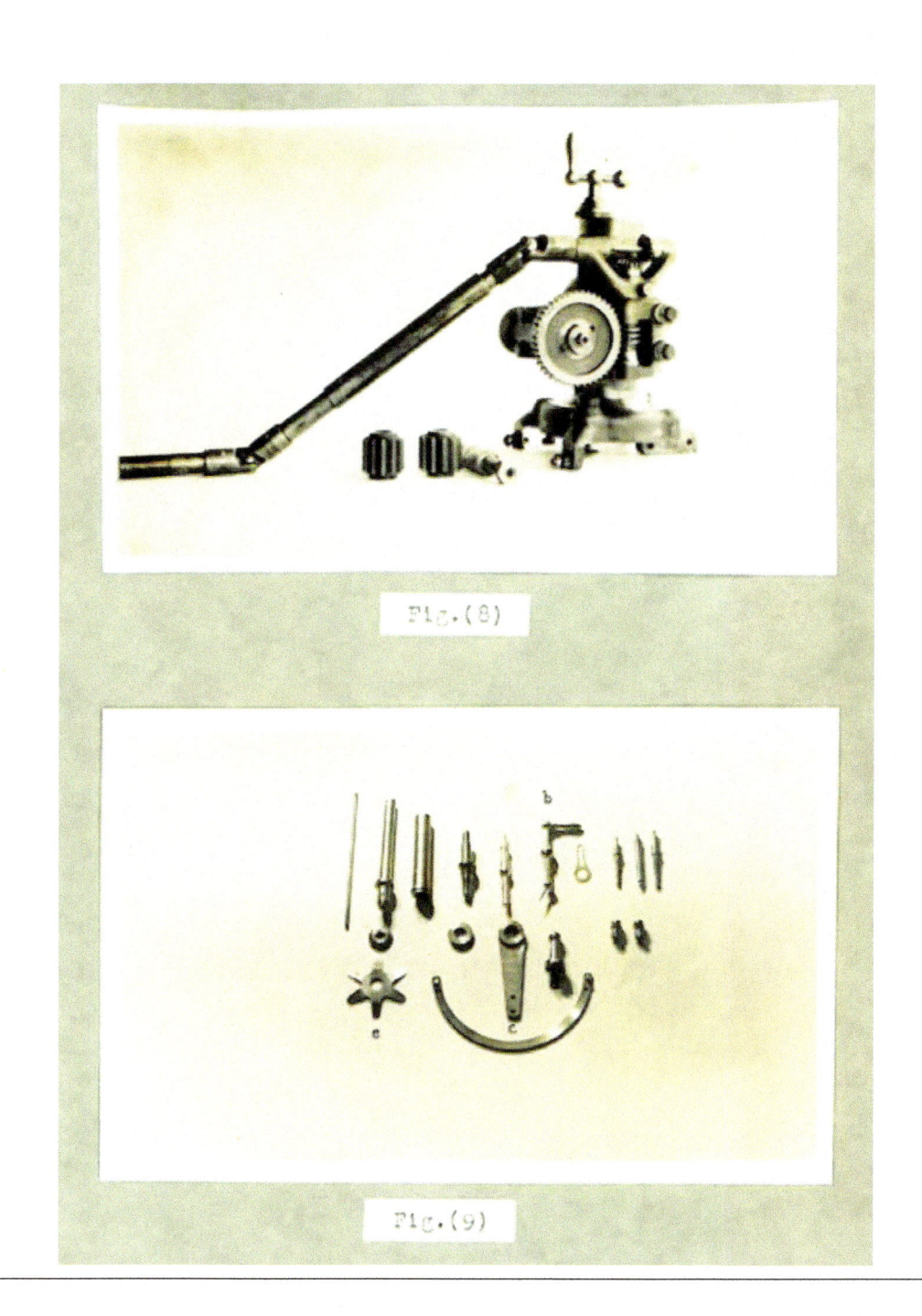

Fig.(9)

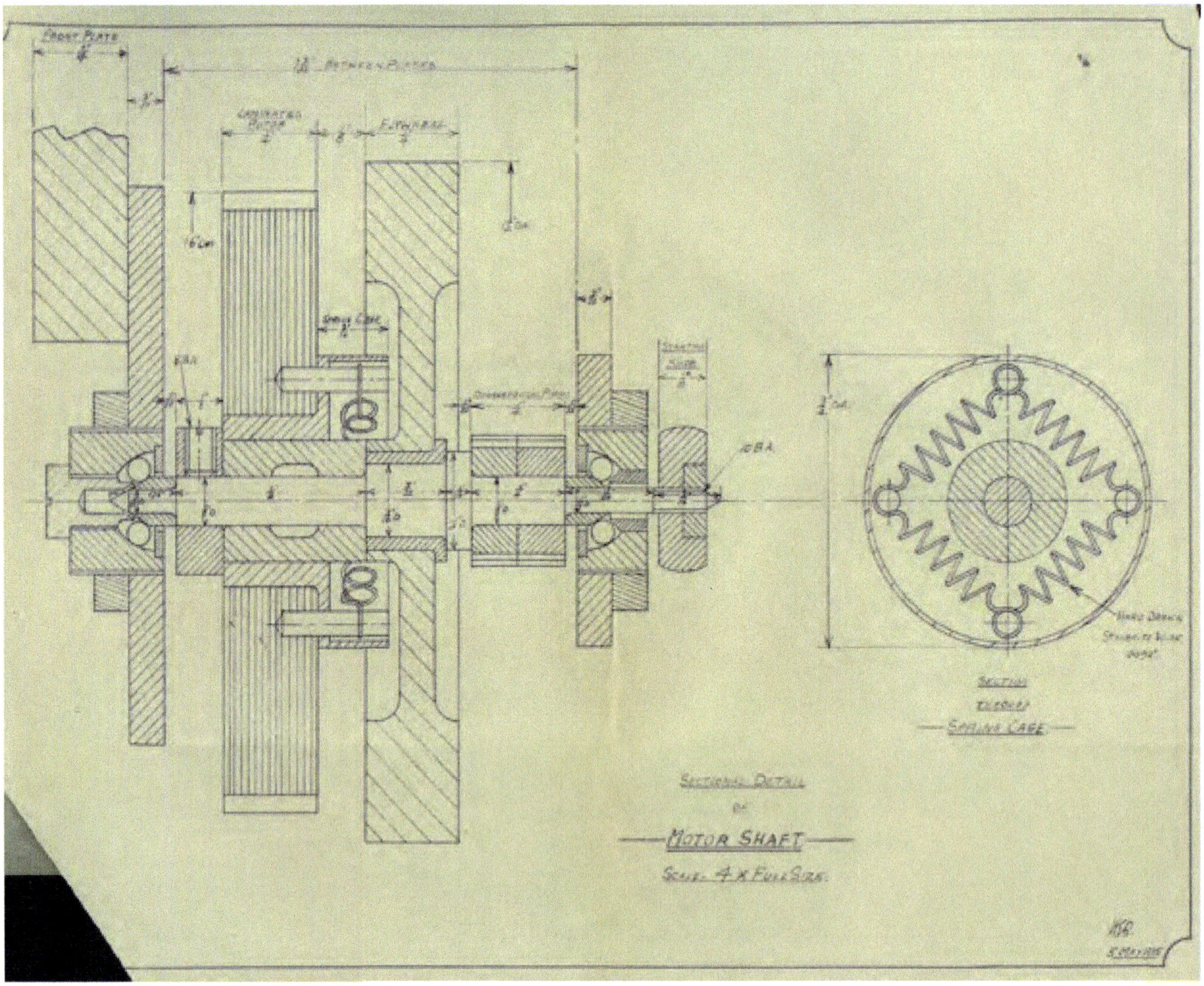
MOTOR SHAFT
SPRING CAGE

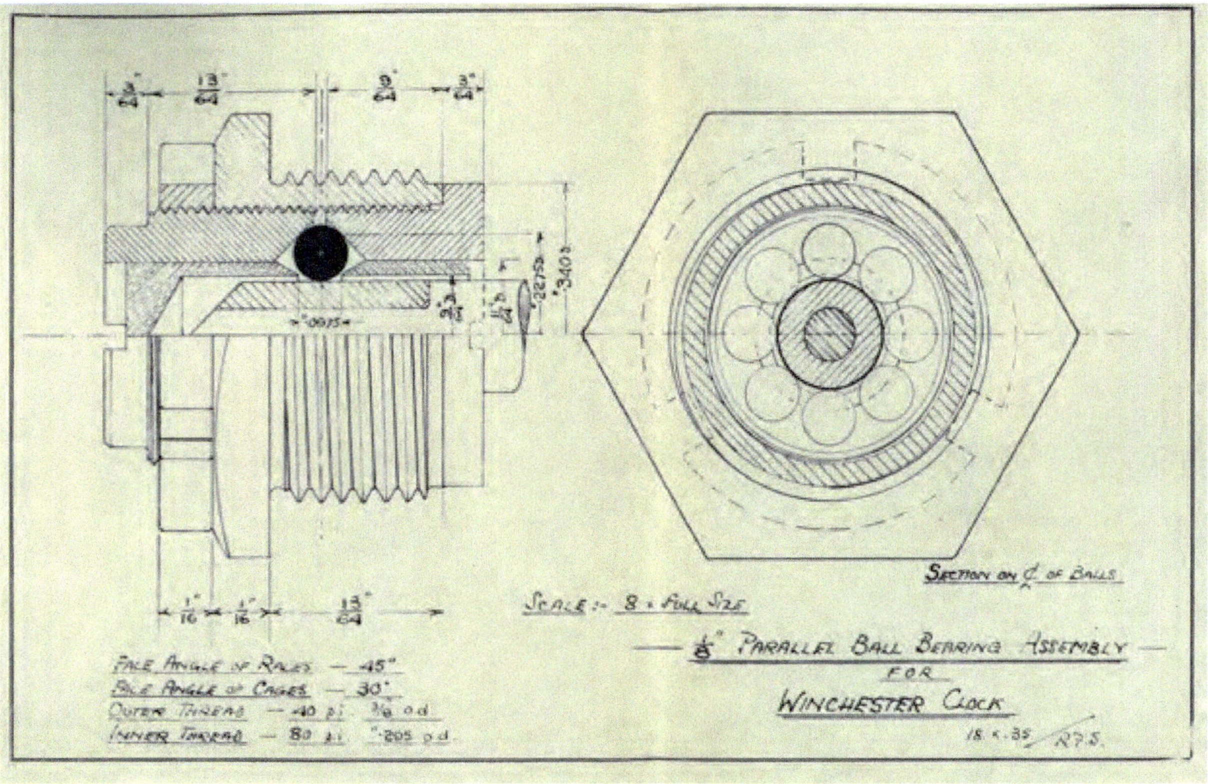

SECTION ON ℄ OF BALLS
SCALE :- 8 × FULL SIZE
1/8" PARALLEL BALL BEARING ASSEMBLY
FOR
WINCHESTER CLOCK
FACE ANGLE OF RACES — 45°
FACE ANGLE OF CAGES — 30°
OUTER THREAD — 40 p.i. 3/16 o.d
INNER THREAD — 80 p.i. ·205 o.d

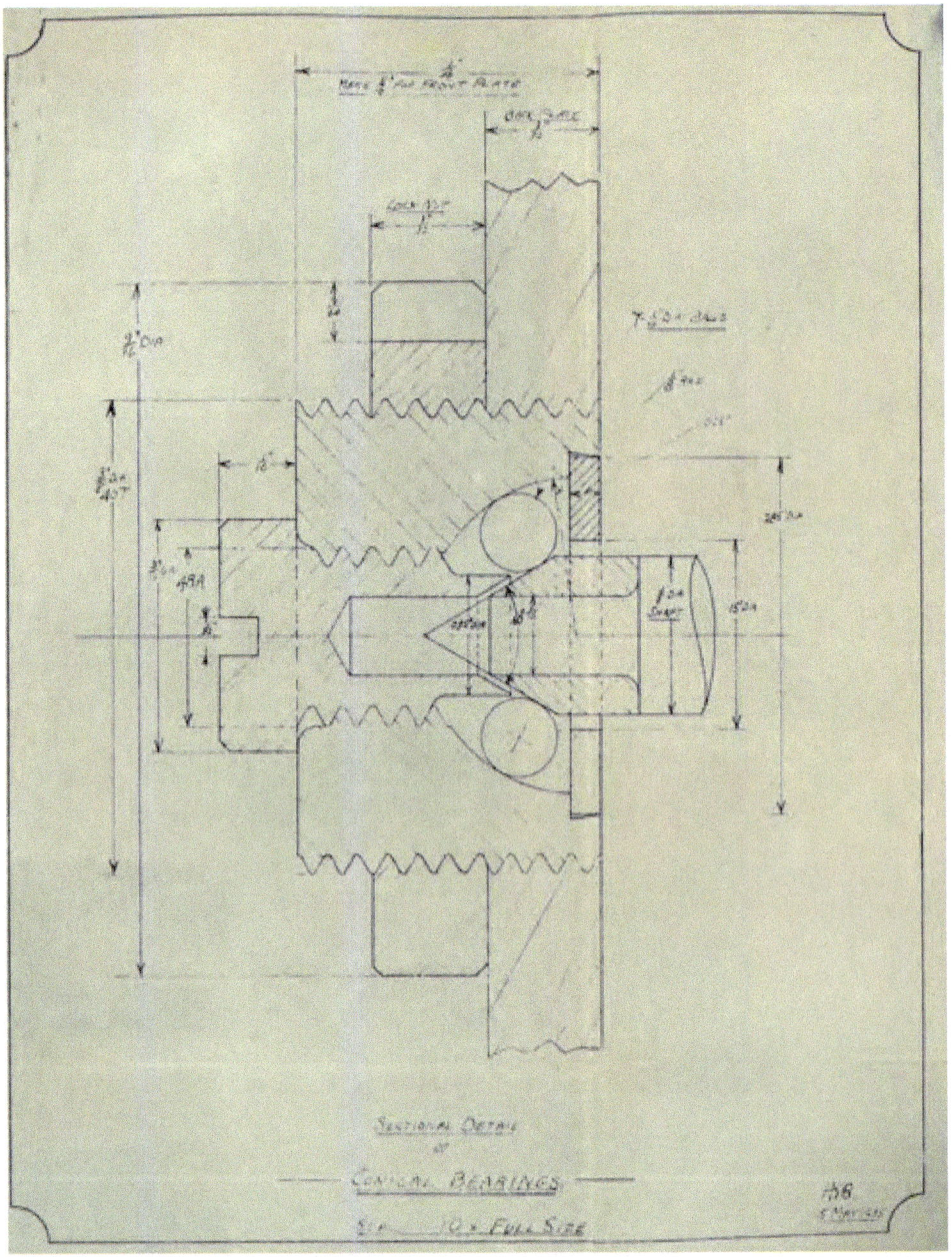
Sectional Detail
of
Conical Bearings
10 x Full Size

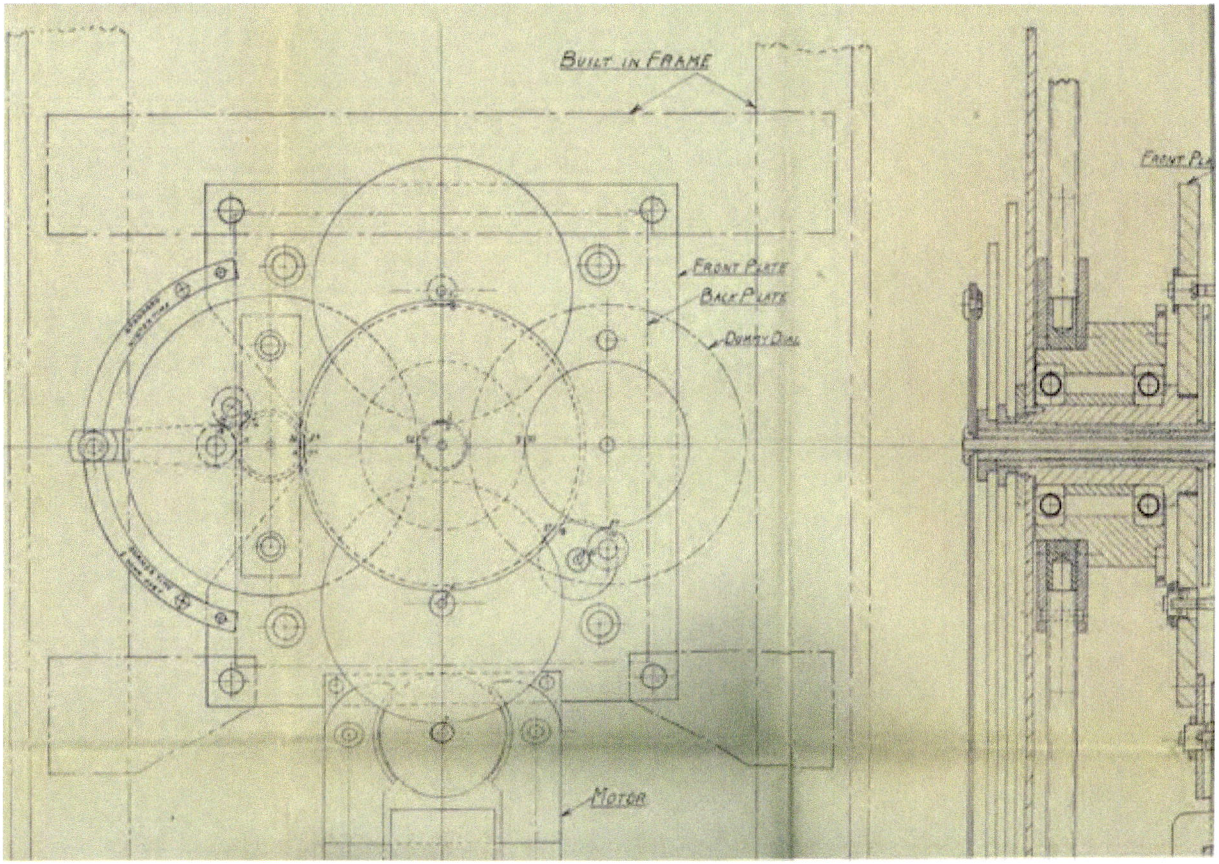
BUILT IN FRAME
FRONT PLATE
BACK PLATE
DUMMY DIAL
MOTOR

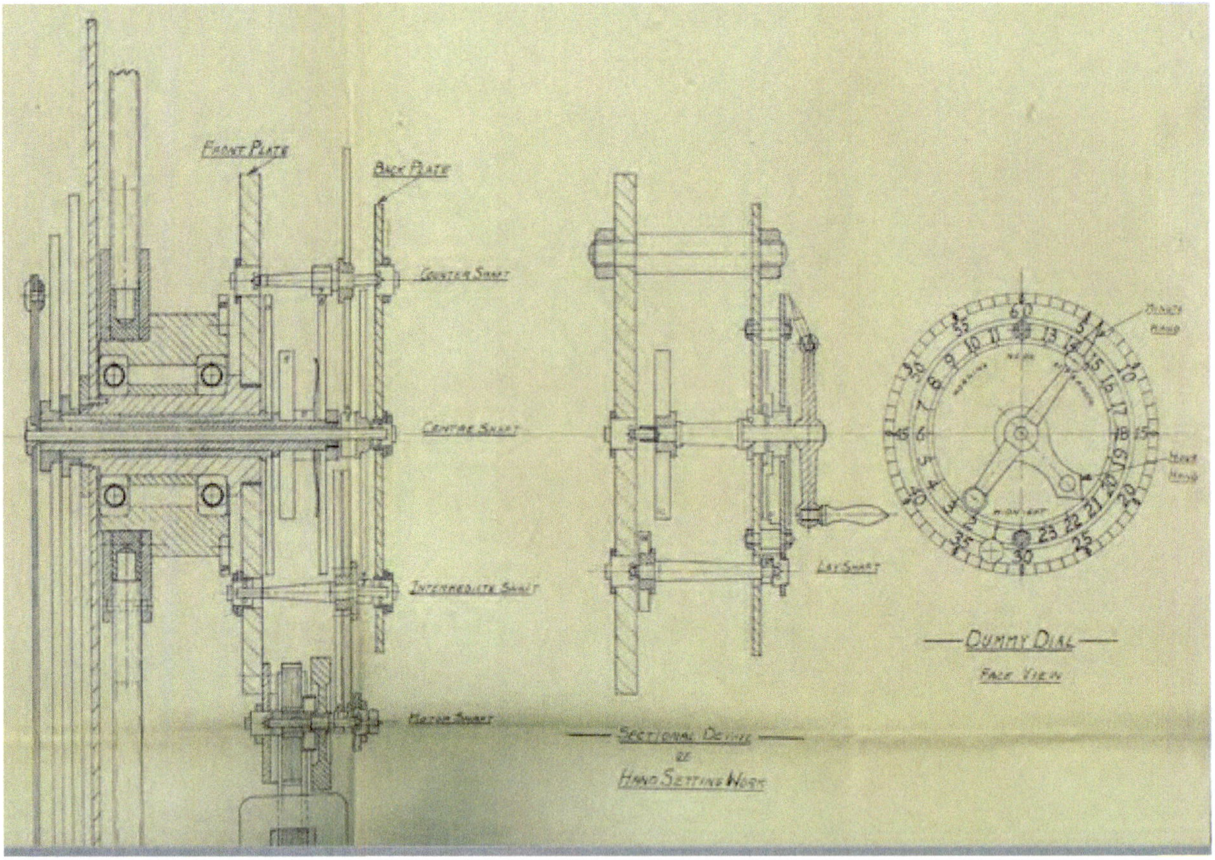
FRONT PLATE
BACK PLATE
COUNTER SHAFT
CENTRE SHAFT
INTERMEDIATE SHAFT
MOTOR SHAFT
LAY SHAFT
HAND SETTING WORK
DUMMY DIAL
FACE VIEW

DUMMY DIAL
FACE VIEW

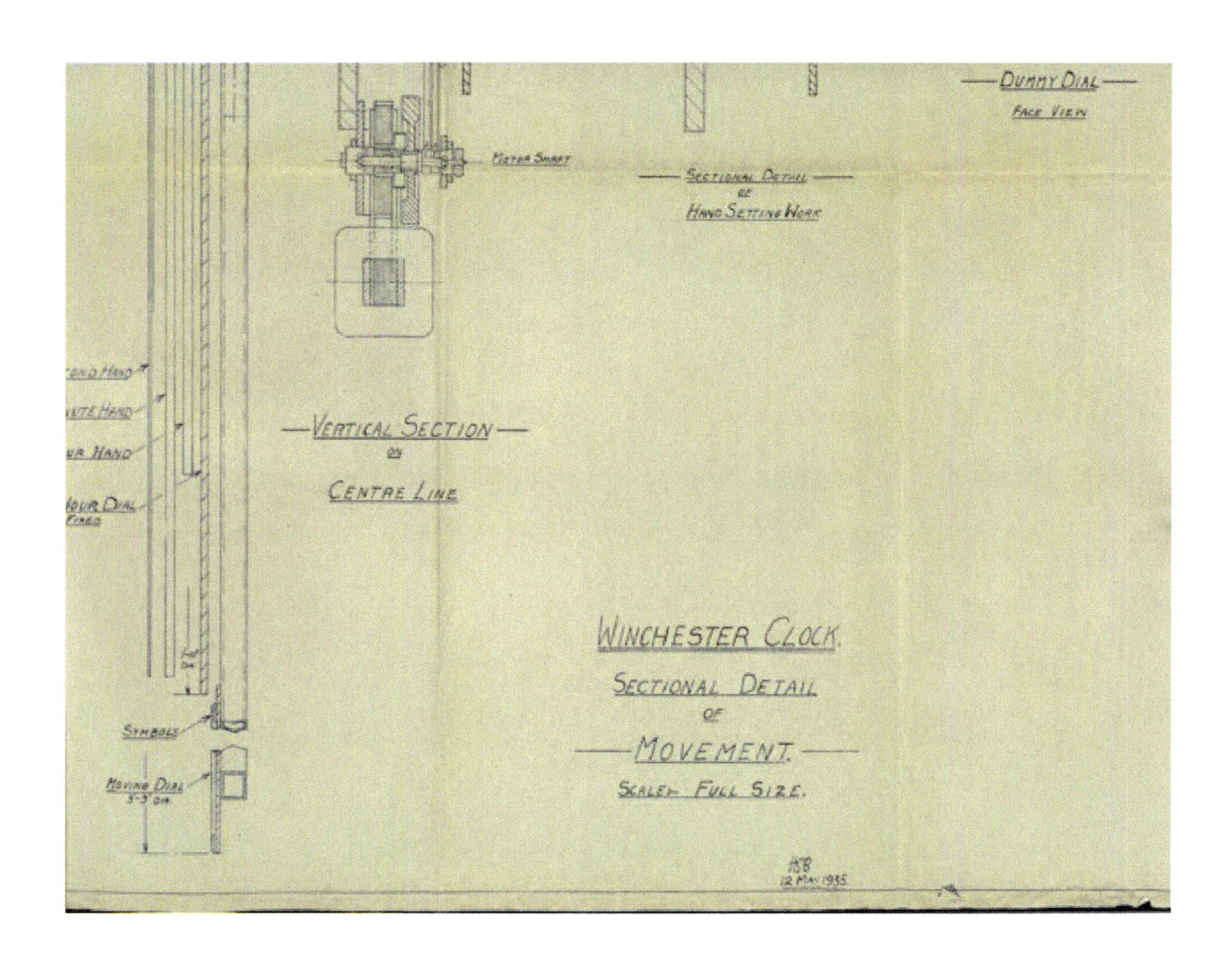

MOTOR SHAFT

SECTIONAL DETAIL
OF
HAND SETTING WORK

VERTICAL SECTION
ON
CENTRE LINE

SECOND HAND
MINUTE HAND
HOUR HAND
HOUR DIAL
FIXED

SYMBOLS

MOVING DIAL
5'-3" DIA

WINCHESTER CLOCK.
SECTIONAL DETAIL
OF
MOVEMENT.
SCALE:— FULL SIZE.

HB
12 MAY 1935

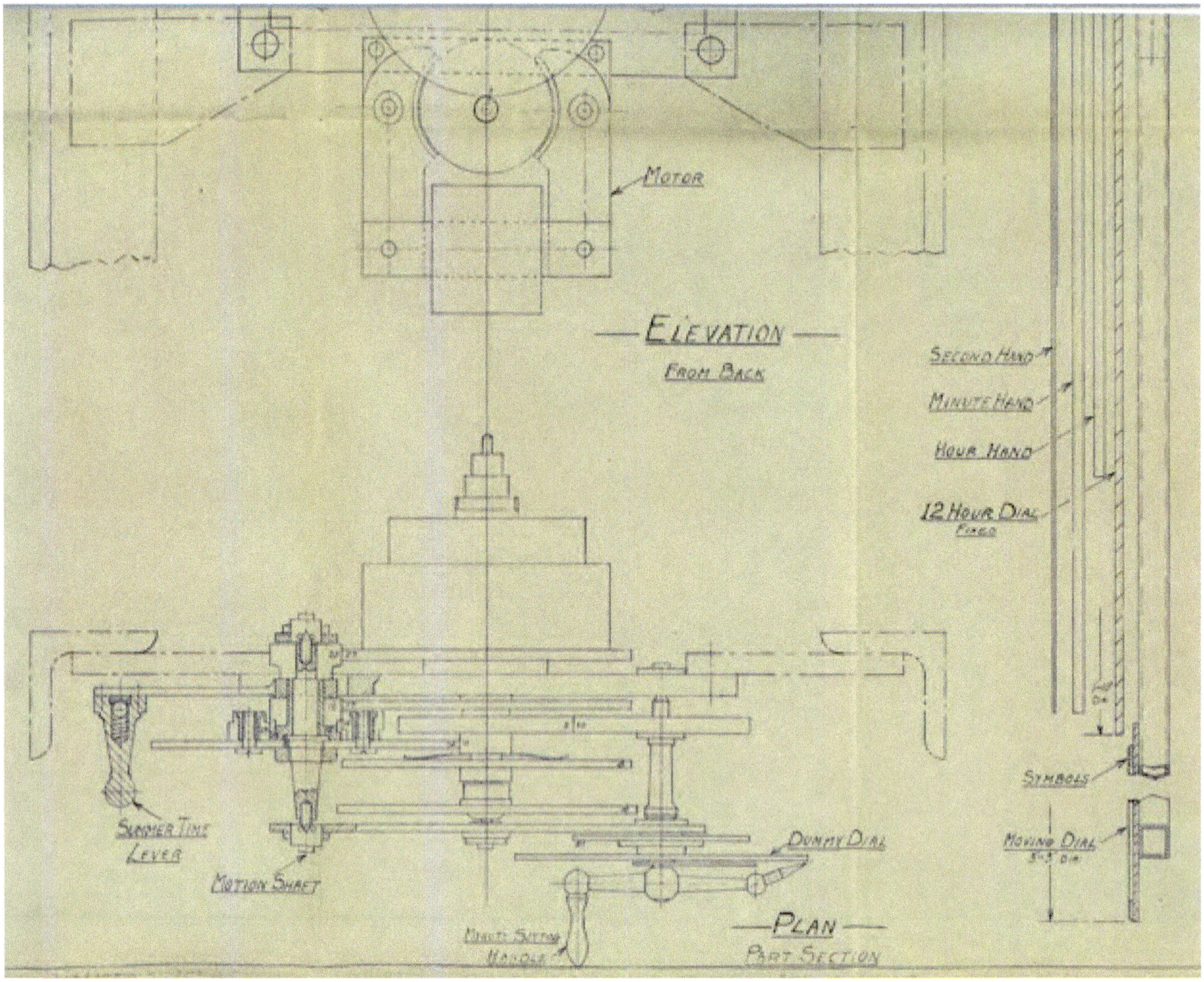

MOTOR
ELEVATION
FROM BACK
SECOND HAND
MINUTE HAND
HOUR HAND
12 HOUR DIAL
FIXED
SYMBOLS
MOVING DIAL
SUMMER TIME
LEVER
MOTION SHAFT
DUMMY DIAL
PLAN
PART SECTION

BACK VIEW OF COMPLETE MOVEMENT.

SIDE VIEW OF COMPLETE MOVEMENT.

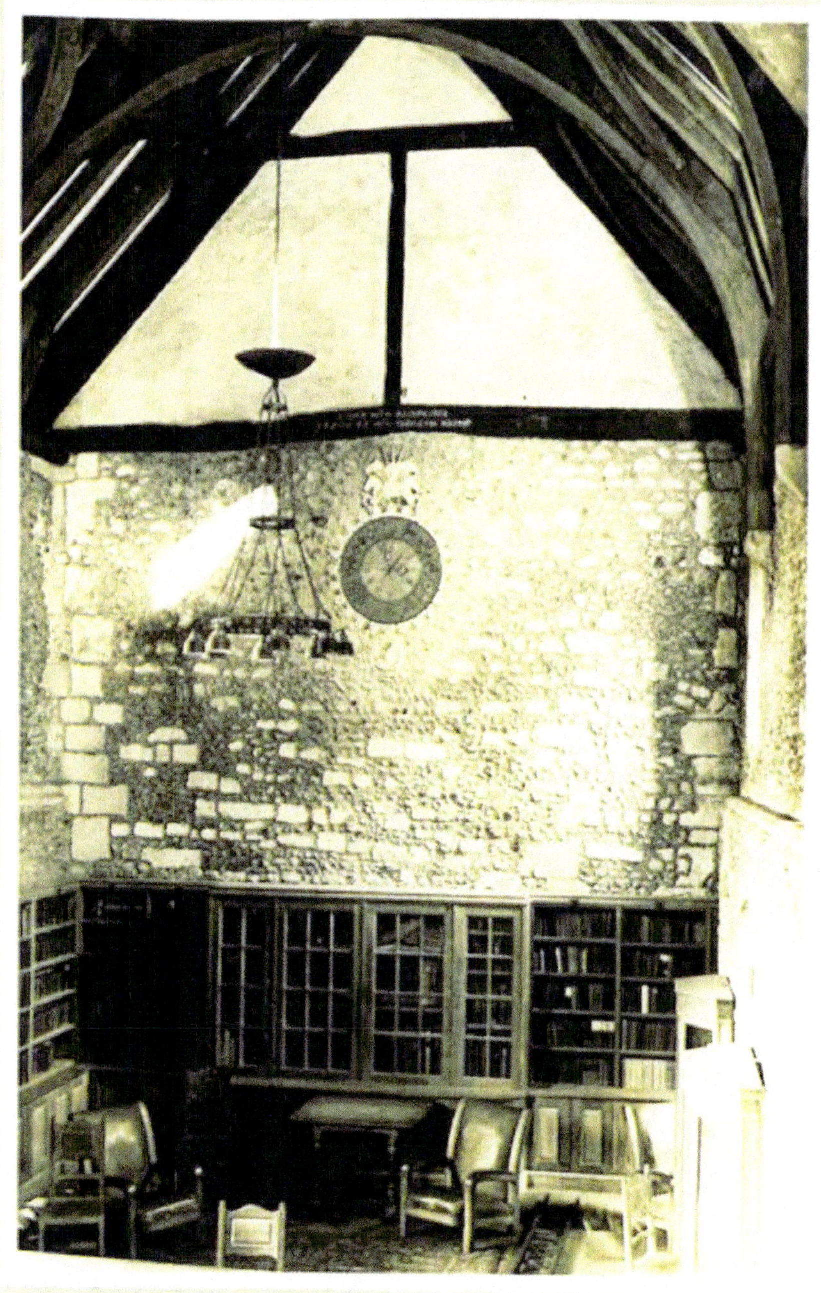

ΣΩΜΑ ΜΕΝ ΑΝΘΡΩΠΟΙ
ΨΥΧΗΝ ΔΕ ΜΟΙ ΩΠΑΣΕΝ ΑΙΘΗΡ

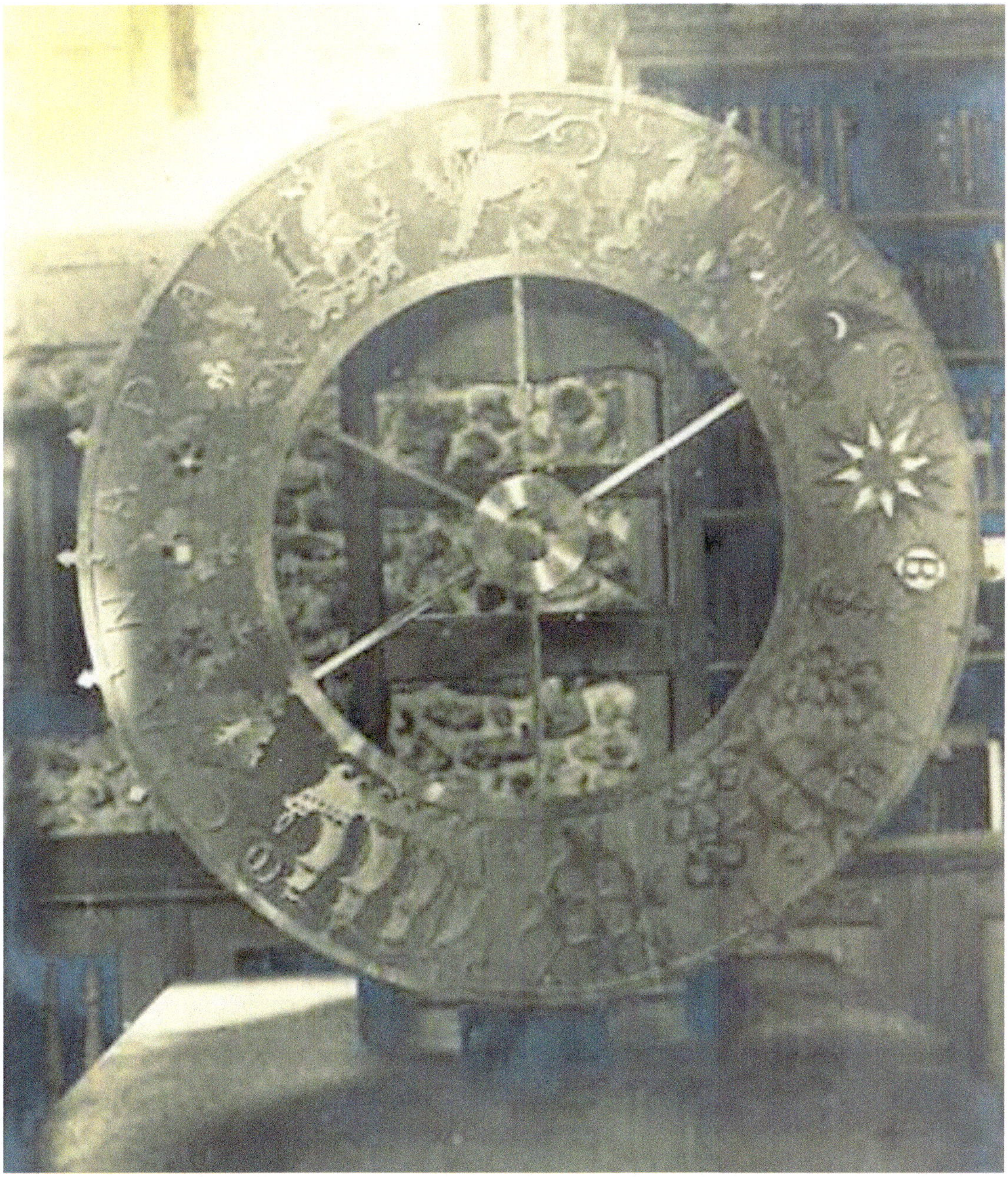

ABOUT THE AUTHOR

Paul R. Secord, as an undergraduate at the University of New Mexico, Albuquerque, spent the summer of 1970 as a "digger" on the Winchester Excavation Committee's Project in Winchester, and was subsequently engaged in an independent studies program in England. After completing his undergraduate degree in Anthropology and Geology he earned a graduate degree in geology (MA), also from the University of New Mexico. In 1974 he completed a Master's Degree in Public Administration (MPA) from the University of Southern California and began a professional career as an environmental planning consultant specializing in historic evaluations and cultural resource management. Prior to retiring, he maintained active membership in the American Institute of Certified Planners (AICP). He is a member of the Society for American Archaeologists (SAA). Since moving permanently to New Mexico in 2010, he has been involved in a number of history and archaeology projects and is the author or editor of several books pertaining to archaeology, architecture, and mining history in New Mexico. Restricted to his computer in 2020, he undertook several projects focused on Winchester College. The result are *The Patterned Tiles of William Tyelere of Otterbourne*, *19th Century Winchester College Notion Book Illustrations from the Winchester College Archives*, and *The Trusty Servant*.

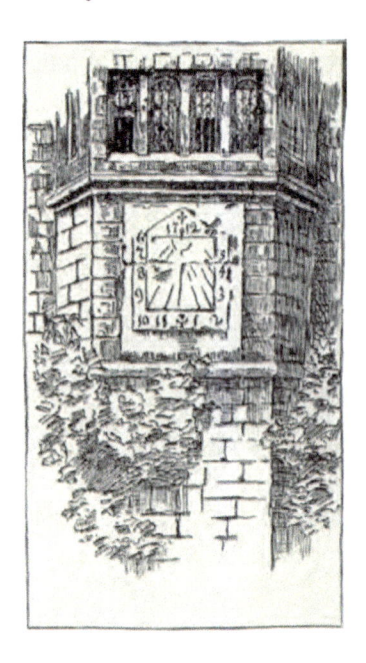

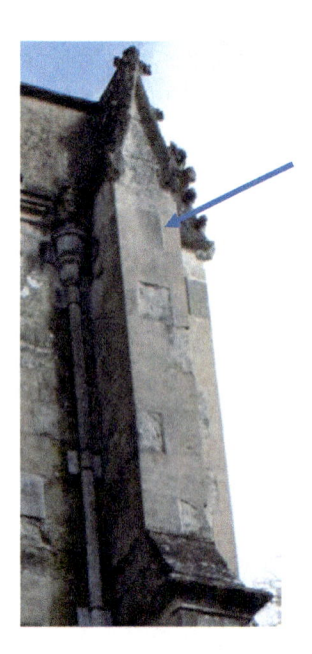

Possible sundial location on a Fromond Chantry buttress.

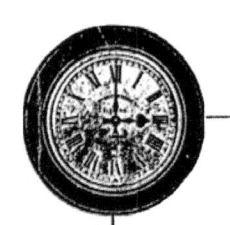

TO BE KEPT FOR REFERENCE.

INSTRUCTIONS
for
ERECTION and MANAGEMENT
OF
Synchronome
ELECTRIC
Time-Circuits

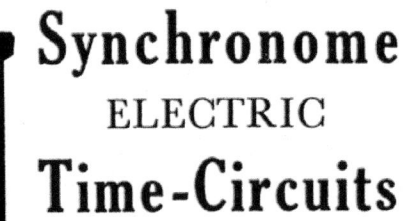

In Great Britain our prices generally include a visit of inspection to make sure that all the clocks are properly erected and in good order and adjustment. If erected by our staff we accept full responsibility for their safe-going and time-keeping, but we ask that they be put in the hands of a competent assistant provided with a copy of these instructions

THE SYNCHRONOME CO., Ltd.,
ABBEY ELECTRIC CLOCK WORKS,
WOODSIDE PLACE,
ALPERTON, MIDDLX.

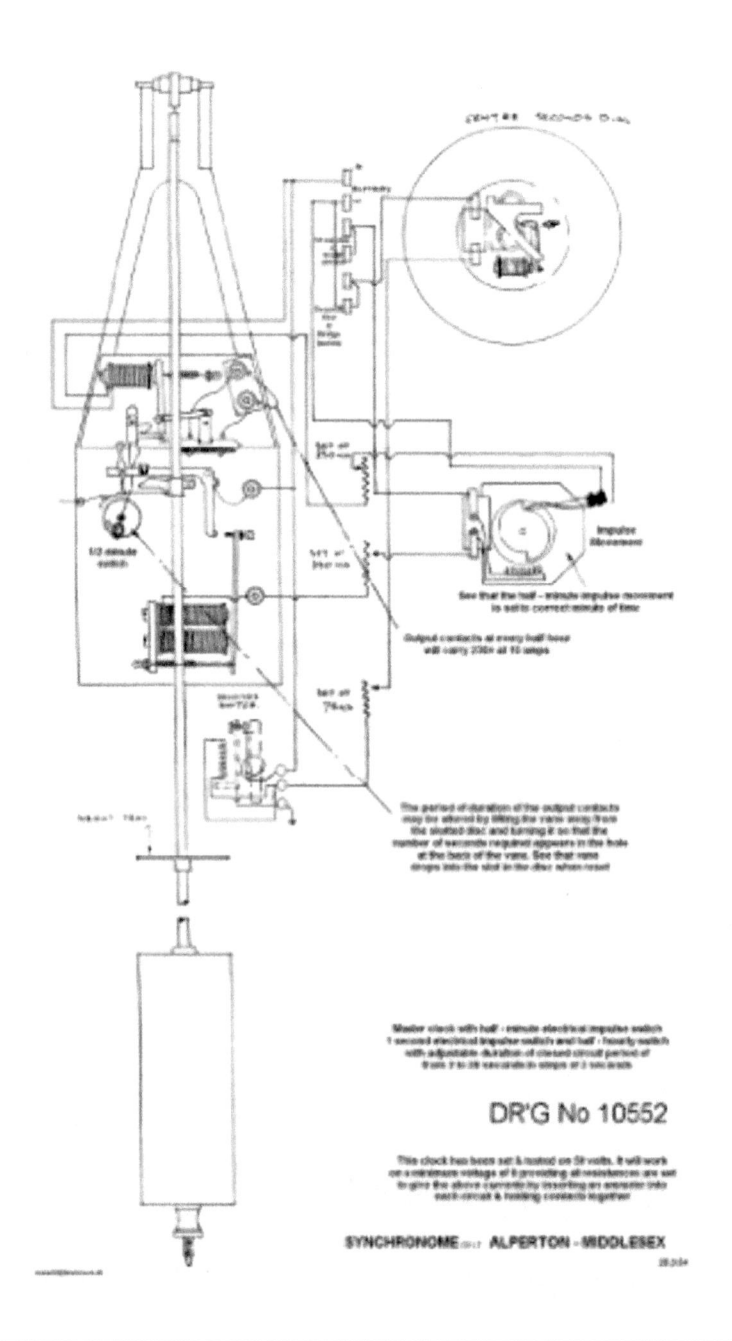

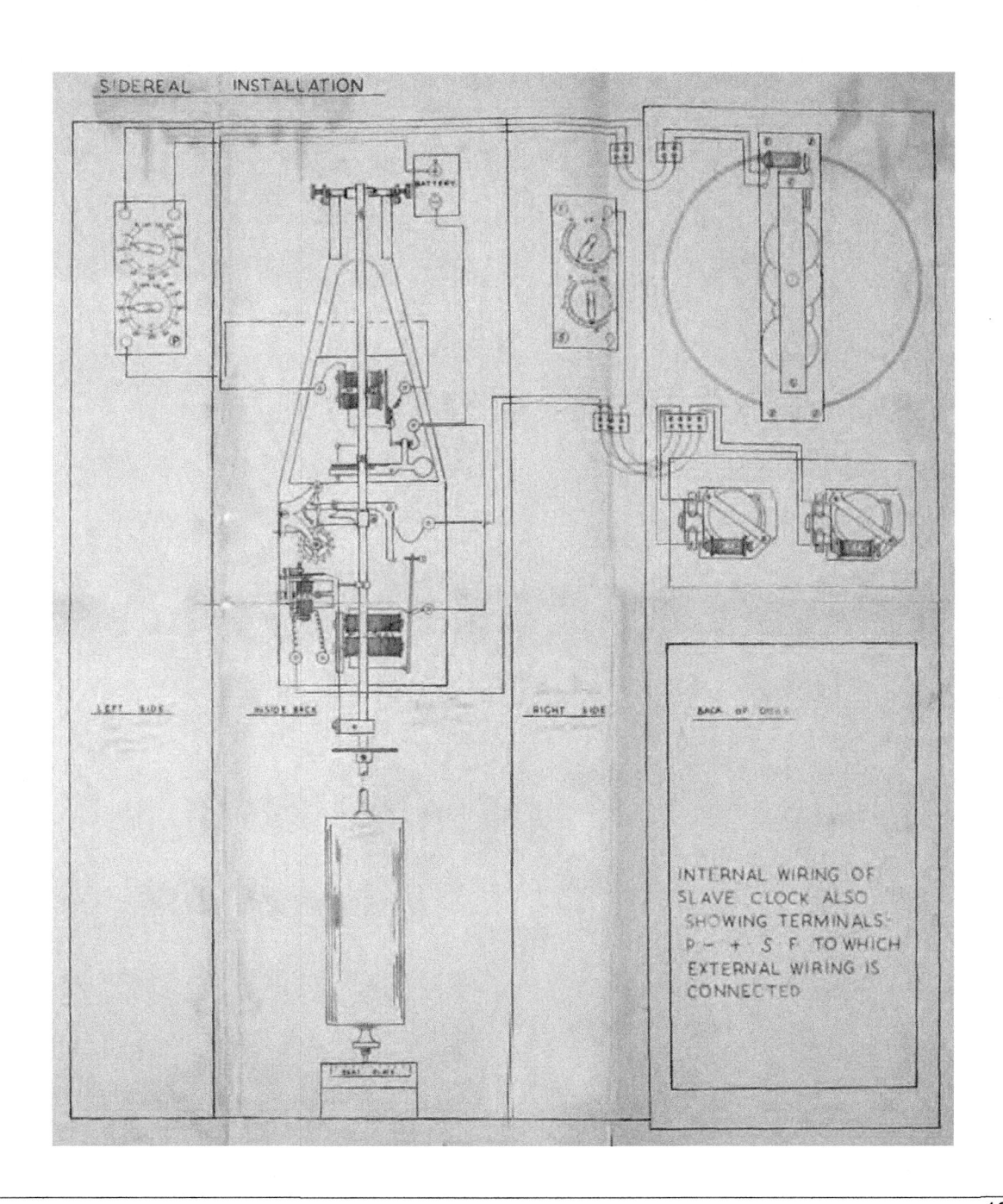

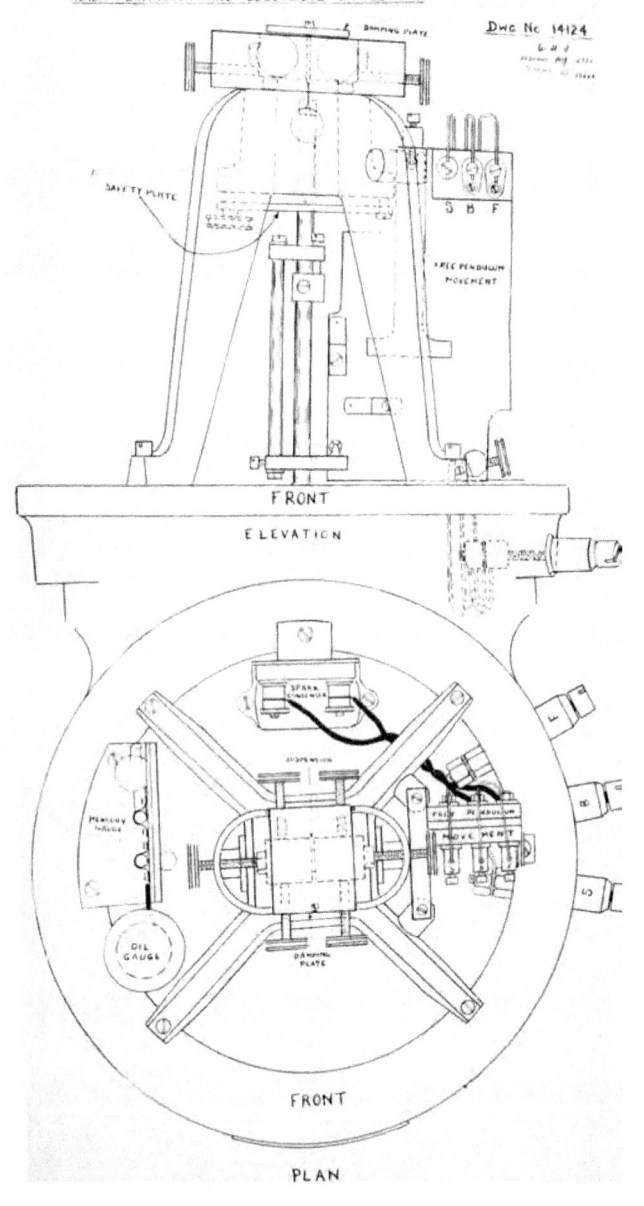

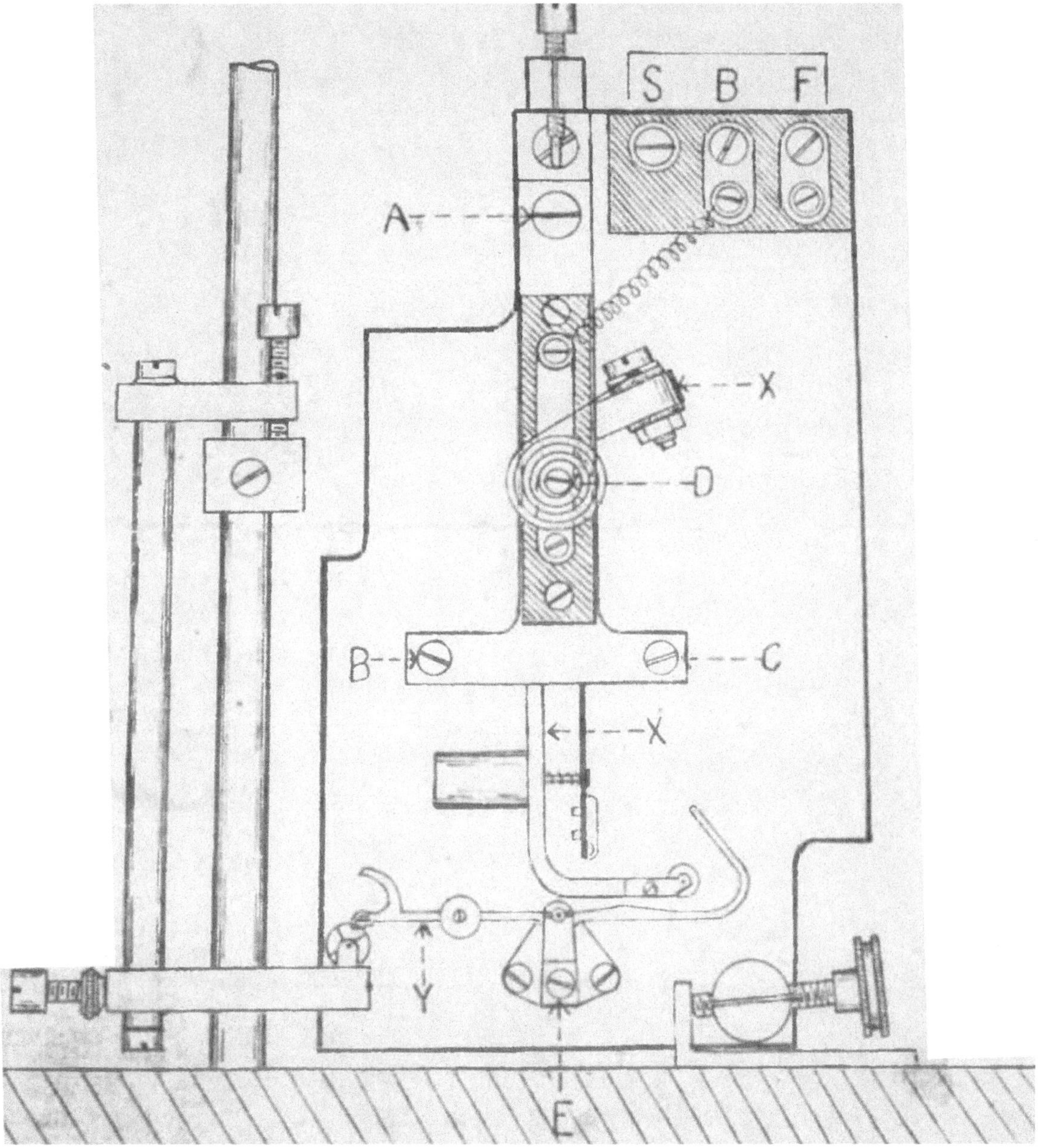
S B F
A
X
D
B
C
X
Y
E

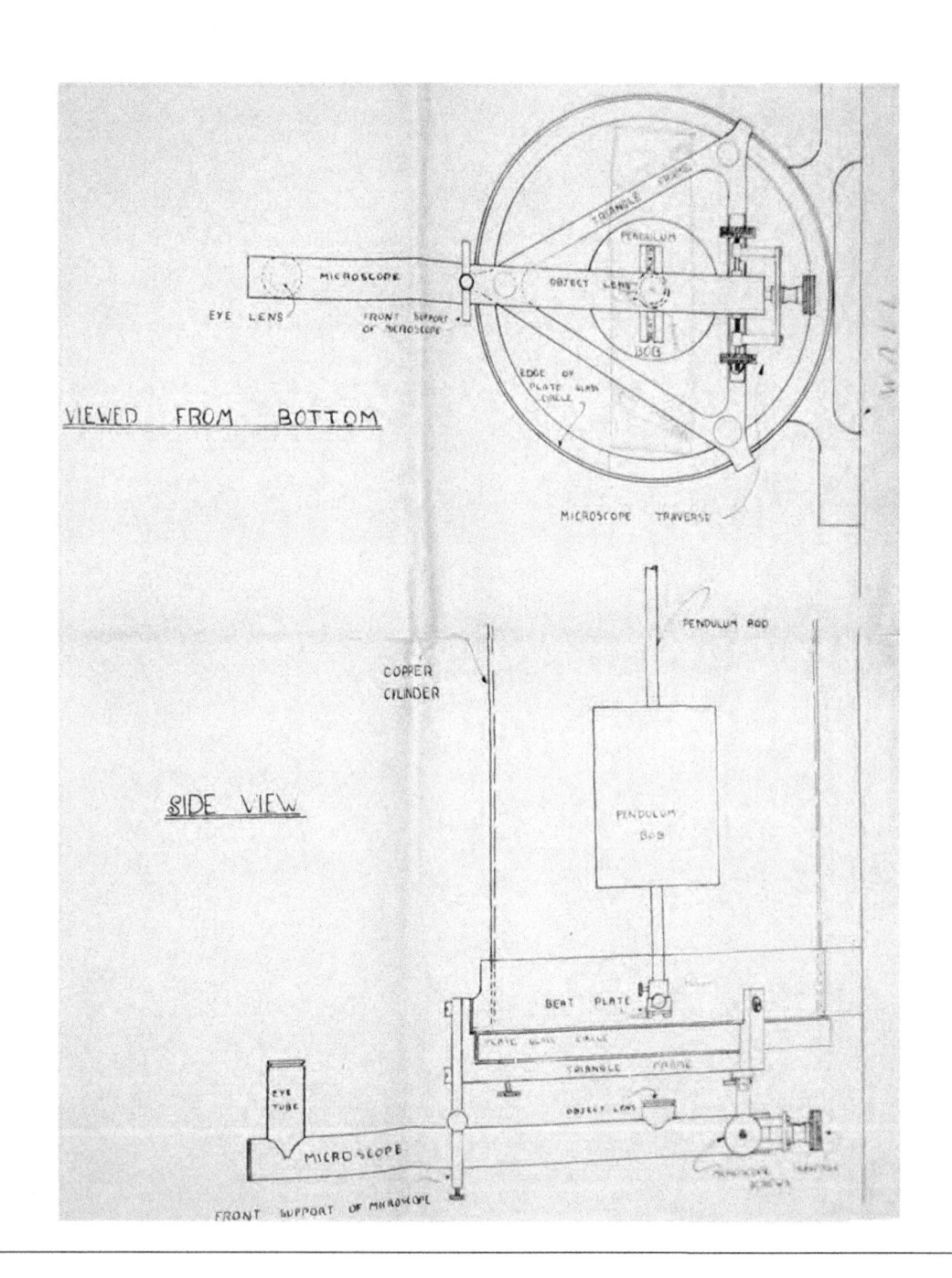

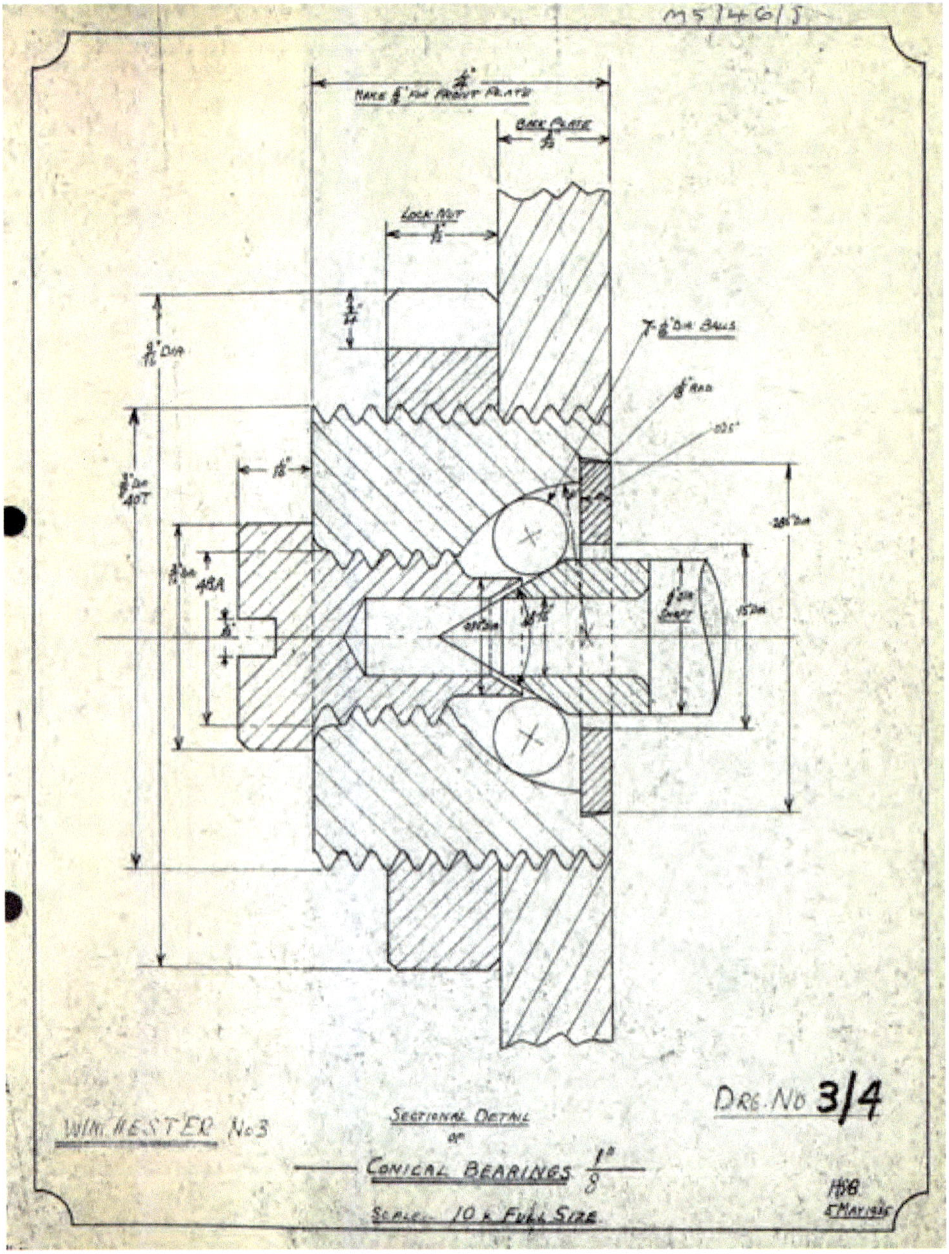

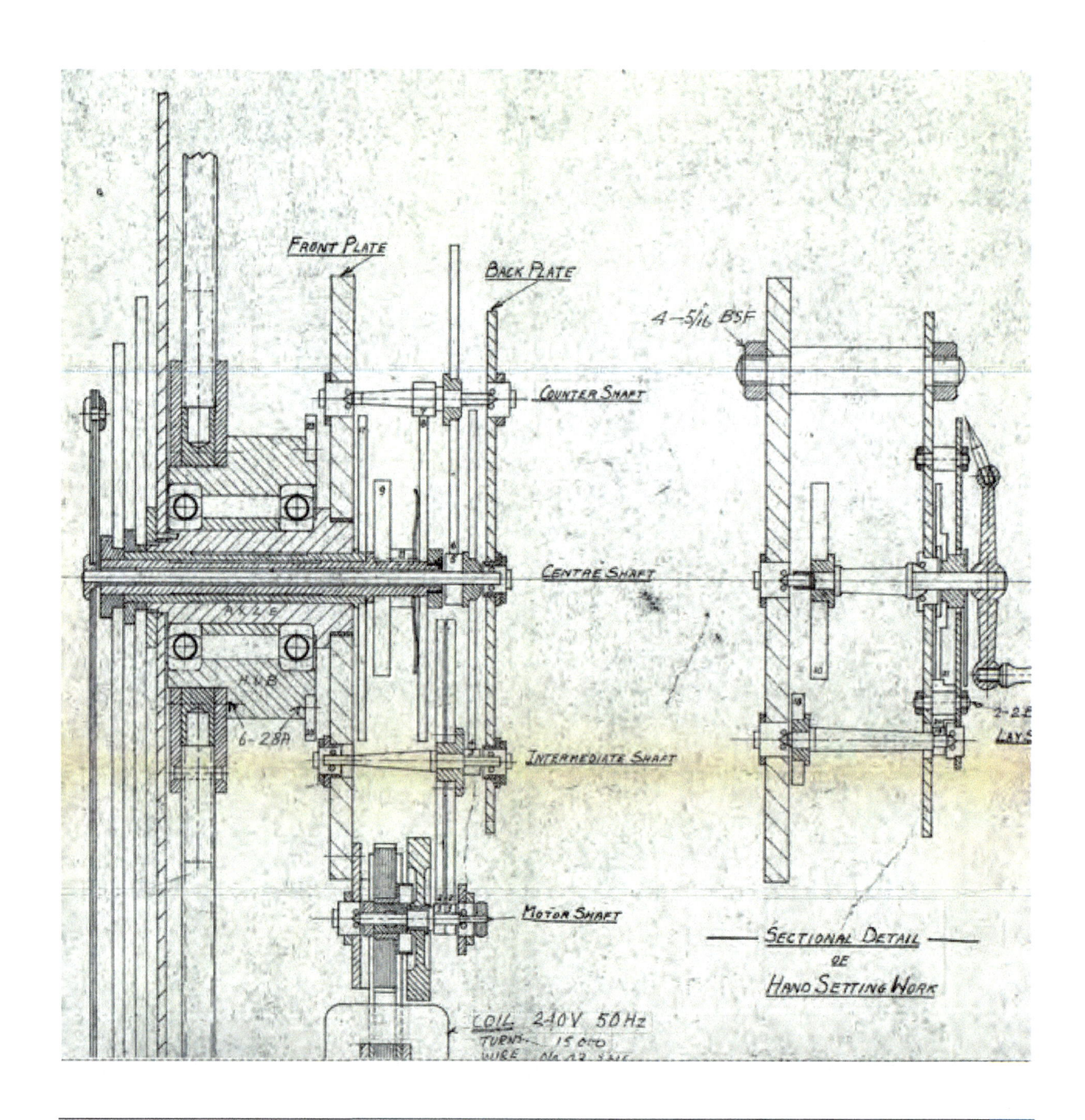

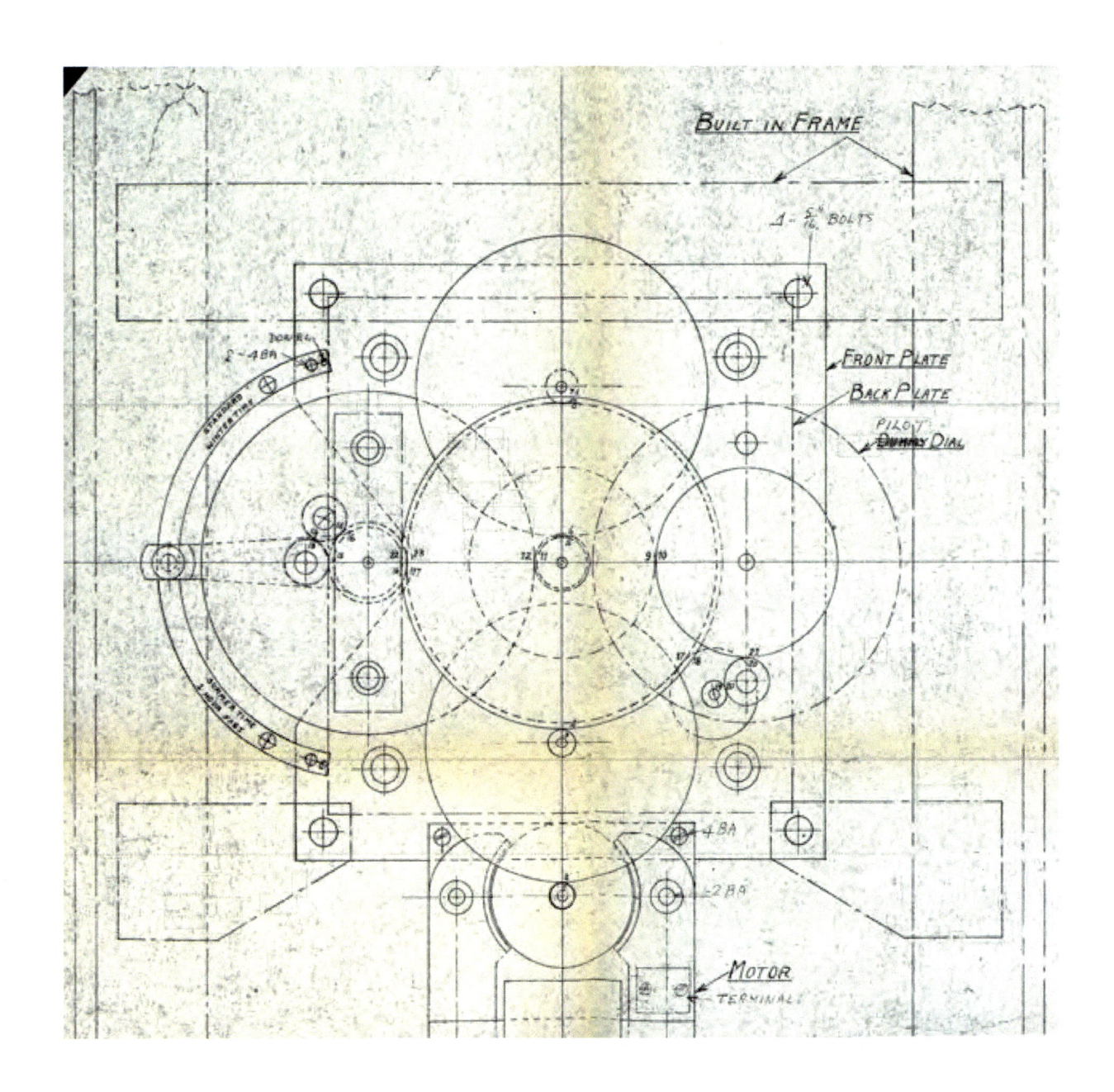

FRONT PLATE
BACK PLATE
PILOT
DUMMY DIAL

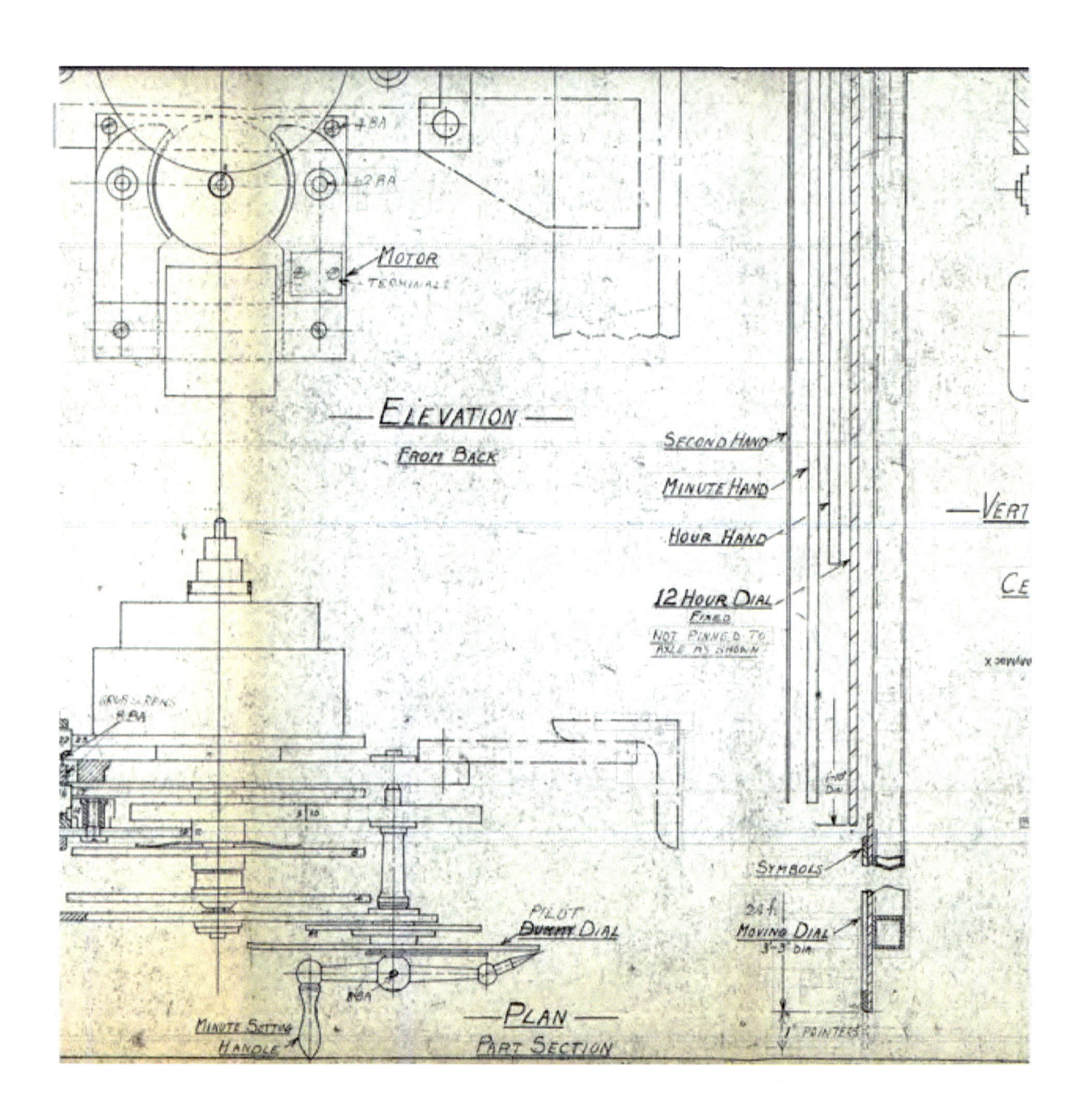

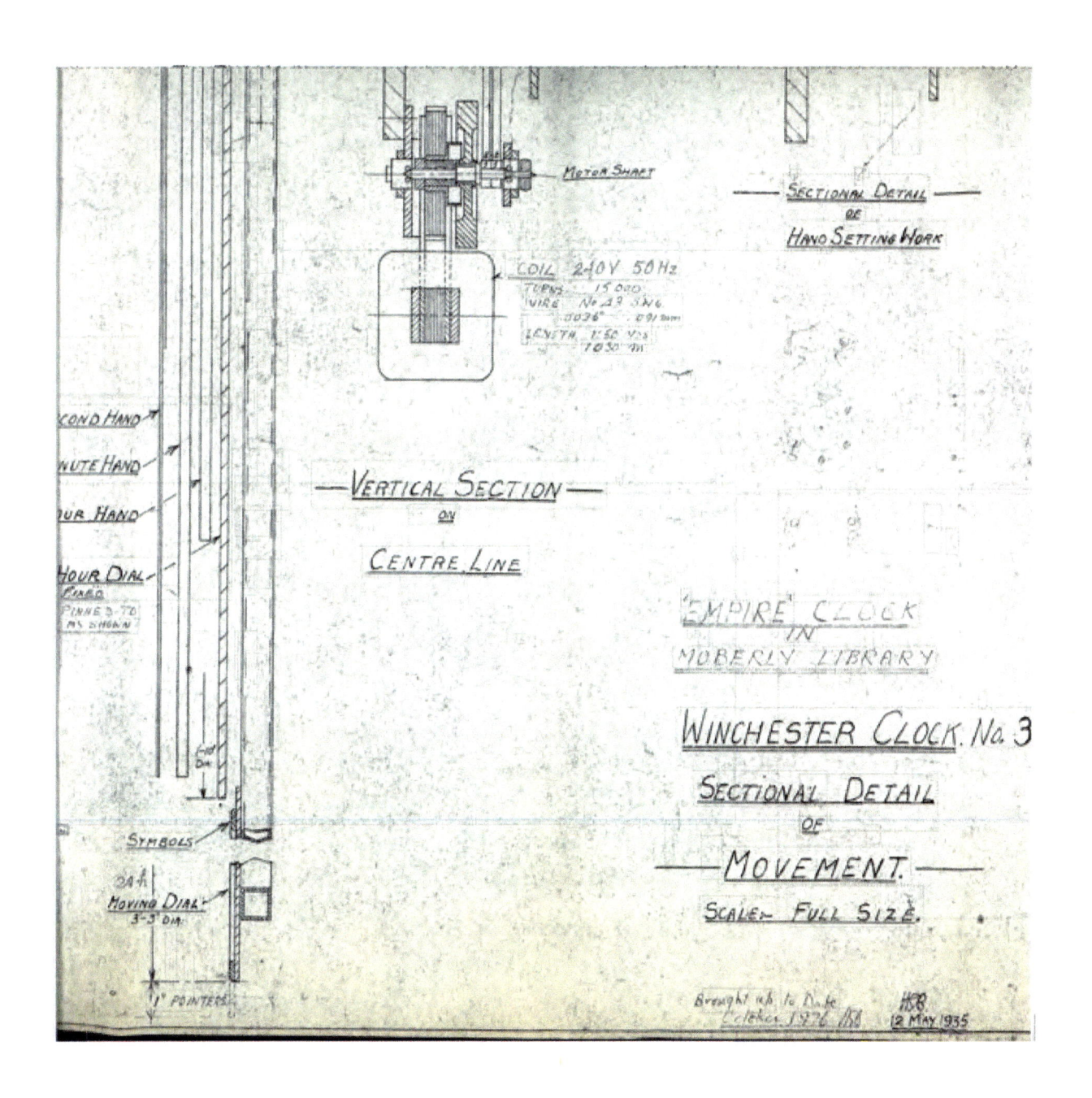

Sectional Detail of Hand Setting Work

Coil 240V 50Hz
Turns 15 000
Wire No 49 SWG
.0036" .091 mm
Length 7750 yds 7030 m

Vertical Section on Centre Line

"Empire" Clock in Moberly Library

- Second Hand
- Minute Hand
- Hour Hand
- Hour Dial Fixed, Pinned 3-70 as shown
- Symbols
- 24 h Moving Dial 3-3 Dia.
- 1" Pointers

Brought up to Date October 1976 HSB / 12 May 1935

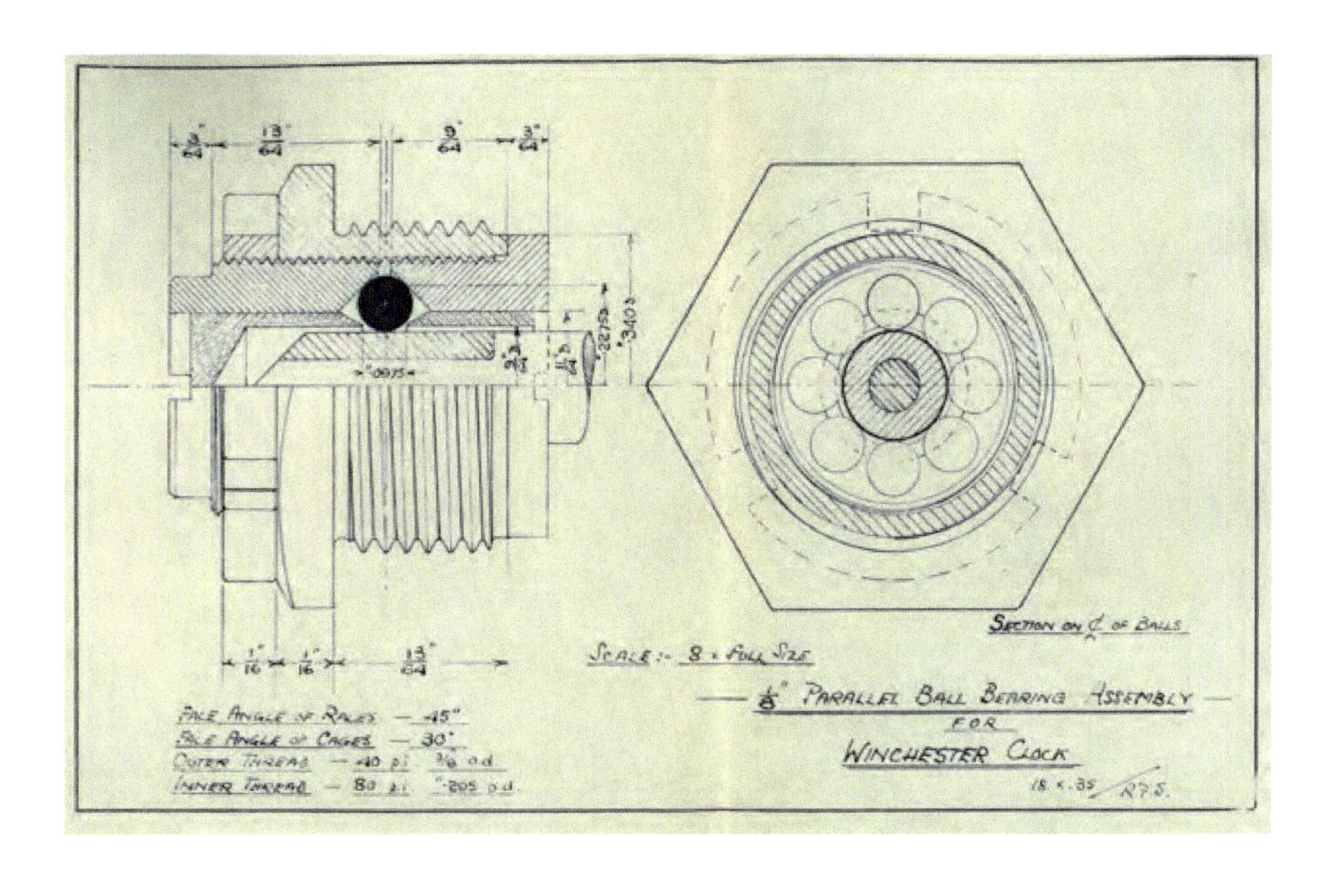

Sectional Detail
of
Conical Bearings

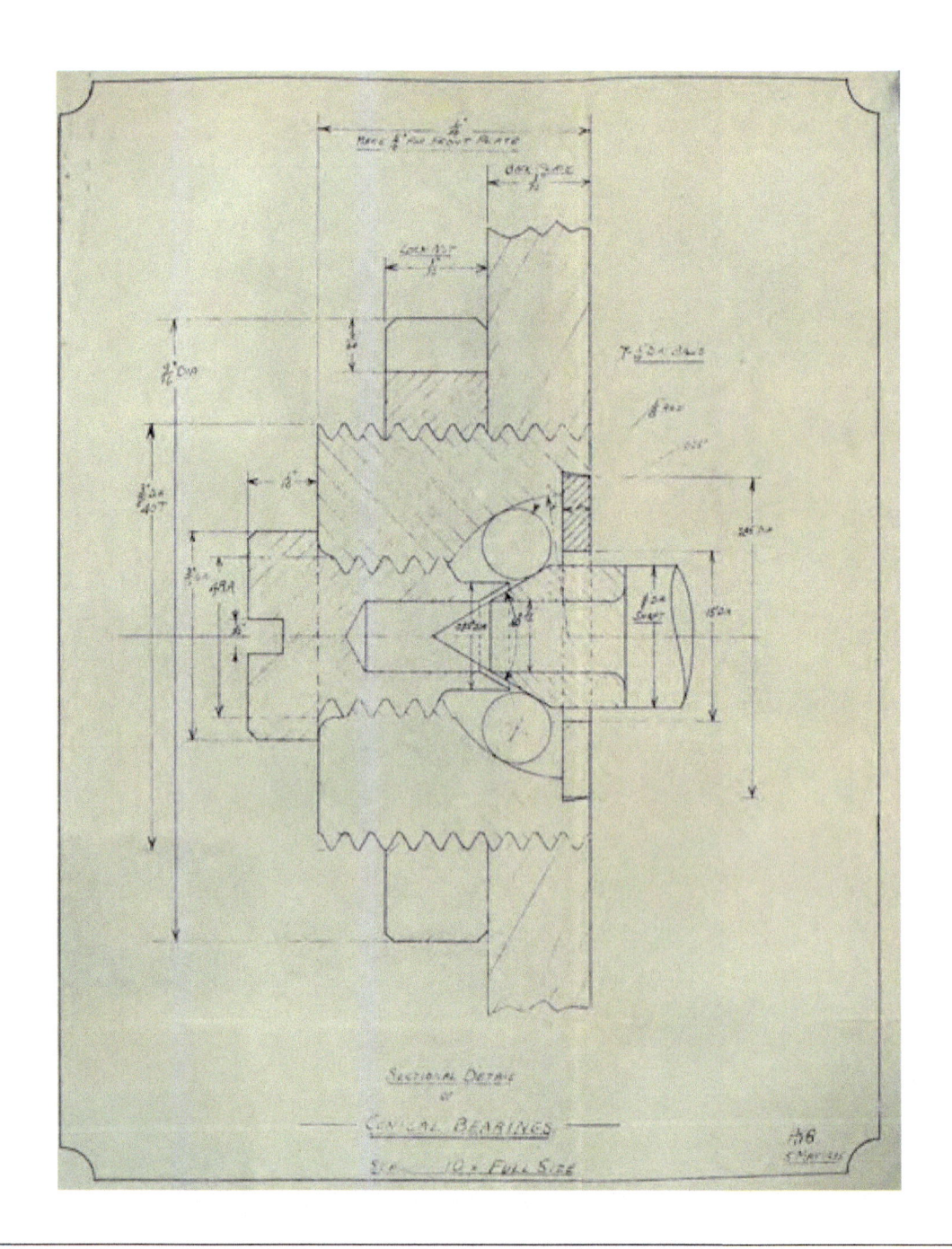

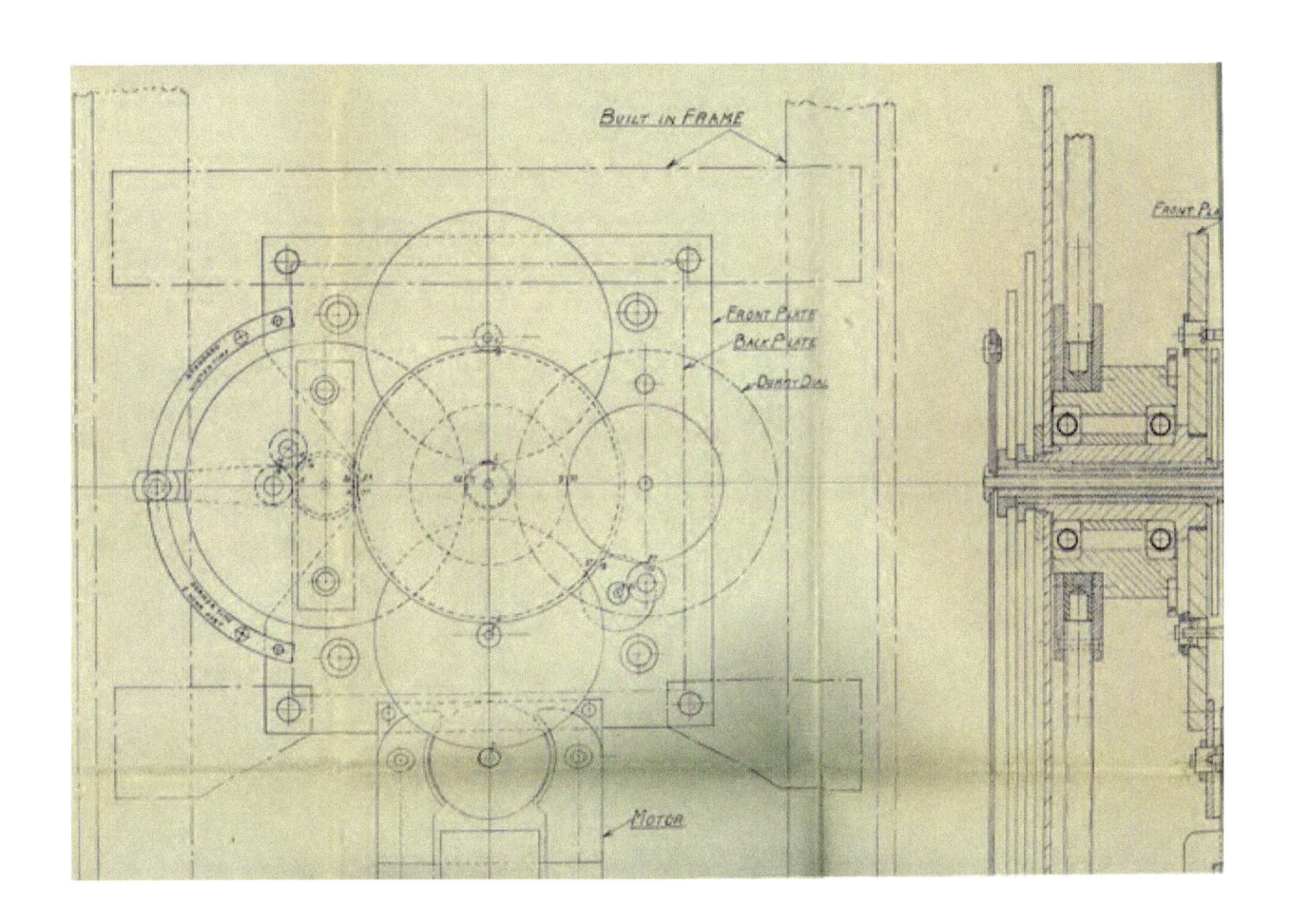

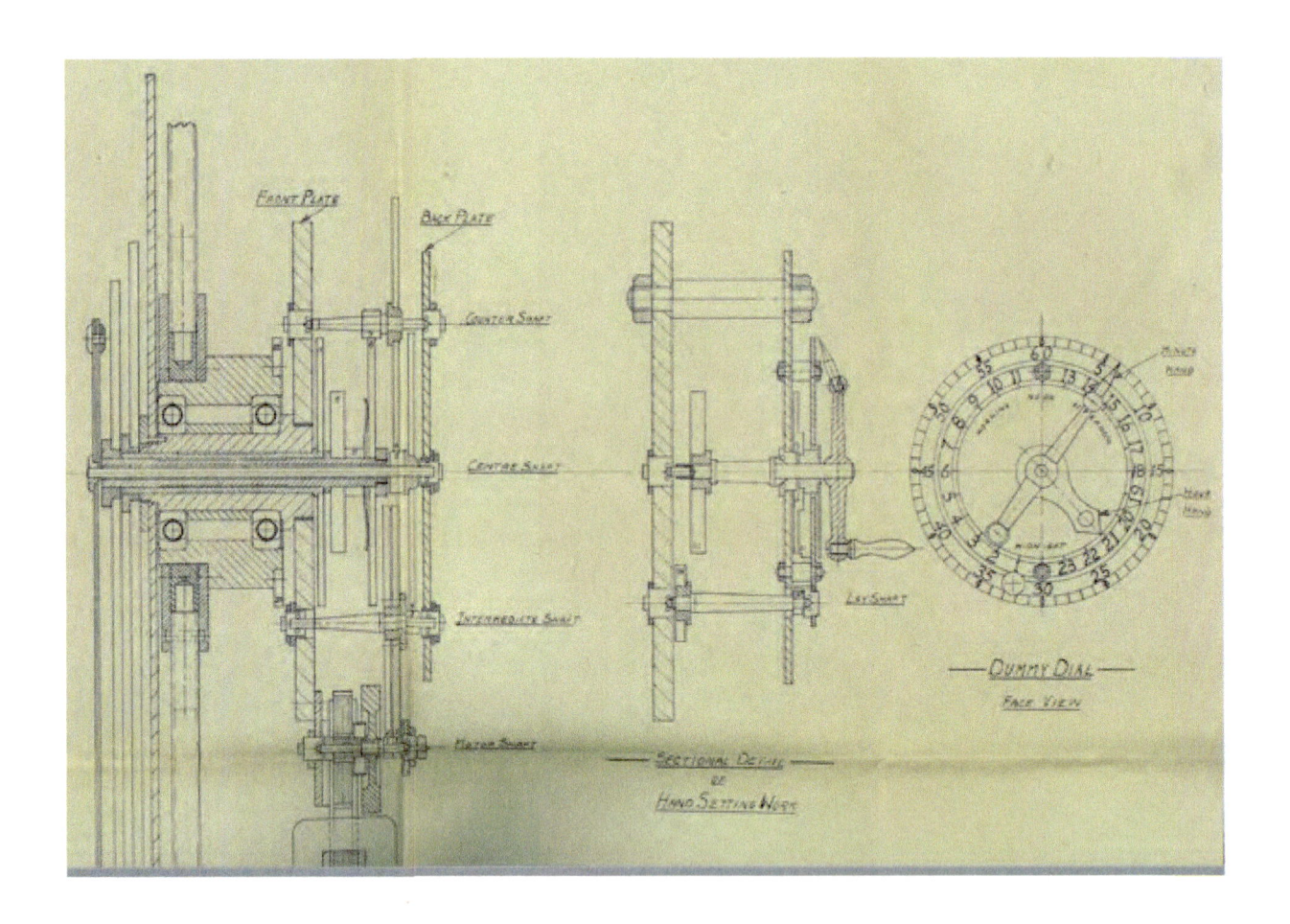

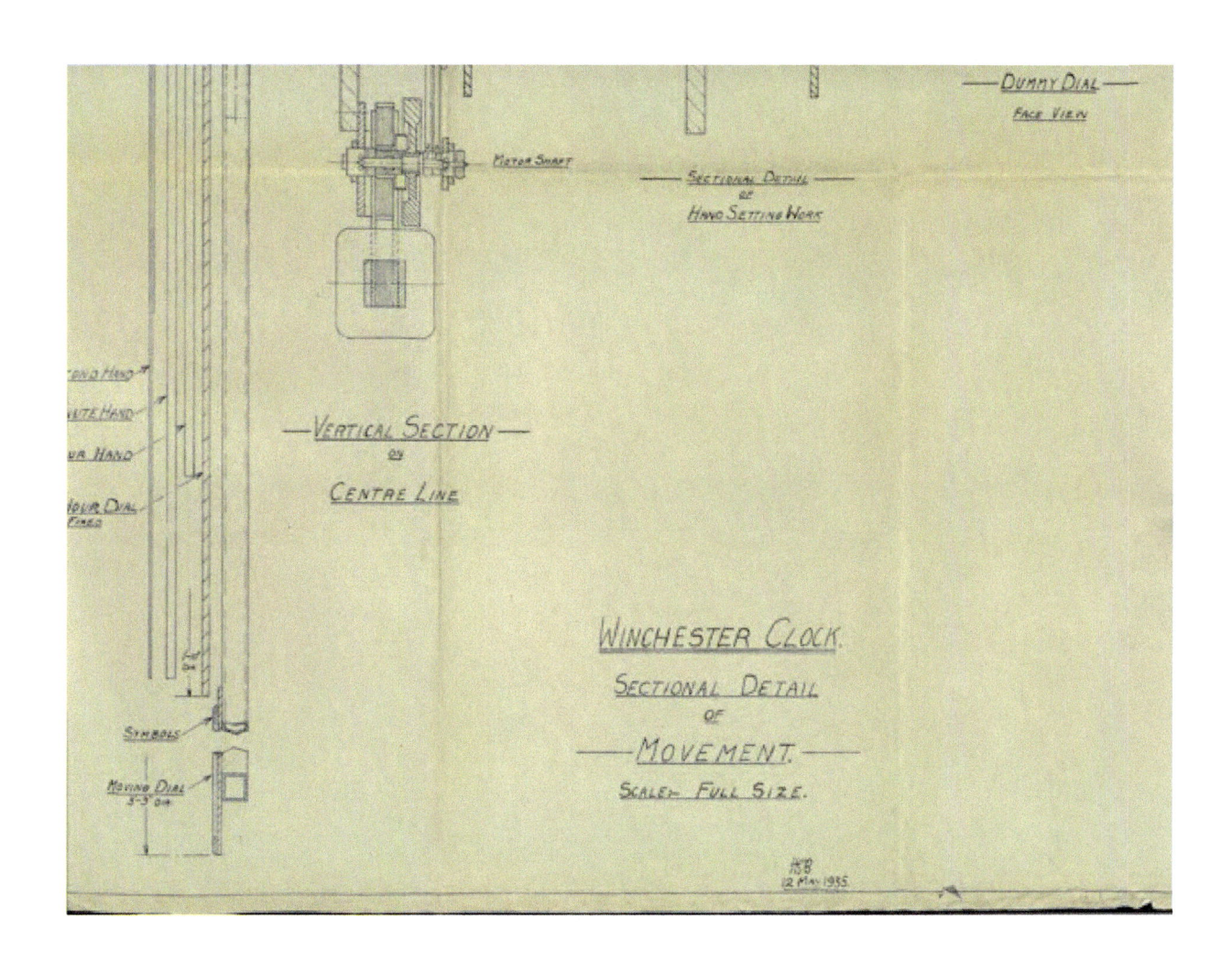

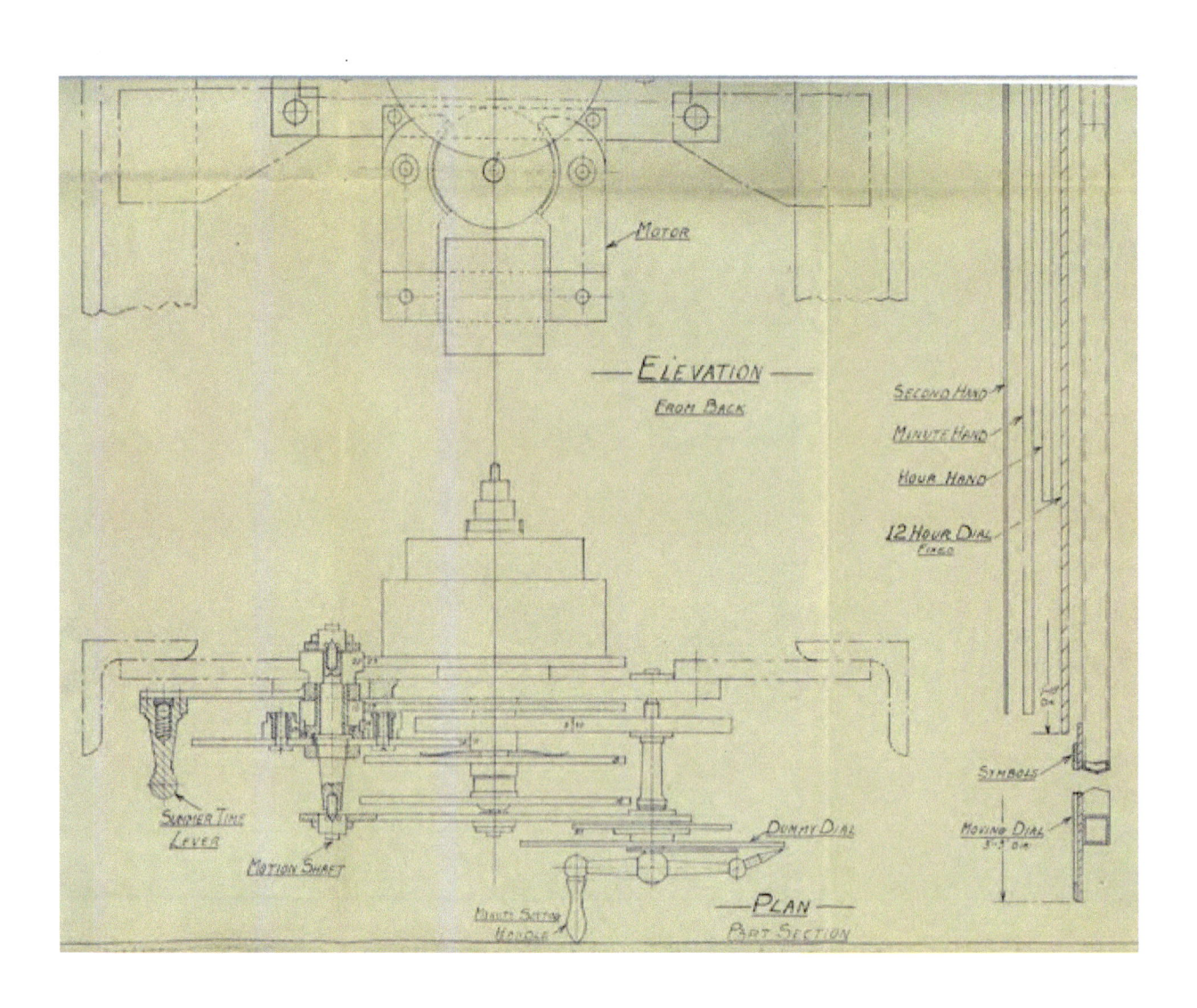